Die Bundesrepublik Deutschland · The Federal Republic of Germany · La République Fédérale d'Allemagne

FOTOGRAFIEN: LOTHAR UND ANDREAS KASTER
EINLEITUNG: RUDOLF HAGELSTANGE

DIE BUNDESREPUBLIK DEUTSCHLAND

THE FEDERAL REPUBLIC OF GERMANY
LA REPUBLIQUE FEDERALE D'ALLEMAGNE

UMSCHAU VERLAG · FRANKFURT AM MAIN

Die Einleitungen zu den Teilen „Der Norden", „Die Mitte", „Der Süden" verfaßte Gerhard Roth

Übersetzung ins Englische: Derrick O. Michelson und Pro Interpret
Übersetzung ins Französische Gerhard Steinborn und Pro Interpret
Gestaltung: Lothar Kaster und Fred Kaspruk

The introductions to the sections "The North", "The Central Area" and "The South" were written by Gerhard Roth

English translation: Derrick O. Michelson and Pro Interpret
French translation: Gerhard Steinborn and Pro Interpret
Layout: Lothar Kaster and Fred Kaspruk

L'auteur des aperçus introduisant les parties « Allemagne du Nord », « Allemagne moyenne » et « Allemagne du Sud » est Gerhard Roth.

traduction anglaise : Derrick O. Michelson et Pro Interpret
traduction française : Gerhard Steinborn et Pro Interpret
façonnement : Lothar Kaster et Fred Kaspruk

Unveränderter Nachdruck 1989
© 1980 Umschau Verlag Breidenstein GmbH · Frankfurt am Main

Alle Rechte der Verbreitung, auch durch Film, Funk, Fernsehen, fotomechanische Wiedergabe, Tonträger jeder Art, auszugsweisen Nachdruck oder Einspeicherung und Rückgewinnung in Datenverarbeitungsanlagen aller Art, sind vorbehalten
Datenerfassung: dateam Vertriebsgesellschaft mbH + Co KG · Frankfurt am Main
Gesamtherstellung: Brönners Druckerei Breidenstein GmbH · Frankfurt am Main

Alle Aufnahmen dieses Buches wurden mit Asahi-Cameras 6 × 7 und Takumar-Objektiven von Asahi auf Agfacolor Negativfilm 80 S Professional fotografiert

ISBN 3-524-63020-0 · PRINTED IN GERMANY

CIP-Titelaufnahme der Deutschen Bibliothek

Die Bundesrepublik Deutschland = The Federal Republic of Germany / Fotogr.: Lothar u. Andreas Kaster. Einl.: Rudolf Hagelstange. [Die Einl. zu d. Teilen „Der Norden", „Die Mitte", „Der Süden" verf. Gerhard Roth. Übers. ins Engl.: Derrick O. Michelson u. Pro Interpret. Übers. ins Franz. Gerhard Steinborn u. Pro Interpret]. — Unveränd. Nachdr. — Frankfurt am Main: Umschau-Verl., 1989
ISBN 3-524-63020-0
NE: Kaster, Lothar [Ill.]; Hagelstange, Rudolf [Mitverf.]; PT

| EINLEITUNG | INTRODUCTION | INTRODUCTION |

Die Teilung Deutschlands ist das historische Ergebnis des zweiten Weltkrieges und der totalen Niederlage des Deutschen Reiches. Nach der bedingungslosen Kapitulation des Deutschen Reiches übernahmen die vier Siegermächte die oberste Gewalt in Deutschland. Die deutschen Gebiete östlich der Oder und Neiße wurden unter polnische und sowjetrussische Verwaltung gestellt. Bald aber nahm der Ost-West-Konflikt und mit ihm die Teilung Europas in zwei antagonistische Staatensysteme Gestalt an. Damit wurde die Teilung Deutschlands nach einem Schwebezustand, der bis 1948 andauerte, Wirklichkeit. Das deutsche Volk lebt seitdem in zwei Staaten, die sehr verschieden voneinander sind, aber durch Sprache, gemeinsames geschichtliches und kulturelles Erbe und — wie wir hoffen dürfen — durch gemeinsames Wünschen und Sehnen und die fortschreitende Demokratisierung der Welt eines Tages wieder zu *einem* Ganzen zusammen- und zurückfinden werden. Dieser Wunsch ist selbstverständlich und legitim. Das vorliegende Buch stellt nur einen Teil unseres Vaterlandes dar, die Bundesrepublik Deutschland und das freie Berlin, also nur den Teil der alten Reichshauptstadt, der zum freiheitlich demokratischen Deutschland gehört.

Die Bundesrepublik ist kein gewachsener Staat, sondern durch irreguläre, gewalttätige und später machtbedingte Verhältnisse entstanden. Ihre geographische Gestalt hängt letztlich mit der Aufteilung der Besatzungszonen zusammen, die nach Kriegsende abrupte und sinnlose Korrekturen zugunsten der Sowjetunion erfuhr, welche zum Beispiel meine Heimatstadt Nordhausen, welche amerikanisch besetzt war, noch nachträglich (mit einem Teil Thüringens) den Sowjets überantworteten. Abgesehen von der Reformation und dem Zerfall des Heiligen Römischen Reiches Deutscher Nation durch die Angriffskriege Napoleons brachte der Ausgang des von Hitler entfesselten zweiten Weltkrieges die *schmerzlichsten* Folgen für unser deutsches Schicksal und unsere Geschichte. Denn trotz aller Verluste und Bußen, die der verlorene erste Weltkrieg ausgelöst hatte, war unsere so mühsam und spät errungene deutsche Einheit doch erhalten geblieben. Mit der — beinahe zwangsläufigen — Etablierung der

The partition of Germany is the historical result of the Second World War and the total defeat of the Third Reich. After its unconditional surrender, the four Allied Powers took over the government of Germany. The areas of Germany east of the Oder and Neisse were placed under Polish and Soviet administration. Soon after, however, the east-west conflict took shape, and with it the division of Europe into two opposed systems of nations. The partition of Germany crystallised from a transitional state that lasted until 1948. Since then the German people have been living in two separate states which are quite distinct, both politically and socially, yet which, by virtue of language, their common historic and cultural inheritance and — we hope at least — their common hopes and desires, as well as the increasing democratisation of the world, will one day again come together as ONE single unit. This desire is self-evident and legitimate. This book presents only part of our Fatherland, the Federal Republic of Germany and Free Berlin, although only that part of the former Reichs Capital that belongs to the liberal democracy of Germany.

The Federal Republic is not a country that has grown; rather has it emerged as a result of unusual circumstances involving force and, later, factors of power. In the final analysis its geography came about as the result of the distribution into occupation zones which, after the war's end, were subjected to abrupt and senseless corrections in favour of the Soviet Union which, for example, meant that my own home town Nordhausen, first of all U.S. occupied, was subsequently transferred to Soviet influence, along with a part of Thuringia. Apart from the reformation and the disintegration of the Holy Roman Empire resulting from the imperialistic wars of Napoleon, the outcome of Hitler's Second World War produced painful consequences for the fate of Germany and our history. Otherwise, in spite of all losses and sacrifices brought about by the First World War, our German unity which had been achieved so late and at such cost would have remained intact. The

Le partage de l'Allemagne résulte historiquement de la deuxième guerre mondiale et de la défaite totale du Reich allemand. Après sa capitulation sans conditions, les quatre puissances alliées allaient se partager le pouvoir suprême et les territoires allemands situés à l'est de l'Oder et de la Neisse soumis à l'administration polonaise et soviétique.

Très tôt, le conflit Est-Ouest qui allait diviser l'Europe en deux camps antagonistes devait prendre forme. Ainsi, le partage de l'Allemagne, en instance jusqu'en 1948 allait devenir réalité et le peuple allemand condamné à vivre, depuis la fin de la deuxième guerre mondiale, dans deux états aux régimes totalement différents. Seuls leur langue, leur histoire, leur culture tout comme leurs espoirs et leurs souhaits communs accompagnés des progrès de la démocratie dans le monde — et nous y croyons — devrait leur permettre, un jour, de retrouver leur unité. Ce désir et ce but sont évidents et légitimes. Cet ouvrage ne présente qu'une des deux parties de notre patrie, la République fédérale d'Allemagne ainsi que la partie de notre ancienne capitale, Berlin qui appartient à l'Allemagne démocratique libre. La R.F.A. n'est pas un état traditionnel. Elle est le produit d'un conflit brutal ayant abouti plus tard à une confrontation de forces. Géographiquement, elle résulte du partage de l'Allemagne vaincue en quatre zones d'occupation administrées militairement qui devaient subir, après la fin de la guerre, des modifications aussi abruptes que dépourvues de sens à l'avantage de l'Union soviétique : ma ville natale, par exemple, Nordhausen, qui était située en zone américaine, fut abandonnée ultérieurement, avec une grande partie de la Thuringe, aux occupants soviétiques.

En dehors de la Réforme et de la désintégration du Saint-Empire romain germanique provoquée par Napoléon, la deuxième guerre mondiale est certainement l'événement historique aux conséquences les plus graves pour notre destin.

En effet, après le premier conflit mondial, en dépit des pertes territoriales et économiques

unter westalliierter Besetzung stehenden Zonen zur Bundesrepublik und der bald nachfolgenden Gründung der Deutschen Demokratischen Republik wurde dann die Teilung besiegelt.

Freilich beide Staaten zusammengenommen, waren jetzt kleiner als die Weimarer Republik. Beinahe ein Viertel der alten (1935 um das Saargebiet legal vergrößerten) Fläche und ein Siebentel der ehemaligen Bevölkerung war verlorengegangen. Immerhin leben von etwa 80 Millionen Deutschen fast 60 Millionen in der Bundesrepublik. Sie hatten, seit 1949 eine freie Presse, einen Bundestag, elf Länderparlamente, einen demokratischen Staat also, der als föderative Republik wieder handlungs- und bündnisfähig wurde. Das bis dahin geltende Besatzungstatut wurde auf eine rechtsförmliche Grundlage gestellt. Die letzten Einschränkungen der Souveränität entfielen dann 1955 mit dem Inkrafttreten des sogenannten Deutschlandvertrages und der Verträge über den Eintritt der Bundesrepublik in die Westeuropäische Union und den Nordatlantik-Pakt.

Man muß wohl nicht eigens darauf hinweisen, daß die ersten Jahre nach dem verlorenen Krieg entbehrungsreiche, harte Jahre waren. Der älteren und mittleren Generation dürften die Bilder der Zerstörung für ihr Leben eingeprägt bleiben. Aber über alle Not und Entbehrung hinaus wuchs an den Aufgaben des Wiederaufbaus eine neue Widerstandskraft, eine neue „Moral" im leidgeprüften Volk, und als eine neue Währung eingeführt und der verfassungsmäßige Rahmen eines freiheitlich demokratischen Staates geschaffen war, begann jene Entwicklung ihren Anfang zu nehmen, die später dann als das deutsche „Wirtschaftswunder" hinreichend Lob und Selbstlob hervorrief. Aus den Ruinen wuchsen neue Häuser und Fabriken, zerstörte oder doch gelähmte Städte und Wirtschaftszweige lebten wieder auf, und da deutsche Tüchtigkeit und deutscher Fleiß Vertrauen weckten, blieb auch die Hilfe des — früher meist verfeindeten — Auslands nicht aus. Innerhalb zweier Jahrzehnte hatte sich die Bundesrepublik, welche der Gegenstand unserer Betrachtung und Darstellung ist, eine geachtete Position in Europa erarbeitet. Über eine ganze Reihe von Jahren hin hatte sie in der Welt den deutschen Namen und die deutschen Interessen repräsentiert. Es vergingen Jahre, bis die DDR, der zweite deutsche Staat, der sich in enger Anlehnung an die Sowjetunion gebildet hat, allmählich weltweit anerkannt wurde. Zwischen der Bundesrepublik Deutschland und der DDR kam es zu Gesprächen, Verhandlungen und Vereinbarungen auf Regierungsebene, offizielle Vertretungen wurden eingerichtet, der Besucherverkehr kam allmählich in Gang — das Miteinander der einzelnen Men-

partition was sealed as a result of the almost forced establishment of the Western Allies' zones in the form of the Federal Republic, followed almost immediately by the setting up of the German Democratic Republic.

In any case both parts taken together were then smaller than the Weimar Republic. Almost a quarter of the former area (including the legal incorporation of the Saarland in 1935) and a seventh of the population had been lost. Nevertheless, out of some 80 million Germans, just on 60 million live in the Federal Republic. Since 1949 they have had a free press, a parliament, eleven state assemblies, in other words a democratic state which as a federal entity was again empowered to make its own decisions and its own alliances. The occupation statue, until then operative, was given a legal basis. The remaining limitations to sovereignty were removed in 1955 with the implementation of the so-called German Covenant and the agreements on the entry of the Federal Republic into the Western European Union and the North Atlantic Treaty.

It is superfluous to point out that the early years following the lost war were filled with hardship and privation. The image of devastation will lifelong remain stamped on the middle and older generations. But a new power of resistance arose out of this want and privation, stamped with the idea of rebuilding — a new moral value in this sorely tried people. And when a new currency was introduced and the constitutional framework of a liberal democracy established, the development got under way which did not fail to evoke praise and even self-praise. New houses and factories arose out of the ruins, maimed and destroyed towns and industries regained life, and thanks to the fact that German hard work and industry encouraged confidence, foreign help,, often from former enemies, was not lacking. Within two decades the Federal Republic which we are now discussing had worked itself into an enviable position in Europe. For a great number of years it had represented the name of Germany and German interests. It was many years before the GDR, the other German State, which had become a supporter of the Soviet Union, gradually achieved international recognition. Discussions between the Federal Republic of Germany and the GDR grew into negotiations and agreements at government level, official representations were set up, human interchange slowly got moving, a factor which gained pre-eminence above the differences between the two German states. The exchange of goods and other economic interchange were already under way.

qui en résultèrent, l'unité relativement récente de l'Allemagne lui resta acquise.

Après la deuxième guerre mondiale, avec l'établissement des zones d'occupation et la formation de « länder ou pays » administrés par les Alliés d'où devaient naître la R.F.A. et la R.D.A., le partage de l'Allemagne devenait un état de fait.

Evidemment, cette Allemagne des deux états avait perdu, comparée à la République de Weimar, un quart de son territoire, y compris la Sarre, revenue cependant légalement à l'Allemagne en 1935, et un septième de sa population, bien qu'actuellement, la R.F.A., à elle seule, compte environ 60 millions d'habitants contre 80 millions en Allemagne d'avant-guerre. Elle jouit, depuis 1949, de la liberté de la presse, d'un parlement fédéral, le « Bundestag », et de onze parlements fédéraux les « Landtag ». Elle est donc un état démocrate. La République, redevenu libre de ses actions et de ses alliances et le statut d'occupation qui régissait l'Allemagne jusqu'alors recevait ainsi une base juridique formelle. Les dernières restrictions à sa souveraineté devinrent non avenantes en 1955 par la signature de la Convention sur les Relations entre les trois Puissances et la République fédérale d'Allemagne ainsi que celles de la Convention d'admission de la R.F.A. au sein de l'Union de l'Europe Occidentale et de son admission dans l'Organisation du Traité de l'Atlantique Nord (O.T.A.N.).

Il est évident que les premières années d'après-guerre furent très dures et marquées de nombreuses privations. Les contemporains de l'époque n'oublieront jamais l'image de ces villes allemandes dévastées et détruites. Mais malgré la misère et les privations, une force nouvelle de résistance, une nouvelle morale devaient naître au sein du peuple affligé. Et après une réforme monétaire stabilisatrice, l'état nouveau allait recevoir le cadre constitutionnel d'un état démocratique libre. La voie était ouverte à une évolution qui devait devenir célèbre sous l'appellation de « miracle économique ». Fabriques et immeubles nouveaux allaient renaître des cendres des cités allemandes de la défaite. La reconstruction des villes paralysées et détruites allait avancer à pas de géant et l'économie allait retrouver son activité. Et la qualification comme l'assiduité des Allemands allaient leur faire rapidement regagner la confiance universelle et l'Etranger — composé essentiellement d'anciens pays ennemis — allait leur offrir son aide. Il ne fallut qu'une vingtaine d'années à la R.F.A. pour occuper une position d'importance en Europe occidentale. Pendant toute cette période, elle représentait le nom et les intérêts allemands dans le monde. Il fallut des années à la R.D.A.,

schen wurde über die Gegensätze der beiden deutschen Staaten gestellt. Warenaustausch und andere wirtschaftliche Kontakte waren dem schon vorausgegangen.

Aber auch das konnte nicht verhindern, daß jedermann, wenn er einigermaßen über die politisch-staatliche Aufgliederung der Welt im Bilde war, wußte, was mit der DDR und mit der Bundesrepublik gemeint war, zumal es Felder gab, auf denen *beide* deutschen Staaten rivalisierend auftraten und eine exakte Kennziffer geradezu herausforderten. Eines der am häufigsten die Alternativfrage stellenden Gebiete war der internationale Sport, in dem beide deutsche Staaten durch ihre Leistungen seit langem ein gewichtiges Wort mitsprachen. Auf dem olympischen Felde hatte es da sogar vorübergehend eine *gesamtdeutsche* Mannschaft gegeben. Auf den ersten Olympischen Spielen in Deutschland nach dem Kriege — in München 1972 — standen sich aber schon zwei getrennte Mannschaften gegenüber: Wenn man von dem heimtückischen Anschlag der Palästinenser auf israelische Sportler absieht, gehörten diese Spiele zu den gelungensten der Nachkriegszeit. Sie wurden damit auch zu einer glücklichen Selbstdarstellung unserer Bundesrepublik.

Mit dem Stichwort Selbstdarstellung sind wir am neuralgischen Punkt dieses Buches, das nicht mehr und nicht weniger versucht, als ein verhältnismäßig sachgerechtes, stellvertretendes Bild zu vermitteln von diesem Land und seiner Bevölkerung, seinen geographischen, wirtschaftlichen und kulturellen Schwerpunkten, der Verschiedenheit seiner Stämme und Landschaften, von baulichen Anziehungspunkten und den wichtigsten, ältesten und reizvollsten Siedlungen seiner Menschen, die so verschieden sind in ihrem Wesen und ihren Dialekten wie ein Fischer von der Kieler Förde und ein Bauer im oberbayerischen Gebirgsdorf oberhalb des Hintersees.

Diese Verschiedenheit der Stämme, welcher die föderalistische Verfassung mehr Rechnung trägt als gelegentlich nützlich und vernünftig erscheinen mag und die in zurückliegenden Jahrhunderten auch ihren Teil zu den langdauernden Wehen und der schwierigen Geburt der deutschen Einheit beigetragen haben dürfte, ist andererseits auch wieder ein Guthaben, aus dem fremdländische Besucher der Bundesrepublik ihren Gewinn ziehen können. Das trifft sowohl für engere Nachbarn zu, welche — wie Niederländer, Flamen, Dänen — oben im Norden und Nordwesten dem anheimelnden Platt begegnen, oder sich, wie Elsässer und Schweizer, auf ein geselliges Alemannisch mit den Bewohnern Südwestdeutschlands (vorwiegend Schwaben) einigen können. Der Weg von den Niederbayern zu den Oberösterreichern

But all this was still unable to suppress the fact that anybody in any way familiar with the national political division of the world knew very well what was meant by GDR and West Germany, not the least of reasons being that there were many areas in which *both* Germany states entered the scene as rivals, thus providing the need for a clear-cut differentiation. One of the most frequent areas in which this need arose was in the international sporting arena where, on account of their long-standing performance, both German states had a powerful say. In the Olympics there had even been a transitional period where a combined German team had taken part. At the first Olympic Games in Germany after the war, 1972 in Munich, two separate teams opposed each other: if we close our eyes to the underhanded and most unhappy blow struck by the Palestinians against the Israeli sportsmen, the latter Games were among the most successful since the war. In this way they also turned out to be a happy projection of the image of our Federal Republic.

The word image brings us to the very nerve centre of this book, which in fact seeks to do no more and no less than to present as far as ever possible a factual, representative picture of our country and its inhabitants, its vital points of geographical, economic and cultural significance, the differences between its ethnic groups and its landscapes, its architectural attractions and its most important, oldest and most exciting human communities, all of which are so varied in their intrinsic being and their dialects as a fisherman from the Kiel fjord from a farmer in an Upper Bavarian village beyond the Hintersee.

These variations among its people, which the Federal Constitution often appears to respect to a greater degree than might be considered useful and sensible, and which in past centuries also played a part in the protracted sufferings and the laboured emergence of German unity, is also a form of capital from which the visitor from abroad can profit. This also holds for close neighbours who, in the case of the Dutch, Flemings and Danes in the North and North-West, encounter a homely "Plattdeutsch", or in the case of the inhabitants of south-west Germany (mostly Swabians), the Alsatians and the Swiss, who are able to exchange ideas on a basis of a sociable form of the Allemanic tongue. It is also but a short step from Upper Bavaria to Lower Austria. The frontiers often present less of a

ce deuxième état allemand qui s'était formée avec l'appui de l'Union soviétique, pour être reconnue universellement. Des rencontres, reconnue universellement. Des rencontres, des délibérations et des accords eurent lieu à officielles des deux états furent installées, les communications et échanges de visites améliorés, le tout déjà précédé d'échanges de marchandises et autres relations économiques. Les milieux plus ou moins bien informés des courants politiques du monde tenaient compte de ce partage de l'ancienne Allemagne entre les deux blocs occidental et oriental, les deux états se retrouvant en rivaux dans certains secteurs d'activité exigeant des prises de position précises. Un de ceux-ci était celui des rencontres sportives. Une équipe commune olympique allemande fit même son apparition, bien que les premiers Jeux olympiques organisés en Allemagne après la guerre à Munich en 1972, virent déjà les deux équipes allemandes de la R.F.A. et de la R.D.A. s'affronter. Abstraction faite du lâche attentat palestinien qui coûta la vie à plusieurs sportifs israéliens, ces Jeux de Munich comptent parmi les mieux réussis de l'après-guerre. Ils permirent à la R.F.A. de se présenter avec succès au monde entier.

Nous en arrivons ainsi au point névralgique de cet ouvrage qui ne veut que donner une image relativement objective de la R.F.A. et de sa population, de ses centres géographiques, économiques et culturels, de ses ethnies et de ses sites, de son architecture et de ses agglomérations, villes et villages les plus importants, les plus anciens et les plus pittoresques comme de ses habitants avec leur façon de vivre et leurs patois aussi différents que celui des pêcheurs de la côte de la Baltique par rapport à celui des paysans de Haute-Bavière.

Cette disparité des ethnies dont notre fédéralisme tient parfois plus compte qu'apparemment utile et raisonnable — et qui avait déjà rendu si difficile et si problématique la naissance de l'unité nationale allemande — offre cependant certaines facilités à nos voisins étrangers se déplaçant en R.F.A. et ceci, tout aussi bien pour les Flamands, Néerlandais ou Danois et autres qui y retrouvent les dialectes bas-allemands que pour les Alsaciens comprennent le dialecte de Bade ou pour les Suisses avec leur dialecte alémanique apparenté à celui des habitants de l'Allemagne méridionale et plus particulièrement des Souabes. Et les Autrichiens ne sont pas fort éloignés de la Basse-Bavière. Pour toutes ces ethnies voisines, les frontières sont moins existantes que pour les politiciens. Et les minorités allemandes s'exprimant dans d'autres langues sont toutes représentées

ist auch nicht weiter. Für einfache Nachbarn sind Grenzen oft weit weniger tabuisiert als für Politiker.

Wo es anderssprachige Minderheiten gibt — wie in Schleswig-Holstein —, sind sie parlamentarisch vertreten und leben respektiert und gleichberechtigt mit den Deutschen zusammen. Die Insel-Region dieser Landschaft mit Sylt, Helgoland und der Norddeich vorgelagerten Inselkette einerseits und Fehmarn andererseits läßt Brückenschläge zu, die in dänischer und schwedischer Richtung gern erwidert werden.

Eine Einrichtung wie die „Kieler Woche" zum Beispiel bringt alljährlich — über das Segelsportliche hinaus — die „Wikinger" der verschiedenen Nordnationen an einen Tisch und ist längst wieder zu einem Völkertreff geworden, der aus dieser Region nicht mehr fortzudenken ist. Flensburg ist unsere nördlichste Stadt, und Lübeck, das alte, ist durch seinen schreibfreudigen Sohn Thomas Mann nicht nur im deutschen Bewußtsein fest verankert. Den Vogel in der Nordregion schießen freilich die beiden Stadtstaaten Hamburg und Bremen ab. Nicht nur, daß Hamburg mit fast zwei Millionen Einwohnern neben Berlin die volkreichste Stadt in Deutschland ist; ihr Hafen — zumal mit dem internationalen Ruf genießenden Vergnügungsviertel St. Pauli —, der sich über 15 Kilometer erstreckt, bewältigt den Löwenanteil unseres Seehandels mit der Welt. Und auch im Geistigen und Künstlerischen ist Hamburg eine weltoffene, fortschrittliche Stadt gewesen und auch geblieben. An baulichen Höhepunkten ist sie freilich, wenn man von der Michaelskirche absieht, dem weitaus kleineren, aber charaktervollen Bremen unterlegen, dessen Rathaus und Ratskeller, dessen Gildehaus und Böttcherstraße zu den interessantesten Attraktionen norddeutscher Baukultur zählen.

Man darf jedoch nicht meinen, charaktervolle eigenwillige Bauweise beschränke sich im Norden auf ein paar Hanse- beziehungsweise Paradestädte. Von Theodor Storms Husum und dem idyllischen Friedrichstadt über den einstigen Maler-Wallfahrtsort Worpswede bis hinunter nach Celle, ins Niedersächsische hinein, stößt man immer wieder auf private oder „amtliche" Bauten, die von anheimelnder norddeutscher Originalität sind; bescheidene, aber zugleich anmutige, gesellige, aber letztlich individuelle Behausungen eines zurückhaltenden, aber immer zuverlässigen Menschentyps.

Das Wort „Menschentyp" läßt vielleicht die Frage aufkommen, ob sich denn im Laufe von gut drei Jahrzehnten so etwas wie ein Typ des Deutschen in der Bundesrepublik herausgebildet haben mag. Gewisse Reaktionen

barrier to the simple neighbour than they do the politician.

Where there are minorities with a different tongue — as in Schleswig-Holstein — they have parliamentary representation and live on a basis of equal rights with the Germans. The island regions of this area, Sylt, Heligoland and the chains of islands opposite the Northern Dyke and Fehmarn form links with the Danes and the Swedes.

An event such as the "Kiel Week" brings, quite apart from yachtsmen, every year "Vikings" from all the nothern nations together and has long been a meeting of the peoples of the region whose loss would be unthinkable. Flensburg is our most nothern city, and old-world Lübeck is firmly fixed in German and world thought by virtue of the eloquent pen of its son Thomas Mann. The City States Hamburg und Bremen round off the northern region. Not alone is Hamburg with almost two million inhabitants with Berlin the most populous town in Germany — its dockland, flanked by the world-famed St. Pauli amusement area, stretches along more than nine miles — it also accounts for the lion's share of our world trade. In matters of art and culture too. Hamburg is a broad-minded, progressive city, and it has always been such. It is, to be sure, lacking in architectural highlights — if we overlook the Church of St. Michael — in which respect it is no match for the far smaller, character-filled Bremen whose Rathaus (Town Hall) and Ratskeller, Guild House and Böttcherstrasse are among the most interesting North German architectural attractions.

It should not, however, be imagined that character-filled and unique architecture in the north is limited to a couple of Hanseatic and elite towns. From Husum, home town of Theodor Storm, and idyllic Friedrichstadt through the one-time mecca of painters, Worpswede, right down to Celle and into Lower Saxony, one again and again encounters either private or public buildings of typical North German originally. They take the form of modest and at the same time charming, "sociable" yet individual dwellings for a type of people which is reserved yet essentially to be relied upon.

The term "type of people" gives rise to the question as to whether in the course of three decades a generalised form of Federal German citizen has evolved. Certain reactions and forms of expression from immigrants from the East or later refugees from East Ger-

aux parlements des « länder », à égalité de droits avec leurs autres compatriotes comme, par exemple, les peu Danois du Slesvig-Holstein. Les îles de Sylt et de Helgoland, l'archipel au large de Norddeich en mer du Nord et l'île de Fehmarn, dans la Baltique sont d'ailleurs autant de ponts reliant l'Allemagne au Danemark et à la Suède.

Une manifestation annuelle de première importance, la « Semaine de Kiel », est devenue, le sport de la voile mis à part, un rendez-vous populaire et traditionnel des descendants des Vikings des différentes nations scandinaves. Flensbourg, la ville la plus au nord d'Allemagne, et la vieille ville de Lubeck, berceau de l'écrivain allemand Thomas Mann, sont connues bien au delà des frontières de notre pays. Les deux villes et « länder » hanséatiques de Hambourg et Brême sont particulièrement célèbres. Hambourg, avec ses quelques deux millions d'habitants est avec Berlin la plus grande ville d'Allemagne. Son port, par où transite la majeure partie de notre trafic maritime de marchandises, avec son quartier d'amusement universellement connu, Saint-Pauli, s'étend sur une superficie de plus de 15 kilomètres carrés. Hambourg a toujours été et reste une ville d'art cosmopolite et intellectuelle, moderne, amante du progrès. Malgré certains monuments, comme l'église Saint-Michel, par exemple, elle ne rend cependant pas la pareille à Brême dont l'Hôtel de ville et sa célèbre cave-restaurant, la Maison des Métiers et les édifices de la Boettcherstrasse sont caractéristiques pour l'architecture de l'Allemagne septentrionale.

Celle-ci ne se concentre cependant pas seulement sur quelques édifices publics de villes hanséatiques particulièrement représentatives. De Husum, ville chantée par le poète Theodor Storm, à la petite ville si pittoresque de Friedrichstadt en passant par l'ancienne colonie de peintres de Worpswede pour aller à Celle, en Basse-Saxe, partout on retrouve ces édifices privés comme publics empreints de cette originalité toute intime de l'architecture de l'Allemagne du Nord : des habitations modestes et cependant charmantes, au caractère d'individualité propre aux habitants du Nord.

Mais, après les quelques trente années d'existence de la R.F.A., est-il possible d'en caractériser un « type » de citoyen. Certaines réactions et réflexions d'immigrés venus de l'est ou de réfugiés arrivés récemment de la

und Redewendungen von Zuwanderern aus dem Osten oder späten DDR-Flüchtlingen, die sich schwer tun mit ihrer Einbürgerung, könnten das vermuten lassen.

Natürlich haben der neue Wohlstand, die wiedererlangte Geltung im europäischen Verband die Menschen der Bundesrepublik etwas selbstzufrieden werden lassen, und das Fehlen von andrängender Not, der Mangel an ernsthafter politischer Pression, die beide in den Ostblockstaaten zwangsläufig zu einer engeren menschlichen Solidarität nötigen, lassen sich ganz gewiß in gelasseneren bis gleichgültigeren Verhaltensweisen erspüren — auch der „Einheimische" stellt dergleichen zuweilen mit einigem Bedauern fest. Aber ernsthalt typenbildend haben sich die Verhältnisse doch kaum ausgewirkt, kaum auswirken können. Einmal sind gewisse scheinbare Sicherheiten längst wieder fragwürdig geworden — die siebziger und achtziger Jahre haben der Wirtschaft weltweit Krisensituationen beschert, und die Verflochtenheit und Abhängigkeit der Staaten untereinander nimmt da keinen Partner aus. Nicht nur die jüngere Generation — aber diese mit Vorrang — hat bemerkt, daß es keinen unendlichen Aufwärtstrend gibt, und sie am ehesten kleidet sich „typisch" und prägt das allgemeine Bild entscheidend mit. Dieses läuft mehr aufs Härene-Poppige hinaus — die Blue jeans haben fast eine Uniformität bewirkt, die allerdings mehr international als deutsch ist. Ansonsten wirkt das äußere Bild in den Städten einheitlich, um nicht zu sagen langweilig. Der rasche Wechsel der (Frauen-)Mode trägt seinen Teil dazu bei. Wohl im ganzen europäischen und amerikanischen Teil der Welt regiert das Laisser-faire, und wenn wir uns nach besonderen Akzenten umsehen wollten, müßten wir schon in den einzelnen Bundesländern nach Kundgebungen der Stammestemperamente forschen, die durch die föderalistisch verbürgte Kulturhoheit mit einer gewissen Pflege rechnen können. Aber es hat den Anschein, als machten sich auch die sogenannte „Volkstums"bekundungen im Alltag — von Bayern vielleicht abgesehen — immer rarer. Trachten werden fast nur noch für Festtage und Sonderveranstaltungen angelegt, dann freilich meist in sonntäglicher Güte und Perfektion. Aber freilich: Unter dem Alltagsgewand behauptet der Schwabe und der Badener, seit längerem im Südweststaat auf gleiche Ration gesetzt, ebenso selbstverständlich wie der Pfälzer oder der Saarländer seine Eigenheit. Auch ein echter Kölner oder ein gewachsener Westfale wird sich nicht seiner Eigenart begeben wollen, wenngleich in dem volkreichsten Bundesland Nordrhein-Westfalen, das rund 17 Millionen Einwohner zählt (Hessen gut 5½, Bayern fast 11, das Saarland gut 1 Million), durch die vorwiegend industriellen Tätigkeiten das Volkstümliche leich-

many who have grave problems in settling in, suggest that this is so.

Naturally the new-found high living standards and the recognition in the European Community have made the people of the Federal Republic in some degree self-satisfied, while the lack of pressing necessity and serious political pressure, both of which automatically lead to closer forms of human bonds in the East Bloc states, have their effects in the form of an easy-going attitude bordering in to indifference, an attitude often regarded with some dismay even by the "natives". Nevertheless, these conditions have proved to have little to do with producing a type, and it is hard to see how they could. On the one hand certain apparent security has again become questionable. The seventies gave rise to world-wide economic crisis situations, and the close-knit interdependence of the nations allows no state to stand aloof. It is not only the younger generation that has seen clearly that there is no such thing as a never-ending upwards trend. It seems to clad itself accordingly, even "typically," and plays a decisive part in setting the scene. This is primarily expressed in "pop ideas," and here too blue jeans have almost produced a uniformity, which is of course more to be regarded as international than German.

In other respects the face presented by the towns is uniform, not to say boring. Swift shifts in women's fashion have played their part. To be sure, laisser-faire rules the whole of the European and American world, and if we are seeking characteristic accents we would have to turn to events in the individual Federal States which give expression to regional temperament which, thanks to the federalistic cultural sovereignty guaranteed by the State, are relatively preserved. Nevertheless it would appear that everyday expressions of the so-called "folk inheritance," Bavaria being a possible exception, are becoming ever more scarce. The Tracht now comes out almost only on highdays and holidays, and then only in its Sunday freshness and immaculate order. The Swabian and the Inhabitant of Baden who are nowadays classified together, as well as the person from the Palatinate or the Saarland, all find it possible to maintain their individuality in everyday attire. A genuine "Cologner" too, or a dyed-in-the-wool Westphalian will not fail to betray his origins, even though North-Rhein-Westphalia, the most populous state with some 17 million inhabitants (Hessen some

R.D.A. et ayant des difficultés à s'intégrer pourraient le faire croire.

La prospérité nouvelle, la crédibilité retrouvée au sein de la communauté européenne, ont certainement donné aux habitants de la R.F.A. un certain sentiment d'autosatisfaction. La misère inexistante, l'absence de cette oppression politique qui fait peut-être parfois naître un sentiment de solidarité commune parmi les habitants des pays du bloc Est, s'expriment par une certaine indifférence que même les « indigènes » de la R.F.A. constatent avec quelque regret. L'évolution de ces trente années d'existence de la R.F.A. n'a laissé qu'une empreinte relativement faible. D'abord, la sécurité générale apparente semble plus douteuse. Et les années soixante-dix et quatre-vingt ont doté notre économie de crises n'épargnant aucun pays en raison de leur interdépendance. Non seulement les jeunes — et ceux-ci avant tout autres — se sont aperçu qu'il n'existe pas d'essor à l'infini. Ils s'habillent peut-être en conséquence et leurs « blue-jeans » leur confèrent une uniformité plus internationale qu'allemande. Cette exception faite, l'image de nos villes apparaît non-conformiste, pour ne pas dire insipide bien que les changements rapides de la mode féminine y posent ses accents. En Amérique comme en Europe, le principe du laisser-faire domine.

Et pour rencontrer un certain caractère d'individualisme, il nous faudra aller à la recherche des usages populaires des différentes ethnies dans les « länder » fédérés. Or, il apparaîtrait qu'à l'exception de la Bavière, ces usages se perdent. Les costumes régionaux, dans toute leur splendeur et leur richesse, ne sont plus portés qu'exceptionnellement à l'occasion de festivités ou de grandes manifestations. Des différentiations se font cependant jour : sous leur aspect quotidien, les Souabes et les habitants du pays de Bade, réunis au sein d'un « land » commun, sauvegardent leur personnalité tout comme ceux du Palatinat ou de la Sarre. Il en est de même des habitants de Cologne ou de Westphalie bien qu'ils se perdent quelque peu dans la masse de la population du pays de Rhénanie-du-Nord-Westphalie, important « land » industriel avec 17 millions d'habitants, la densité la plus importante de la R.F.A. A titre de comparaison, la Hesse compte un peu plus de 5,5 millions, la Bavière, près de 11 millions et la Sarre dépasse de peu le million d'habitants.

ter anonymisiert wird als anderswo. Hinzu kommt, daß in dem Straßenbild, zumal der „arbeitsamen" Städte und Großstädte, sich seit einer ganzen Reihe von Jahren Hunderttausende von Angehörigen anderer, zum Teil außereuropäischer Nationen bewegen, die mit Kind und Kegel und sogar älterer Anverwandtschaft unter uns leben und wohnen und dem Bilde, das ein Besucher der Bundesrepublik sich von ihren Bewohnern und Bürgern machen will, nicht geringe fremd-völkische Farbtupfen verleihen. Insofern wird es schwer fallen, einen „Bundesrepublikaner" ausfindig zu machen, geschweige denn als Typ auf den Schild zu heben. Wer Näheres von uns wissen will, der muß schon unter die Türen der einzelnen Stämme treten und an ihren Tischen Platz nehmen; denn auch die Küche der verschiedenen Pappenheimer sagt nicht wenig über ihr Temperament und ihre Eigenschaften aus.

Im großen und ganzen haben sich die Akzente der Stämme freilich etwas entschärft im Laufe der letzten Jahrzehnte — 14 Millionen Vertriebene aus Schlesien, Ost- und Westpreußen, Flüchtlinge aus der DDR und ausgewanderte Volksdeutsche aus den Ostblockstaaten haben das angestammte Element aufgelockert und zugleich durchlässiger und toleranter werden lassen, und aller landsmannschaftlichen Reminiszenz und Wiederbelebung zum Trotz schreitet die Verschmelzung der deutschen Stämme langsam, aber unaufhaltsam fort. Was an sich noch kein Nachteil sein muß. Das mehr auf dem Lande wurzelnde Stammes- und Volkstum steht ohnedies seit dem Wiederaufbau unter dem Einfluß einer enormen Industrialisierung, die natürlich auch die Landwirtschaftsbetriebe nicht vergessen hat. Aber eben: Je mehr Maschinen den Menschen entbehrlich machen, um so weniger Menschen kann das Land halten. Auch der Deutsche ist auf dem Wege, vorwiegend ein Stadtmensch zu sein. Das irre Anwachsen der großen Städte in aller Welt zeigt, daß er mit diesem Stadttrieb beileibe nicht allein steht.

Indem wir uns dieser Stadt-Sucht und einiger ihrer warnendsten Beispiele erinnern, stellt sich die Frage, wie die Städte der Bundesrepublik, zum Teil nach teilweiser oder fast gänzlicher Vernichtung, wiederaufgebaut wurden und — des weiteren — wie und ob die leidlich davongekommenen in der zunehmenden Technisierung und Industrialisierung ihr Gesicht bewahren konnten.

Daß sich das Industriegebiet an der Ruhr — im Volksmund seit Ewigkeit als der „Ruhrpott" apostrophiert — nicht mehr idyllisieren läßt, muß niemandem erklärt werden. Immerhin verdient betont zu werden, daß gerade dort, zum Beispiel in Dortmund, wo die Ge-

5½ million, Bavaria just on 11, and the Saar around one million) would be more likely to lapse into anonymity on account of its primarily industrial nature. There is the additional factor that the street scene in the "industrious" towns and cities has for a long while had an injection of colour as a result of the hundreds of thousands of members of other nations, in part extra-European, who have moved into the areas complete with offspring and even with older members of the family, to become a part of them, meaning that a visitor to the Federal Republic seeking to gain an impression of the inhabitants and citizens will also discover this trace of foreign "colour." It is thus very difficult to encounter the "Federal Republican" as such, on to whom to hang the label "typical." Anybody who wishes to get to know us better will have to gain entry to the houses of the people and sit at their table — the fare offered by the different groups often says much about their temperament and their idiosyncrasies.

By and large the individual regional characteristics have, in the course of recent decades, become blunted. Fourteen million outcasts from Silesia, East and West Prussia, refugees from East Germany and people of German descent who have cleared out of the East Bloc countries have infiltrated and diffused the local elements and at the same time made them far more tolerant. In spite of all regional affection for the past and its rebirth, the process of German ethnic integration proceeds, slowly and irresistibly, and this need not be a bad thing. The acceptance of folk tradition and custom, more a part of rural life, is, notwithstanding, being subjected in an enormous degree to industrialisation, and this has not left the farm untouched. On the contrary, the more the machine can replace the human hand, the fewer the people needed on the farm. The German citizen is on his way to becoming primarily a town dweller. The wild growth of all the world's big cities shows that he is far from being alone in this rush to the big city.

When we think of this "urban urge" in its most ominous manifestations the question presents itself, how can the cities of the Federal Republic, to an extent rebuilt after partial or complete destruction, continue to retain their face in the light of ever increasing technological advance and industrialisation.

It is unnecessary to explain to anybody why it would now be impossible to create an idyll out of the Ruhr industrial area, colloquially

Depuis plusieurs années, la vie quotidienne des villes de toute importance de la R.F.A. est marquée par des centaines de milliers d'immigrés venus en partie de pays non-européens avec leur famille, souvent père et grand-père y compris. Peut-être, l'image ainsi offerte aux visiteurs étrangers y a-t-elle gagné en coloris quelque peu exotiques.

Il semble donc plutôt difficile d'établir un portrait typique du « Républicain fédéral allemand ». Et pour en savoir plus de la vie quotidienne de notre jeune République, on se verra obligé de pénétrer quelque peu dans son intimité et de prendre place à la table de ses citoyens, les cuisines régionales en révélant plus que tout autre description de leur caractère et de leur personnalité.

Dans leur ensemble, la diversité des différentes ethnies allemandes est moins prononcée qu'il y a encore quelques dizaines d'années. Quatorze millions de réfugiés venant de Silésie, de Prusse orientale et occidentale, de la R.D.A. ou encore d'origine ethnique allemande venant des pays du bloc Est ont influencé l'identité des ethnies indigènes qui, malgré leurs traditions, font preuve de compréhension, de tolérance et favorisent ainsi une fusion peut-être très lente mais progressive des ethnies allemandes en général. Une constatation positive. L'identité et le folklore des ethnies ont toujours été plus enracinés dans les campagnes que dans les villes. Et cependant, l'industrialisation qui gagne progressivement du terrain dans l'agriculture exerce une très forte influence dans ce secteur. Les machines remplaçant de plus en plus la main d'œuvre humaine, celle-ci émigre de plus en plus vers les villes. Les Allemands deviennent de plus en plus des citadins. L'augmentation croissante du chiffre des populations citadines dans le monde prouve que cette tendance est universelle.

En évoquant celle-ci, la question se pose naturellement de savoir comment furent reconstruites ces villes de la R.F.A. partiellement ou totalement détruites pendant la deuxième guerre mondiale et jusqu'à quel point l'essor technique et industriel leur ont laissé leur aspect traditionnel.

Il va sans dire qu'un centre industriel comme celui du bassin de la Ruhr ne pourrait que difficilement se métamorphoser en pastorale, bien que les résultats obtenus là où les dangers de l'industrialisation pour la qualité de vie étaient les plus flagrants soient remarquables. Citons l'exemple de Dortmund avec ses nombreux jardins publics aménagés au cen-

fahren am drohendsten waren, das Rettende (bewußte Auflockerung und Begrünung) nicht ausblieb, nicht versäumt wurde. Daß Hannover seine Kriegsschäden durch einen besonnenen und gezielten Wiederaufbau mehr als wettmachen würde, konnte von einem Aufmerksamen schon recht früh beobachtet werden. Und wenn es mit München zunächst recht langsam zu gehen schien mit dem Wiederaufbau, so darf das Endergebnis, die heutige Stadt also, ihrer Anziehungskraft auf viele Besucher aus aller Welt sicher sein. Die schönen Künste haben dort nicht nur eine Akademie, sondern nach wie vor eine allgemein freundliche und großzügige Heimstatt, und nicht nur alteingesessene und bierselige Feste lassen sich in ihr feiern. Das Olympiajahr 1972 hat München die Chance gegeben, eine ebenso technisch gelungene wie liebenswürdige Gastgeberrolle mit Bravour zu spielen.

Wer die Stadt Frankfurt in den dreißiger Jahren kennen und lieben gelernt hat, mag es heute schwer haben, die alten Gefühle wieder aufzurufen — hier hat eine Reihe von Auflagen (gleich nach dem Zusammenbruch), Rollen und Entwicklungen eine Silhouette bewirkt, die dem einst musischen Charakter der Mainstadt und Hessenmetropole allzu forsch absagt. Aber die verschiedenen Messen, nicht zuletzt die von aller Welt besuchte Buchmesse im Herbst, und der Flughafen und anderes mehr machen Frankfurt zu einem unentbehrlichen oder unumgänglichen Anziehungs- und Mittelpunkt. Vielleicht hat das „kölsche" Panorama seine großen Züge da glücklicher bewahrt, und auch die Stuttgarter wußten ihrer vielfältig gegliederten Stadt die ärgsten Versuchungen und Bauabenteuer zu ersparen.

Im Grunde können wir schon von Glück und freundlicher Fügung sprechen, daß uns die modernen Stadtmonster erspart blieben. Die Bundesrepublik hat zwar — und in dieser Art und Dichte als Unikum in der Welt — ein Industriegebiet, in welchem sich Großstadt an Großstadt reiht; aber selbst dort und gerade dort, so möchte man sagen, ist ein vielfältiges kulturelles Leben gefordert. Essen, Bochum, Duisburg, Hagen, Wuppertal-Barmen, Recklinghausen —, beinahe jeder dieser Städtenamen ist mit irgendeiner besonderen kulturellen Bemühung oder Einrichtung verbunden. Und von dieser ganz offenbar dem Ausgleich dienenden Neigung und Anfälligkeit sind nicht weniger auch die kleineren und mittleren Städte dieser Region „befallen". In den fünfunddreißig Jahren meiner Vortragstätigkeit habe ich keine deutsche Provinz so bis in die entlegenste Kleinstadt studieren

known as the "Ruhrpott". It is, however, worthy of note that in this very region, in Dortmund where the dangers were most ominous, rescue came in the form of decentralisation and green belts, just in time. Those who are observant very quickly recognised the fact that Hanover was quickly on the way to do more than just make good the war damage by clear-sighted and well-considered reconstruction. And even though progress in Munich at first appeared slow, the final result, the city of today, can rest assured of its attraction for hosts of visitors from the world over. Not only have the belles-arts an academy there, it is also a friendly and broad-minded city where festivals take place, and not only traditional ones. The 1972 Olympics gave Munich the opportunity of presenting itself not only as a hearty host, but also of demonstrating its technical ability.

Anybody who knew Frankfurt in the thirties and who grew attached to it may today find it difficult to conjure up to the old feelings. A number of demands which occurred right after the war, the roles it was called on to play and attendant developments have produced a silhouette which has rudely destroyed the once poetic character of the Hessen metropolis on the Main. But the manifold fairs, not the least important being the Book Fair attracting people from all over the world each autumn, the Rhein-Main Airport and many other things make Frankfurt an inescapable or at least an unavoidable point of attraction. Possibly the Cologne panorama has succeeded better in preserving its major characteristics, and Stuttgart too managed to save its many-sided city image from the most wild temptations and architectural adventures.

Basically we can thank our luck and a happy way of combining for the fact that we have been spared from modern urban monsters. To be sure, the Federal Republic boasts an industrial area that is unique in the world, both in extent and density, where big town crowds up to big town, but even there, in fact right there, a richly diversified range of cultural activity is promoted. Essen, Bochum, Duisburg, Hagen, Wuppertal-Barmen, Recklinghausen — almost every one of these place names is associated with some sort of special cultural effort or establishment. The smaller municipalities too have become imbued with this inclination an affinity which quite obviously serve as a form of compensatory equalisation. In thirty-five years of lecturing activity I have been able to study no German

tre de la ville. Ou Hanovre réparant méthodiquement ses dommages de guerre. Et si la reconstruction de Munich fut lente, les résultats obtenus assurent à cette ville une séduction s'excerçant sur ses visiteurs venant du monde entier. Les beaux-arts ne s'y concentrent pas seulement sur une Académie : toute la ville est un centre culturel et ses fêtes et autres manifestations traditionnelles ne sont pas seulement le fait de ses célèbres brasseries. Les jeux Olympiques de 1972 ont donné à Munich l'occasion de se présenter au monde sous son véritable aspect d'amphitryon capable et aimable.

Ceux qui firent la connaissance de Francfort-sur-le-Main et apprirent à l'aimer dans les années trente y retrouveront difficilement l'ambiance de l'époque. Les nécessités de l'évolution de l'après-guerre ont modifié la silhouette de la métropole de Hesse, domicile des Muses, bien que ses nombreux salons, foires et expositions internationaux, n'oublions pas ici la Foire du Livre, la plus importante du genre au monde, son aéroport et tant d'autres facteurs en aient fait un grand centre de commerce et de communications.

Peut-être Cologne est-elle restée plus fidèle à sa tradition et a-t-elle mieux préservé son aspect traditionnel et les habitants de Stuttgart affichent-ils un plus grand respect pour la silhouette traditionnelle de leur ville évitant ainsi l'écueil d'une restructuration facilement négative lors des travaux de reconstruction de leur cité.

Au fond, nous devons être reconnaissants au destin de nous avoir épargné les monstruosités d'une architecture citadine trop moderne. La R.F.A. possède une agglomération très dense et peut-être unique au monde de grandes villes industrielles. Et cependant, on y rencontre de nombreuses activités culturelles. Essen, Bochum, Duisbourg, Hagen, Wuppertal-Barmen, Recklinghausen, oui, la plupart des villes de la R.F.A. possèdent quelque institution culturelle importante. Cette tendance compensatrice se fait également jour dans les localités de moindre importance de ces régions industrielles. Mes trente-cinq années de conférences et de déplacements, m'ont permis d'acquérir une connaissance plus approfondie de ce bassin de la Ruhr que d'autres provinces allemandes. Ainsi ai-je constaté que, parfois, le besoin plus que l'aisance décide du niveau culturel des populations.

können wie diesen voreilig gescholtenen Ruhrpott. Manchmal bestimmt eben nicht die Wohlhabenheit das Niveau, sondern das Bedürfnis. Oder beides.

Aber vielleicht gibt es – jenseits von Größe und Idyllik, Einwohnerzahl und wirtschaftlichen Schwerpunkten – Städte in dieser Bundesrepublik, die eine verschwiegene Anziehungskraft ausüben, in der sich Gestalt und Erbe, Stammesprofil und gesellschaftliche Rolle wechselseitig ergänzen oder ablösen... Natürlich zählen gewisse Universitätsstädte dazu wie Würzburg oder Münster, Freiburg oder Tübingen, Aachen oder Heidelberg oder Marburg, Darmstadt, Trier, Braunschweig... Jedoch auch Paderborn, die „altmodische" Bischofsstadt, wie das vielgeplagte und mit Recht vielgerühmte Nürnberg, wie das hübsche Fulda, wie Passau oder Bamberg, Hildesheim, Kassel, Osnabrück, Konstanz...

Man muß betonen, daß es hier weder um Rangordnung noch um Vollständigkeit gehen kann. Die Reisekataloge sind voll von Namen, und die geläufigsten versperren nicht dem spürigen Alleingänger den Weg zu ungenannten, aber nicht minder anziehenden und nennenswerten Zielen. Wer den Weg moselaufwärts schon einmal gefahren ist, der weiß, was ihn an charaktervoller und einmaliger Landschaft erwartet, denn gerade die Fluß-Siedlungen, zumal wenn das Gewerbe der Weinbauern ihr Schwerpunkt ist, zeichnen sich durch verschwiegene Reize und Besonderheiten aus. Wer des öfteren den Weg nekkaraufwärts nehmen muß oder dem Main entlang reist (er kann dies sogar auf einer Bahnfahrt von Würzburg nach Hanau schon erfahren), der lernt einsehen, daß er da einige der schönsten und intimsten Landschaften wahrnimmt, die nicht umsonst das alte rühmende Lied „Bald gras' ich am Neckar, bald gras' ich am Main..." herausgefordert haben. Wie lange brauchte es, bis ich die Schönheiten des Odenwaldes kennenlernte, der gewissermaßen von den Hauptverkehrsadern umgangen wird. Das alte originale Stelzen-Rathaus von Michelstadt ist nur einer der vielen Reizpunkte, die dieses verschwiegene Mittelgebirge aufweist, das mich immer wieder an meine Heimatlandschaft, den Harz, erinnert, der leider durch eine willkürliche Grenze gehälftet wurde. Aber wer die alte Kaiserstadt Goslar aufsucht, der wird nicht nur einen Hauch der Landschaft, sondern auch unserer Geschichte verspüren. Ob ich an Aschaffenburg denke, an das hochgelegene Wimpfen, an das köstliche Landshut, an gewisse Orte am Niederrhein – nein, es herrscht in dieser Bundesrepublik kein Mangel, weder an reizvoller, abwechslungsreicher Landschaft noch an anziehenden Städten und Städtchen. Wer alle Schönheit aufspüren und anschauen wollte, der wäre für sein halbes Leben vollauf mit Ausflugszielen versorgt.

province so closely, right down to the most remote small town, as I have this rather rashly criticised "Ruhrpott." Very often it is not well-being that determines the status, but rather the need. Or the two.

But above and beyond either size or idyllic attraction, population or economic gravitation, there are possibly towns in the Federal Republic with a hidden power of attraction in which substance and inheritance, type of people and their role in society play interchangeable parts. To these belong such university towns as Würzburg or Münster, Freiburg or Tübingen, Aachen, Heidelberg or Marburg, Darmstadt, Trier, Braunschweig. But even Paderborn, the "old-fashioned" episcopal city, the much tortured and rightly renowned Nuremberg, the charming Fulda, Passau, Bamberg, Hildesheim, Kassel, Osnabrück, Constance...

It must be emphasised that there can be no question here of either order of ranking or completeness. The tourist catalogues are full of names which are commonplace, but this does not prevent the person determined to go his own way and with a feeling for what he wants from finding attractive destinations less known. Anybody who has once travelled up the Mosel knows about the unique landscape filled with character that awaits him. Riverside communities, particularly where wine growing prevails, have countless hidden charms and peculiarities. Anybody repeatedly journeying up the Neckar or along the Rhein (even a run from Würzburg to Hanau is evidence enough) will readily see that he is taking in some of the most beautiful and intimate of landscapes which conjure up thoughts of the old song in their praise "Bald gras' ich am Neckar, bald gras' ich am Main..." (Soon I will "graze" on the Neckar, and soon on the Main...). It was a long time before I got to know of the beauty of the Odenwald, which is to a large extent by-passed by the main traffic routes. The old and original Stelzen-Rathaus (Town Hall on Stilts) in Michelstadt is only one of the many charms of the secluded Mittelgebirge (Central Mountains) which again and again remind me of my homeland, the Harz, now regretfully split in two by an arbitrary frontier. The visitor to the Imperial Town of Goslar will be fascinated not only by the landscape, he will also absorb something of our history. Whether I think of Aschaffenburg, of high-up Wimpfen, of the charms of Landshut or of many spots on the Lower Rhein I am forced to say that our Federal Republic is in no sense lacking in variety of landscape and attractive towns and townships. To discover and experience all this beauty would fill half a lifetime.

Mais peut-être existe t-il encore en R.F.A., indépendamment de leur superficie, de leur population, de leur charme et de leur importance économique, des villes qui séduisent par leur ambiance discrète, leur patrimoine culturel et leur tradition. C'est, bien sûr, le cas de villes universitaires telles que Wurtzbourg, Münster, Fribourg, Tubingen, Aix-la-Chapelle, Heidelberg ou Marbourg bien qu'il y en ait encore beaucoup d'autres. Citons ici Paderborn, ville détruite mais célèbre à juste titre, Fulda, si jolie, Passau, Bamberg, Hildesheim, Kassel, Osnabrück ou Constance...

Et cette énumération certainement incomplète ne tient pas compte d'un ordre de grandeur ou d'importance. Nos dépliants touristiques débordent de noms de villes, de villages et de localités dont les plus connus ne sont pas toujours les plus attrayants. Le voyageur ayant remonté le cours de la Moselle connaît ces sites innombrables aussi charmants que pittoresques cachés dans ces régions fluviales et vinicoles. Il en est de même des touristes remontant peut-être en train le cours du Neckar ou du Main et qui seront surpris de découvrir entre Wurtzbourg et Hanau ce site, un des plus intimes et aussi des plus beaux d'Allemagne fédérale, ayant inspiré au barde sa célèbre ballade : « Tantôt, je me baguenauderai sur le Neckar, tantôt, je me baguenauderai sur le Main... ». Bien trop tard, je fis connaissance des beautés du massif de l'Odenwald, abrité à l'écart des grandes voies de communication.

Le vieil hôtel de ville de Michelstadt avec ses arcades n'est qu'un des nombreux centres d'attraction de cette région qui me rappelle ma contrée natale de ce massif du Harz, malheureusement partagé, lui aussi, par une frontière politique arbitraire.

Qui visite la vieille ville impériale de Goslar ne se retrouvera pas seulement dans un site des plus attrayants mais encore au centre d'un grand passé historique.

Et si je pense à Aschaffenbourg, en Basse-Franconie, comme à Wimpfen, perchée sur les hauteurs, ou à Landshut sur l'Isar ou encore aux nombreuses localités du Bas-Rhin allemand, c'est pour constater que notre République fédérale d'Allemagne ne manque pas de sites, de villes, de localités, de villages plus charmants les uns que les autres. Pour découvrir toutes les beautés de l'Allemagne fédérale, je crois qu'on devrait y consacrer la moitié de sa vie.

Même si son choix en tant que capitale fut d'abord accueilli çà et là avec quelque scepticisme, avec le temps, Bonn ne s'est pas seu-

Auch wenn die Wahl zur Bundeshauptstadt da und dort zunächst mit leiser Skepsis aufgenommen worden sein mag — im Laufe der Jahre hat Bonn, und nicht nur rein äußerlich, durch imponierende neue Bauten, durch neue Straßenanlagen, durch die Folgen der Bundesgartenschau, ein unbestreitbares Format gewonnen — die Stadt ist auch politisch und nicht zuletzt durch die Persönlichkeit führender Staatsmänner, die in ihr wirkten, oder sie zu entscheidenden Gesprächen immer wieder aufsuchen, ganz natürlich zu einem Schwerpunkt erster Ordnung geworden. Es kommt ja nicht — siehe Washington — auf Einwohnerzahlen an, sondern auf Schwerpunkte und Anziehungskraft. Zudem sind Rhein und Siebengebirge eine denkbar gelungene Kulisse für die politische Bühne Bonn.

Berlin ist eine Insel inmitten der DDR. Räumlich getrennt von der Bundesrepublik ist Berlin (West) der Bundesrepublik innerlich verbunden durch demokratisches Bekenntnis und politische Praxis. Es ist in die Rechts-, Wirtschafts-, Finanz-, Währungs- und Sozialordnung der Bundesrepublik integriert. Es wird durch wirtschaftliche Hilfe unterstützt. Das Berlinabkommen der vier Mächte von 1971 brachte eine Reihe von Erleichterungen für die Stadt mit sich. Der Verkehr auf den Straßen, Schienen und Wasserwegen zwischen Berlin (West) und der Bundesrepublik Deutschland hat durch das Abkommen eine sichere Rechtsgrundlage erhalten. Nach dem Grundgesetz ist Berlin (West) ein Land der Bundesrepublik, aber es darf aufgrund der fortbestehenden Viermächtehoheit über Berlin nicht durch den Bund regiert werden. Die Vertreter Berlins im Bundestag und Bundesrat haben nur beratende Stimmen.

Berlin (West), das 481 Quadratkilometer groß ist, sollte nach dem Willen der UdSSR und der DDR, längst „einverleibt" sein; die tragisch bewegten Monate der Berliner „Luftbrücke" sind und werden nicht vergessen. Es ist dem vereinten westlichen Widerstand gelungen, diese Insel der Freiheit lebensfähig zu erhalten, und der Wille, dies fortzusetzen, darf auch nicht angezweifelt werden. Eine andere Frage ist es, ob wirtschaftliche Hilfe allein genügen wird, diese langsam abnehmende 2-Millionen-Stadt auf weite Sicht lebenskräftig und zukunftsträchtig zu erhalten. Nach wie vor ist ihr Charme, ihre Lebendigkeit ungebrochen, und die Anstrengungen, die Stadt durch Neuerungen — zuletzt ein enormes Kongreß-Zentrum — attraktiver und international populärer zu machen, sind beträchtlich. Obgleich wir in Bonn eine durchaus liebenswerte und schon keineswegs mehr provisorische Bundeshauptstadt besitzen, gilt unsere besondere Zuneigung und Sorge der alten Reichshauptstadt Berlin. Wer wären wir auch, wenn wir uns anders verhielten, als sich die

Even if the choice of Bonn was greeted at first with a certain irony, over the years the city has acquired an undisputed eminence, and not only in merely external terms, the result of imposing new buildings, new roads, and the Federal Horticultural Show. The city has grown naturally into a political centre of the first order, not least through the leading statesmen who have been active there or who have repeatedly chosen it for critical negotiations. As the example of Washington shows, it is not the number of inhabitants that matters, but the attractions and institutions having their base there. The Rhein and the Siebengebirge area provide a magnificent setting for the political life of the capital.

Berlin is an island in the middle of the GDR. Separated geographically from the Federal Republic, Berlin (West) remains an inherent part of it by virtue of its commitment to democracy, and its political approach. In terms of its legal, commercial, financial, currency and social system, it is integrated into the Federal Republic, from which it receives economic support. The 1971 Berlin Four-Power Agreement brought a number of improvements to the city: one effect was to lay a secure legal foundation for road, rail and water traffic between Berlin (West) and the Federal Republic of Germany. Under the Fundamental Law, Berlin (West) is a State of the Federal Republic, but the continuation of the Four-Power Administration of the city means that it may not be governed by the Federal Government. The city's representatives in the Bundestag and the Bundesrat have only an advisory capacity.

Berlin (West), with an area of 481 sq. km (185 sq. miles) should, according to the willl of Soviet Russia and East Germany, long since have been "incorporated" into that area. The months of hardship during ther Berlin "Air-Lift" are not, and will never be, forgotten. The resistance of the West has successfully preserved the means of existence of this island of freedom, and there can be no doubt of the will to maintain it. It is another question as to whether or not economic help alone will suffice to maintain this slowly diminishing city of two million people alive and progressive. Its charm and vivacity still remain unbroken and the efforts of the city towards making it more attractive and internationally popular by means of innovations — the latest being a gigantic Congress Centre — are extensive. Although Bonn provides us with an attractive official capital which has long outlived any temporary status, our inclinations and our concern are directed towards the old Reichs Capital Berlin. What could we say for our-

lement affirmée par ses bâtiments et ses nouvelles voies de communication ou les complexes édifiés à l'époque pour la grande exposition horticole : Bonn a acquis un format international. Politiquement comme par la personnalité des hommes d'état qui y œuvrent, qui y séjournent et y reviennent pour discuter des décisions à prendre, la ville de Bonn est devenue un centre politique de première importance dont la valeur ne dépend pas — comme Washington — du chiffre de sa population, mais de ses points cruciaux et de sa fascination. Et le Rhin comme les collines du massif de « Siebengebirge » forment un décor des plus réussis pour ses jeux de scène politiques.

Berlin est un îlot au sein de la R.D.A., bien que Berlin-Ouest dépende de la R.F.A. Et bien qu'aucune frontière commune ne l'y rattache, exception faite du sentiment démocratique de ses habitants et de sa pratique politique, l'ancienne capitale du Reich est intégrée à la R.F.A. par sa législation, son économie, ses finances, sa monnaie et son ordre social. De plus, elle profite d'une aide économique de la part de l'Allemagne fédérale.

Des accords de Berlin conclu en 1971 entre les quatre grandes puissances résulta une amélioration du régime de la partie occidentale de la ville. La circulation par voie routière, fluviale et par chemin de fer entre Berlin-Ouest et la R.F.A. fut désormais soumise à une réglementation basée sur une juridiction bien établie.

D'après notre Constitution, Berlin-Ouest est un « land » de la R.F.A., bien que celle-ci ne puisse le gouverner, en raison de l'exercice de la souveraineté des quatre puissances. Les représentants de Berlin-Ouest auprès du Parlement et du Conseil fédéral allemand à Bonn ne jouissent que d'un statut consultatif.

L'Union soviétique et la R.D.A. auraient voulu depuis longtemps annexer Berlin-Ouest avec ses 481 kilomètres carrés de superficie. La période tragique et agitée du « pont aérien » est et restera toujours inoubliable. La vitalité de cet îlot de liberté a été préservée grâce à l'action commune des puissances alliées occidentales. Et il est indubitable que cette volonté est un gage d'avenir. Une autre question est cependant de savoir si l'aide économique apportée par la R.F.A. suffira à conserver à l'avenir la puissance vitale de cette ville dont le chiffre de deux millions d'habitants va en décroissant. Berlin-Ouest conserve toujours le charme et l'agitation légendaires de l'ancienne capitale allemande et les efforts de sa municipalité pour augmenter son attractivité et sa popularité internationales sont remar-

Franzosen oder Engländer verhalten würden, wenn man ihnen ihr geliebtes Paris, ihr London wegnehmen oder teilen würde?! Und wie würden sich die Italiener im gleichen Falle ihrer traditionsträchtigen Metropole Rom gegenüber verhalten?

Man darf dieser Frage wohl ihren rhetorischen Charakter belassen. Man soll Selbstverständliches nicht zerreden.

Übrigens sollte man, wenn man von Berlin und seinen Vozügen spricht, keinesfalls verschweigen, daß es, von märkischen Seen umgeben, auch landschaftlich außerordentlich begünstigt ist. Ich habe als Student Monate hindurch im Zelt an der Löcknitz gelebt und die fast alle miteinander verbundenen Seen abge„kleppert" im Faltboot, was ein unvergessenes Erlebnis war, das in größerem Stil wohl nur durch eine Fahrt über die verlorengegangenen ostpreußischen oder Masurischen Seen übertroffen wurde. Wassersport und Dampferausflüge wurden in Berlin immer groß geschrieben.

Ein vergleichbares, freilich weitmaschigeres Wasserparadies gibt es da wohl nur noch in Oberbayern, wo die großen Seen dem Alpengebirge weiter vorgelagert und dafür ausufernder angelegt sind, während die eigentlichen Gebirgsseen eben beschränkteren Ausmaßes, aber dafür mit besonderen landschaftlichen Überraschungen ausgestattet sind. Wasser und Gebirge ergeben fast immer kontrastreiche Szenarien — auch die Flüsse haben daran ihren Anteil.

Wenn wir von den strömenden Gewässern den (Vater) Rhein zuerst erwähnen, so gewiß nicht aus hergebrachten patriotischen Gründen, sondern weil er, ab Konstanz gerechnet, ja mit 865 Kilometer Flußlauf im Lande immer noch der größte deutsche Strom ist. Von Elbe und Oder, die etwa 100 Kilometer weniger Weges ins Meer benötigen, gehört uns von der ersteren ein kurzes Stück in unserem Bereich, und die deutsche Donau muß sich mit 647 Kilometer begnügen. Aber wem müßte man sagen, daß der Rhein zwischen Köln und Mainz auf weite Strecken hin (die man sogar mit der Bundesbahn abgelten kann!) ein wirklich „mitreißender" Strom ist? Mit seinen immer wieder einander ablösenden Hügeln und Vorbergen bildet er eine Wasserstraße von immer wieder fesselnder Gestalt. Namhafte Burgen krönen Höhenzüge und Vorsprünge, deren Namen — wie die Loreley — nicht nur in die Landschaftsprospekte Eingang gefunden haben. Wer den Fluß wirklich kennt von seinem schweizerischen Oberlauf durchs Gebirge her, durch den Bodensee dann und danach — über idyllische alte Siedlungen wie Stein am Rhein — über Schaffhausen in den

selves if we did not feel just like the French or the English would if somebody were to deprive them of their beloved Paris or London, or partition them? And what would be the reaction of the Italians if their tradition-rich metropolis Rome were to suffer a like fate?

May this question remain a purely rhetorical one. The obvious should not be torn apart word by word.

By the way, in speaking of Berlin and its assets its must not be forgotten that its aspect, surrounded by the "märkisch" lakes, boasts a variety of charming landscape. As a student I spent months in the Locknitz area in a tent and "explored" most of the interconnected lakes in a portable boat, an unforgettable experience surpassed only by a journey through the lakes of East Prussia, of which we have long since been deprived. Aquatic sports and pleasure-boat excursions have always been big items on the Berlin programme.

Only Upper Bavaria is able to offer a comparative, albeit far more comprehensive, aquatic paradise, where the large lakes have a background of alpine masses often forming their very banks, although the mountain lakes as such are more limited in area and, possibly as a result, far more full of surprises in the form of bewitching scenery. Water and mountains almost always give rise to contrasts in the scenery — the rivers too lend their share. If, in speaking of flowing waters, we refer to (Father) Rhein right at the start, this is certainly not out of time honoured patriotic motives, but simply because its course within Germany, starting at Constance, covers some 540 miles, making it the longest German river. Of the Elbe and the Oder, whose routes to the sea are some 60 miles shorter only a short stretch of the former belongs to our territory, and the German stretch of the Danube covers only 400 miles. But who needs to be told that on long stretches of the Rhein between Mainz and Cologne (along which the railway runs) it is little short of entrancing? With its ever changing hills and outcrops it is a waterway that cannot fail to excite the imagination. Its heights and cliffs are crowned by castles of renown — the Loreley is just one example — and such names are more than just a part of travel prospectuses. Anybody who is really familiar with the river, who knows it from its Swiss source, through the mountains and through Lake Constance, past idyllic old townships such as Stein am Rhein and through Schaffhausen into the German area, also knows that this river has not gained its reputation for nothing.

quables. Citons, entre autres, le Centre de Congrès inauguré il y a quelques années. Néanmoins, et bien que Bonn soit une capitale charmante ayant perdu son caractère de provisoire, notre amour tout particulier et nos soucis vont vers l'ancienne capitale du Reich. En effet, que deviendrait notre valeur morale si nous nous comportions autrement que les Français ou les Britanniques, supposition faite que Paris ou Londres soit partagés entre plusieurs puissances étrangères. Et quelle serait la réaction du peuple italien vis-à-vis de Rome, en pareil cas ?

Il faut, bien sûr, laisser à cette question sa valeur rhétorique et ne pas aveulir l'évidence.

Parler de Berlin et de ses beautés, n'est pas possible sans évoquer celle des lacs de la Marche de Brandebourg qui entourent la ville. Jeune étudiant, j'ai passé des mois à camper sur les rives de la Loecknitz pour sillonner en canot tous ces lacs généralement reliés les uns aux autres. J'en ai gardé un souvenir inoubliable que seules les excursions sur les lacs de Prusse orientale ou de Mazurie, cette Poméranie masovienne, tous territoires allemands désormais perdus, peuvent peut-être encore surpasser. Les Berlinois qui se sont toujours consacrés avec plaisir aux sports nautiques aiment particulièrement les excursions en bateau.

Seuls les lacs de Haute-Bavière, au pied des Alpes, offrent pareils plaisirs nautiques sur un territoire encore plus étendu tandis que les lacs de montagne, de dimensions plus modestes, attendent l'amateur en lui réservant la surprise de paysages encore plus pittoresques où les pièces d'eau forment contraste avec les massifs montagneux.

Le Rhin occupe certainement la première place des fleuves dont il faut encore parler. Non pas par patriotisme ou par chauvinisme, mais parce qu'avec son parcours de 865 kilomètres en R.F.A., à partir de Constance, il est le plus grand des fleuves allemands. Seule une minime partie du cours de l'Elbe et de l'Oder, qui comptent une centaine de kilomètres de moins avant de se jeter dans la mer, passe par notre territoire et le Danube ne parcourt que 647 kilomètres en Allemagne. Il est superflu de parler de la majesté du Rhin entre Mayence et Cologne. On peut même longer son cours en train. Encaissée entre monts et collines, cette voie navigable fascine par la variété de ses paysages. De célèbres châteaux-forts la surplombent et ses saillies, telles la « Loreley », ne jouissent pas seulement de la publicité des dépliants touristiques. Ceux ayant parcouru le fleuve

deutschen Bereich, der weiß, daß dieser Strom seinen besonderen Ruf nicht umsonst erhalten hat.

Es soll nicht übersehen sein, daß hier nicht das Wasser allein den Weg in Sage und Ruhm bestimmt hat. Wie an der Mosel, deren Schönheit schon gerühmt wurde, reifen ja auch an den Höhenzügen, durch die der Rhein seinen Weg nimmt, köstliche Rebsorten, und wer den ausgegorenen Rebensaft zum täglichen Wirk- und Werkstoff seines Lebens erkor, der weiß recht gut, wie viele „Blumen" und „Lagen" dort wachsen und weshalb die Weine, die von hier kommen, in ihrer günstigsten Gestalt Weltruf genießen. Das gilt auch für die Mosel und die Saar. Und auch am Neckar wächst ein *guter Tropfen*, den die haushälterischen Schwaben freilich lieber selbst trinken. An der Nahe reifen achtbare Weine und wo der Rhein den Bogen um den Kaiserstuhl macht ebenso. Und wenn wir an den vielleicht interessantesten See unserer Bundesrepublik denken, den ebenso als Grenze wie als Brücke angelegten Bodan- oder (jetzt) Bodensee, den der junge Rhein durchfließt, so tragen auch die diese Gewässer umhügelnden Hänge einen achtbaren Wein.

Auch der Frankenwein kann sich weitgehend des Geleites von einem anziehenden Gewässer erfreuen; aber in der von Mosel und Rhein umgrenzten Pfalz gibt es zahllose Lagen und Weinberge, die ohne „Wasser" zu Kehlen und Ansehen kommen. Auf jeden Fall füllt der Südwesten unserer Bundesrepublik die Keller mit edelsten und trinkenswerten Sorten, welche um Freunde und Genießer in aller Welt nicht bangen müssen.

Doch daß wir das fließende Wasser im Zusammenhang mit dem flüssigen Silber, dem Wein, und einer schönen Landschaft rühmten, soll uns nicht hindern, auch gewisser Ströme und Gewässer zu gedenken, die ihren Reiz nur aus der Landschaft beziehen, wie etwa der Werra und Weser, der Altmühl, der Isar, des Lechs, des Inn, um nur einige beim Namen zu nennen. Dazu gibt es noch mehr oder weniger stehende Gewässer, die des Menschen Hand in mancher dafür empfänglichen Geographie der Landschaft abgewonnen oder auferlegt hat: gewisse Talsperren und Seen, die zwar keine Parade-Landschaften bewirkt haben, aber bei näherem Zusehen doch von eigenem Reiz sein können. Wer kennt die Biggetalsperre, die Okertalsperre, den Möhnesee, die Aggertalsperre, den Rurstausee in der Eifel...? Wer die westfälischen Wasserschlösser? Wenn die Namen Anholt oder Mespelbrunn genannt sind, so ist damit nur eine Andeutung gegeben. Und manche Gewässer haben sehr verschiedene Gesichter — man sehe nur den

The fact should also not be overlooked that it is not alone the water that has given rise to its legends and its fame. Just the same as on the Mosel, whose beauty has already been extolled, superlative vines grow on the steep slopes of the Rhein's banks, and those who have made the acquaintance of the fermented juices they yield an who has taken them to his heart as a daily stimulant and sustenance knows very well the number of bouquets and vintages the area yields and why the wines it gives up have come to enjoy world status and renown. Of course, this also holds for the Mosel and the Saar, and the Neckar too yields a fine grape, which the economical Swabians prefer to keep to themselves. A grape worthy of mention also grows on the Nahe, as well as at the point where the Rhein curves round the "Kaiserstuhl". And when our thoughts turn to the possibly most interesting lake in our Federal Republic, which fills the role of both a frontier and a link, namely Lake Constance, through which the "young" Rhein flows, we recall the fact that its sloping banks also yield a noteworthy wine. Franconian wine too enjoys the proximity of many waterways, although in the Palatinate, bordered by the Mosel and the Rhein, there are countless vineyards which have won fame and distinction without the aid of "water". At all events, the South West of our Federal Republic fills the wine cellars with the most aristrocatic and notable types which do not lack friends and connoisseurs in all parts of the world.

But the fact that we have praised running water, aristocratic wine and a beautiful landscape in terms of an entity should not prevent us thinking of certain other waterways which owe their charm of the landscape alone, as for example the Werra, the Weser, the Altmühl, the Isar, the Lech and the Inn, to name only a few. And then there are waters which are more or less still, which owe their existence to the hand of man in places favoured by geography, in other words reservoirs and artificial lakes which, although they have failed to give rise to outstanding examples of scenic beauty, certainly have their own attractions. Who is familiar with the Biggetalsperre, the Okertalsperre, the Möhnesee, the Aggertalsperre or the Rurstausee in the Eifel? Who has made the acquaintance of the Westphalian castles in the water? Hints of these are the names Anholt and Mespelbrunn. Many waters can also show very different faces — one need only to see the Black Forest Titisee in its summer and its winter garb! And anybody who was fortunate enough to witness the big 1963 freeze-up on Lake Constance experienced an event of the century.

depuis le Haut-Rhin helvétique, traversé avec lui le Lac de Constance, passé les vieilles agglomérations rhénanes de Stein ou Schaffhouse pour pénétrer ensuite en territoire allemand, savent que la réputation de beauté de ses sites est méritée.

Bien sûr, ce n'est pas seulement le fleuve qui a inspiré la légende et l'a rendue célèbre. De même que, sur les hauteurs des rives de la Moselle et de la Sarre, déjà évoquées précédemment, des vignobles aux noms célèbres s'élèvent en bordure et s'étendent les amateurs de vin y retrouvent des coteaux mondialement réputés. N'oublions pas non plus le Neckar avec ses vins caractéristiques, plutôt consommés sur place par une population souabe réputée pour ses vertus d'économie.

Autres régions vinicoles allemandes bien connues : la Nahe, la région volcanique de la boucle du Rhin près de Kaiserstuhl, le Lac de Constance, un des plus remarquables de la R.F.A., qui fait frontière avec la Suisse et l'Autriche, la Franconie, profitant elle aussi des fleuves et rivières qui la traversent, ou le Palatinat, encaissé entre Rhin et Moselle, avec des vins de haute qualité. C'est tout le Sud-Ouest de la R.F.A. qui produit pareils vins exportés dans le monde entier.

Ces considérations sur des thèmes vinicoles ne doivent pas nous faire oublier les cours d'eau dont le charme naît des sites qu'ils traversent comme la Werra et la Weser, l'Altmuehl, l'Isar, le Lech ou l'Inn, pour ne citer que ceux-ci, sans oublier un certain nombre de plans d'eau, de lacs artificiels et de barrages, qui n'enrichissant peut-être pas toujours la beauté des sites environnants, possèdent cependant souvent un charme particulier. Qui ne connaît pas les barrages de Biggetal, de Okertal, de Aggertal, de « Moehnesee », ou de « Rurstausee », dans le massif de l'Eifel... ? Ou les splendides castels d'eau de Westphalie ? Les châteaux de Anholt ou de Mespelbrunn n'en sont que deux parmi tant d'autres. Et tous ces lacs et étangs aux visages cent fois différents ? Comme le lac de « Titisee » en Forêt-Noire avec ses aspects estival et hivernal. Ceux ayant admiré le spectacle d'un Lac de Constance gelé, au cours de l'hiver 1963, furent témoins d'un événement séculaire.

La situation géographique de la R.F.A. en Europe centrale la dote d'une grande richesse en paysages et végétation. Les étés verts des massifs de la Rhön, du Harz, du Hunsrück ou du Sauerland contrastent avec des hivers blancs, plus rares, ces dernières dizaines d'années.

Titisee im sommerlichen und dann im winterlichen Schwarzwald! Und wer die große Seegefrörne 1963 des Bodensees miterlebte, der hatte teil an einem Jahrhundertereignis.

Überhaupt schenkt uns die mitteleuropäische Lage eine immer wieder überraschende Vielfalt landschaftlicher Reize. Die grünen Sommer in der Rhön, im Harz, im Hunsrück, im Sauerland und anderen Mittelgebirgen haben nicht selten ihre kontrastreiche Entsprechung in den weißen Wintern (auch wenn diese in den beiden letzten Jahrzehnten etwas kürzer bemessen waren). Und wenn man von der Augenweide absieht und es vor allem auf eine Sport-Weide abgesehen hat, dann ist zwar der bayrische Süden, das Alpenvorland, durchaus bevorzugt; aber wenn die „Saison" leidlich ausfällt, haben es auch die Hannoveraner und die Frankfurter nicht allzu weit in den Schnee. Nein, an landschaftlichen Reizen und Varianten mangelt es dieser Bundesrepublik durchaus nicht. Und dort, wo die Landschaft zu längerem Verweilen oder gar zu ständigem Wohnen einlädt, fehlt es auch nicht an weltlichen oder kirchlichen Zieraten: an Schlössern, Rast- und Gasthäusern, an Klöstern und Kirchen. Man muß nicht bayrischer König sein, um in dieser Richtung unternehmend zu sein; auch in anderen Landen und Städten hat man fürstlich oder königlich gebaut. Und wenn wir die Wies nennen oder die Birnau, dann wird uns bewußt, daß auch die kirchlichen Herren und Baumeister es recht gut verstanden, der irdischen Drangsal himmlische Seiten abzugewinnen.

Um jedoch — wie man es volksmündlich oder volksmundig ausdrückt — die Kirche im Dorf zu lassen (wenn es auch nicht die Birnau oder die Wies sein muß), müssen wir nun freilich auf eine sehr nüchterne, reale, gelegentlich bei allen Vorteilen und Vorzügen nachteilige Seite unserer modernen Existenz zu sprechen kommen, die uns nicht wenig „irdische Drangsal" beschert, *uns* und der Natur, in die unser Dasein eingebettet ist: die enorm anwachsende Industrie, die nicht nur unserer Bundesrepublik, sondern auch anderen europäischen Staaten das Kennwort „Industriestaat" eingetragen hat.

Niemand wird auf die Idee kommen, den wirtschaftlichen Aufschwung, der sich bis in die siebziger Jahre fortsetzte und unseren Bürgern unerwarteten Wohlstand schenkte, zu verlästern. Aber jeder weiß inzwischen, daß dieser Gewinn mit Einbußen anderer Art erkauft oder zumindest mitbezahlt werden mußte. Denn wenn wir heute von schönen Flußlandschaften oder von einem imponierenden Rheinstrom reden, so weiß beinahe jedermann, daß in vielen Flüssen die Fische nicht mehr leben und noch nicht sterben können, daß ein einfaches Flußbad den Badenden

The Central European location bestows on us a rich scenic variety that surprises us again and again with its charms. The "green" summers in the Rhön, in the Harz, in the Hunsrück, the Sauerland and other central ranges very often present a glowing white contrast in the white of winter (even though the last two decades have yielded less than usual). And quite apart from scenic beauty as such and more a matter of the sports scene, then the south of Bavaria, the alpine outcrops, certainly has the pull. When the "crop" of snow is poor, winter sport's enthusiasts in Frankfurt or Hanover have to travel fair distances. It bears repeating: this Federal Republic is not lacking in scenic attractions and variety. And where the scenic charms are such as to encourage a long stay, or even a permanent abode there is also no lack of worldly or ecclesiastic embellishments; schlosses, inns and hotels, monasteries and churches. Not only the Bavarian Kings were active in this way, regal edifices also abound in other states and cities. And if we mention the Wies or the Birnau we instantly realise that even those who dictated the construction of churches, as well as their architects, well understood how to combine the heavenly urge with an earthy approach.

However, leaving the church in the village — as the German colloquialism puts it — we are now forced to turn to a very sober, down-to-earth and, in spite of all its assets and advantages, disadvantageous aspect of our modern existence which is intimately linked with "earthy" aspirations. It affects both ourselves and nature, which after all is deeply rooted in our very existence. This is the enormous advance of industry which not only in the Federal Republic, but also in other European countries has led to the term "industrial nation".

Nobody would dream of condemning the economic upswing whitch continued right into the seventies and brought our citizens such unawaited good fortune. But everybody now knows that this advance had to be bought, at least in part, by means of sacrifices of another sort. For when we speak today of beautiful or impressive river landscapes such as the Rhein almost all of use are aware of the fact that the fish in a great many rivers are at the point of extinction, that a simple dip in a river can be a danger to the health and that the reservoirs, often coping with the needs of half a province, are becoming ever more difficult to maintain at the level of purity compatible with human needs. In areas of industrial concentration even our daily living conditions have been influenced. The words "protection of the environment", often reduced simply to "environment", are now among the most used terms in our everyday vocabulary. They have even led to a

Abstraction faite de la beauté de ce spectacle, les amateurs de sports d'hiver de la Bavière méridionale sont favorisés dans les régions des préalpes bien que, si la saison est propice, bien sûr, les habitants de Francfort-sur-le-Main ou de Hanovre ne soient pas, eux non plus, beaucoup éloignés de la neige.

Non, notre République ne manque pas de sites aussi variés qu'empreints de charme. Et là où le paysage invite à un séjour plus prolongé ou même à demeure, jamais ne manquent les monuments d'art séculiers comme religieux, les châteaux, les abbayes, couvents, monastères, églises, restaurants et hôtels. Les rois de Bavière ne furent pas les seuls à enrichir leur pays de monuments culturels et de splendides résidences princières. Evoquons ici les églises de Wies ou de Birnau pour mieux prendre conscience de la splendeur de l'art architectural des maîtres d'œuvre comme des princes de l'Eglise des époques révolues.

Mais il nous faut, pour employer cette expression quelque peu triviale, « laisser l'église au milieu du village », même s'il ne s'agit pas de celles de Wies ou de Birnau, et évoquer encore les aspects, avantages et désavantages de notre vie moderne, nos soucis comme la menace croissante de pollution de l'environnement, non seulement en R.F.A. mais aussi dans tous les pays européens industrialisés.

Il ne viendra à l'idée de personne de dénigrer cet essor économique dont nous avons profité jusqu'au début des années soixante-dix et d'où nacquit l'aisance dont jouissent les citoyens de la R.F.A. Et cependant, nous savons, entretemps, comment se présente son bilan en profits et pertes dont il nous faut maintenant acquitter la facture. Car si nous évoquons la beauté de nos sites fluviaux comme celle de la vallée du Rhin, nous n'ignorons pas, en général, que les conditions de vie des poissons de nombreux cours d'eau ne sont plus tenables et qu'une simple baignade dans nos rivières ou dans nos fleuves peut entraîner de graves conséquences pour la santé et qu'il devient toujours plus difficile de dépolluer les eaux des réservoirs et châteaux d'eau qui desservent certaines régions. Parallèlement, les conditions de vie dans les régions industrielles subissent l'influence de cette pollution générale et les expressions « protection de l'environnement » et « environnement » — sont devenues des plus usuelles de nos jours ayant même réussi à secouer une certaine léthargie des partis politiques traditionnels. Le

oder seine Gesundheit gefährden würde, daß Wasser-Reservoire für halbe Provinzen immer schwieriger und mühsamer auf jenem Reinheitsgrad gehalten werden können, auf den der Mensch angewiesen bleibt, wenn er nicht Schaden nehmen will. Auch unsere alltäglichen Lebensumstände sind in Gegenden, wo sich Industrieunternehmen häufen, nicht verschont geblieben – das Stichwort „Umweltschutz" oder nur „Umwelt" gehört zu den meistgebrauchten Vokabeln unserer Tage und hat selbst das für stabil geltende und eingefahrene Parteiengefüge etwas in Bewegung gebracht. Die Partei der sogenannten Grünen hat ihre Wurzeln ebenso in ernster Besorgnis wie in erwachtem Widerstandswillen. Und da sich die ersten warnenden Stimmen schon vor einem Vierteljahrhundert erhoben, ist es eigentlich erstaunlich, daß Vorsorge und Kontrolle so lange auf sich warten ließen. Inzwischen hat auch der Staat, haben Länder und Kommunen ihre Verantwortlichkeit erkannt und paraphiert, so daß man annehmen darf, daß zumindest den elementaren Notwendigkeiten entsprochen werden wird. Und das ist gut und notwendig so; denn wenn wir die Berufsanteile unserer Bürger in der Bundesrepublik an den wichtigsten Einkommensquellen erfragen, dürfte sich herausstellen, daß nahezu zwei Drittel unserer Berufstätigen in der industriellen Wirtschaft – Fabrikation, Handel, Verkehr – und von ihr existieren. Kaum mehr als jeder Achtzehnte arbeitet in der Land- und Forstwirtschaft, und einen Anteil von etwa 30 Prozent haben die freien Berufe, Sozialberufe und Verwaltungskräfte.

Daran dürfte sich in absehbarer Zukunft auch kaum etwas ändern, selbst wenn da und dort einmal Krisenalarm in der Wirtschaft gegeben wird, wofür nicht in jedem Fall europäische oder eigene Probleme Sorge tragen. Denn wir sind – nicht zuletzt durch unseren immensen Energiebedarf – auch von manchen risikoträchtigen Geschäftspartnern in der weiten Welt abhängiger geworden als uns lieb sein kann: Die achtziger Jahre dürften uns gewiß noch manche Überraschung und manches Kopfzerbrechen in dieser oder jener Hinsicht bereiten.

Wenn wir keine Wolkenkuckucksheimer und keine utopischen Wunschdenker sind, müssen wir uns der technischen Wirklichkeit sachlich stellen und uns bewußt machen, daß hier die Quellen und Ressourcen unserer Kraft, unseres Wohlstands, unserer internationalen Konkurrenzfähigkeit liegen. Es sind zudem „Quellen", die zum größeren Teil schon seit langem „sprudeln", Konsequenzen und Umsetzungen erfolgreicher Wissenschaftlichkeit, Ergebnisse von Denkprozessen, an denen Generationen von Forschern und Praktikern mitwirkten und deren Einsichten und Fortschritte Anteil haben an dem fantasti-

disruption of our hitherto solid and stable parliamentary party system in the shape of the so-called "green" party, which has its roots in serious concern over the problems and an awakened determination to resist. In the light of the fact that the first warning voices made themselves heard a quarter-of-a-century ago it is a surprising thing that protection and control took such a long time to emerge.

In the meantime the Central Government, the States and the local communities have recognized and set out their area of responsibility, so that it may now be assumed that the elementary necessities will be accommodated. And this is right and proper, since a poll of the occupations and major sources of income among the citizens of the Federal Republic would surely demonstrate the fact that close on two thirds of them are active in the industrial economy, in manufacture, trade and transport and that these provide their livelihood. Scarcely more than one eighth of them work in agriculture and forestry, and around 30 per cent belong to the professions, social services and the administrative sector.

Scarcely any changes in this are likely in the foreseeable future, even though alarms signals are now and again to be heard from various sectors of the economy, which are not always soluble at either European or national level. Due in no small measure to our dependence on trading partners throughout the world who in themselves constitute greater risks than we would like. The eighties will doubtlessly provide many a surprise and many a headache in one connection or the other.

If we are not to go chasing the pie in the sky - and if we are not to become utopian wishful thinkers, we have to take a cold-blooded view of technical realities and recognize the fact that these are both the sources and resources of our strength, our well-being and our international competitiveness. They are also "wells" that have been rising for a long, long time — for the greater part — the results and the transformation into practice of scientific effort, of thought processes pursued for generations by researchers and practicians whose insight and whose share in the forward march have led to the fantastic level of technology that has bestowed on us such great benefits which, although they have become thoughtlessly taken for granted, are in reality superb achievements of human intuition and the ability to associate ideas.

nouveau parti des écologistes, en R.F.A., les « verts », tente de profiter de cet état de fait en jouant cette carte. Bien que les premiers avertissements se firent déjà entendre il y a plus d'un quart de siècle, il semble étonnant que des mesures préventives et de contrôle aient été envisagées aussi tardivement. L'Etat comme les « länder » et les communes ont entretemps pris conscience de leurs responsabilités et les premières mesures nécessaires devraient répondre tout au moins à certaines nécessités primordiales, d'autant plus qu'en examinant la structure professionnelle de la R.F.A., nous constatons que près de deux tiers des travailleurs sont employés dans les différents secteurs de l'économie industrielle : fabrication, distribution et communications. Un peu plus d'un travailleur sur dix-huit travaille en R.F.A. dans l'agriculture ou dans le secteur forestier tandis que les professions libérales, sociales et administratives représentent environ 30% de la population active de la R.F.A.

Cette structure professionnelle ne devrait pas subir de modifications importantes dans un avenir plus ou moins proche, même si l'économie allemande se verrait sujette à quelque grave crise résultant ou non de problèmes propres ou se posant à l'échelon européen. De fait, nous dépendons économiquement, non seulement dans le secteur énergétique, de certains partenaires présentant des risques imprévus.

Les années quatre-vingt nous réservent certainement encore quelques surprises et problèmes plutôt mal avenus.

Nous ne pourrons éviter de vivre d'illusions ou d'utopies, qu'en affrontant objectivement les réalités technologiques. Nous devons en prendre conscience afin de comprendre qu'elle est la source de notre puissance économique, de notre prospérité et de notre aptidude concurrentielle, une source nous confrontant depuis longtemps déjà aux conséquences et aux problèmes des secteurs d'applications scientifiques, des résultats de le recherche sur laquelle des générations de savants et de praticiens se sont penchés et dont nacquirent des merveilles techniques devenues pour nous banalité quotidienne.

Nous pourrions établir une longue liste de noms, non seulement d'entreprises ou d'industriels responsables de réalisations, mais aussi de savants et de chercheurs dont certains doivent à leurs succès de se retrouver parmi les lauréats du prix Nobel et que la plu-

schen Stand der Technik, welche uns Errungenschaften beschert hat, die zwar dem Gedankenlosen zur alltäglichen Selbstverständlichkeit geworden sein mögen, die aber in Wahrheit Höchstleistungen menschlicher Intuition und Kombinationsgabe sind.

Es gibt große und vielgenannte Namen, die da erwähnt werden müßten — nicht nur von Unternehmen und Unternehmern, sondern auch von Forschern und Experimentatoren (deren erfolgreichste auch in die Liste der Nobelpreisträger Aufnahme gefunden haben) — sie sind wohl den meisten Bürgern bekannt. Manche dieser weltbekannten Unternehmen sind untrennbar mit Städten oder Großstädten verbunden, deren Gesicht und Gestalt sie zu einem bedeutenden Teil mitgeprägt haben, andere wieder mit gewissen Landschaften oder ganzen Provinzen. Wenn ihrer gerechterweise in diesem Band gebührend Erwähnung getan wird, so überrascht die zwar nicht neue, aber doch oft genug übersehene Tatsache, daß Technik — zumindest im Blickwinkel einer künstlerisch oder fantastisch programmierten Kamera — unerwartete Effekte auslöst, die in diesem so sachlichen Bezirk von vielen nicht vermutet werden dürften. Diese Höhepunkte, zusammen mit der summarischen Realität, ergeben erst die eigentliche „Wahrheit" und vermitteln, jenseits von Tendenz und Theorie, ein Bild der Großmacht Technik, wie es in dieser Art selten gesehen wurde. Eine petrochemische Anlage, ein Braunkohlenabbau, ein Hüttenwerk, die Anlage einer Erdefunkstelle, eine nächtliche Werk-Silhouette ... — was unterscheidet sie im Grunde von einem Stadtspektrum, von dem nächtlichen Hafen, der romantischen Mühle, wenn nur ein künstlerisch beseeltes und geschultes Auge sie wirklich entdeckt, das heißt: die diesen Themen insgeheim innewohnenden Anziehungspunkte freilegt? „Schönheit" ist kein Reservat für Landschaften oder Frauenkörper oder Blumensträuße — sie wohnt in einer Straße, in einer Geste der Arbeit oder des Festes, in einer Kirche, einem Radioteleskop, einem Sportstadion. Ihr sind keine Erscheinungen und Einrichtungen vorenthalten. Wenn dies noch eines Beweises bedurft hätte, so würde ihn dieser Bildband geliefert haben, ohne darauf aus zu sein.

Natürlich mußten wir dem Gesamtphänomen Bundesrepublik bei allem Bemühen um Vielseitigkeit einiges schuldig bleiben. Kultur zum Beispiel ist schwieriger ins Bild zu nehmen als Landschaft; Sport wiederum ist in der Bewegung zu Haus und widersetzt sich dem statischen Kommando; Politik ist nur zum Teil durch einzelne Personen darstellbar. Und gehören zum Gesicht der Bundesrepublik nicht auch die Millionen Gesichter ihrer Bürger?

Aber dies eben kennzeichnet die Grenze, die jedem Unterfangen gleicher Art gesetzt ist:

There are many great and oft-quoted names — not only those of undertakings and entrepreneurs, but also of researchers and experimentalists (the most successful of which belong in the lists of Nobel Prizewinners) — which are worthy of mention. They are known to most people. Many of the world-renowned undertakings are indisolubly associated with towns and cities whose faces they have helped to fashion. Others are associated with specific areas or whole provinces. If the latter are to receive the recognition they deserve in these circles, the by no means newly discovered yet olten overlooked fact that technology, at least as seen through le lens of a camera focussed on that which is artistic or sensational, gives rise to unexpected effects which, in this basically factual area, had never been anticipated by a great many people. These highlights, together with the sum of reality, lead to the "truth" as such and above and beyond simple theory, provide a picture of technology as a major power, in a role in which it is seldom viewed. A petrochemical plant, open-cast lignite workings, a steel mill, a ground communications station a nighttime silhouette of a factory ... what is the basic difference between these and a panoramic view of a town, a dockland by night or a romantic windmill when they are discovered by the artistically trained eye, in other words the sort of vision that penetrates into their innermost being and reveals their attractions? "Beauty" is in no manner the preserve of landscapes, the female body or vases of flowers. It is to be encountered on the street in a gesture at work or at play, in a church, a radio-telescope or a sports stadium. There are no manifestations or institutions in which it is not to be found. If there is any further need of proof of this it is surely to be found in this picture volume without having been in any way contrived.

However hard we may try to deal with all the aspects we cannot aspire to achieving an all-embracing picture of the phenomenon "Federal Republic". It is, for example, far more difficult to illustrate culture than scenery, sport relies on movement and is stubbornly opposed to that which is static, politics can be illustrated only in part, and then by way of individual personalities. And are not the millions of faces of its citizens a part of the overall picture of the Federal Republic?

But this demonstrates the limits imposed on any undertaking of this nature. No two faces are alike — alone the forehead the nose, the cheeks, the mouth or the chin will differ. What is today considered "typical" might tomorrow have become a banal and distorted cliché. What are in fact the hallmarks of a Frenchman, a Swiss, an Englishman or Dane ... ?

part de nos lecteurs devraient connaître. La raison sociale de certaines de ces entreprises connues dans le monde entier sont inséparables des noms de villes et même de grandes villes de la R.F.A. qu'elles ont marquées tandis que d'autres influencent de façon décisive certains sites et régions ou même des provinces entières. Et si, objectivement, il est fait mention de ces entreprises et de ces industriels dans cet ouvrage, il paraît parfois surprenant qu'une réalité, bien que déjà traditionnelle, passe souvent inaperçue : la technique, tout au moins vue sous l'angle d'une caméra artistiquement ou fantastiquement programmée, déclenche des effets tout à fait inattendus dans ces secteurs pratiques. C'est de la confrontation de ces facteurs prédominants que ressort la « vérité » essentielle, au delà de toute tendance et théorie, une image de la puissance de la technologie telle qu'on ne la voit que très rarement. Des installations pétrochimiques, une mine d'extraction de lignite, une fonderie, un émetteur de radio-télégraphie, la silhouette nocturne d'une usine ... Y a-t-il une différence entre ces images et celles de l'ombre d'une ville, d'un port dans la nuit, du romantisme d'un moulin à vent que découvre le réalisme d'un œil d'artiste ? La beauté ne réside pas seulement dans un site, dans un acte féminin ou dans un bouquet de fleurs. Elle ressort d'une rue, d'un geste au travail ou d'une fête comme d'une église, du design d'un radiotéléscope comme d'un stade de sport. Elle ne se réserve aucune exclusivité. Et s'il le fallait encore le prouver, cet ouvrage le démontrerait bien que se ne soit son but.

Il ne nous est naturellement pas possible d'évoquer ici le phénomène R.F.A. dans son entité. Ses aspects culturels sont beaucoup plus difficiles à présenter par l'image qu'un simple paysage. Le sport, lui, se caractérise par le mouvement et ignore l'instantané. La politique n'est que partiellement explicable par des personnages. Et cependant, les millions de visages des habitants de la R.F.A. n'en sont-ils pas un de ses aspects ?

Ces quelques exemples nous font apparaître les limites de pareille entreprise : il n'existe pas deux visages identiques bien que tous se composent normalement d'un nez, d'une bouche, de deux yeux, de deux oreilles, d'un menton et de deux joues. Ce qu'on qualifie encore aujourd'hui de « typique » peut n'être plus demain qu'un cliché banal et faussé. Quelles sont les caractéristiques d'un Français, d'un Suisse, d'un Anglais ou d'un Danois ... ?

Pour le dire tout de go : Je ne connais pas d'Allemand typique et, certains types ethniques marginaux mis à part, je pense aux Sici-

Keine zwei Gesichter sind einander gleich – wiewohl jedes sich auf Stirn, Nase, Wangen, Mund und Kinn beschränkt sieht. Was heute noch als „typisch" gilt, könnte morgen schon ein banales und verfälschtes Klischee sein. Welche kennzeichnenden Merkmale hat ein Franzose, ein Schweizer, ein Engländer, ein Däne...?

Um es unverblümt zu sagen: Ich sehe keinen typischen Deutschen, und von gewissen an den Rändern lebenden Exponenten anderer Völker abgesehen – ich denke an Sizilianer, Türken oder Norweger –, scheinen mir die Prototypen immer weniger und weniger zu werden. Der zweite Weltkrieg hat den Becher mit den Völker-Würfeln (von den Stammes-Würfeln nicht zu reden) kräftig geschüttelt, und der Zug in das Europäisch-Internationale bleibt auch nicht ohne Folgen. Und warum soll mein Landrat keine Griechin zur Frau haben, mein Akademiekollege keine Tschechin, die Tochter meines Reisegefährten B. keinen Franzosen heiraten? Es wäre allzu billig, ein Dutzend Paradetypen vorzuführen, und schon mutiger, eine Parade von Dutzendtypen aufmarschieren zu lassen. In dieser Bundesrepublik gibt es etwa 60 Millionen Staatsbürger, die ein menschliches Antlitz tragen, den Autor dieses Vorwortes eingeschlossen.

Rudolf Hagelstange

To state it bluntly: I can perceive no typical German, and, apart from a very few specific borderline cases in other peoples I am thinking of the Turks, the Sicilians or Norwegians the number of real prototypes appears to me to be becoming less and less. The last war vigorously shook up the dice on which the faces of nations were imprinted, and even set the smallest of the groups into a state of circulation. The move into European internationalism has also had its consequences. Why should my local magistrate not have a Greek wife, my academic colleague a Czech partner of the daughter of my travelling companion not marry a Frenchman? It would be a cheap trick to present a dozen exemplary types; it would be more courageous to stage a parade of average people. There are some sixty million citizens in this Federal Republic, each with a human visage, including the author of this introduction.

Rudolf Hagelstange

liens, aux Turcs, aux Norvégiens, il me semble que les types ethniques caractéristiques deviennent de plus en plus rares.

La deuxième guerre mondiale avec ses exodes a provoqué un mélange de races et d'ethnies et les progrès accomplis par l'idée de la création de l'unité européenne entraînent également leurs conséquences. Pourquoi un préfet allemand n'épouserait-il pas une ressortissante grecque, un collègue académicien, une Tchécoslovaque ou la fille de B., mon compagnon de voyage habituel, un Français?

Il serait peut-être trop simpliste de ne passer en revue qu'une douzaine de représentants « typiques » de différentes ethnies et par contre, il semble plus encourageant de faire défiler des « types à la douzaine ».

Notre République fédérale compte environ 60 millions de créatures à face humaine. L'auteur de ces avant-propos y compris.

Rudolf Hagelstange

	BILDFOLGE	**ILLUSTRATIONS**	**ILLUSTRATIONS**
DER NORDEN	33 Meldorf/Dithmarschen	33 Meldorf/Dithmarschen	33 Meldorf/Dithmarschen
	34/35 Fehmarn	34/35 Fehmarn	34/35 Fehmarn
THE NORTH	Helgoland	Heligoland	Helgoland
	36/37 Arnis	36/37 Arnis	36/37 Arnis
ALLEMAGNE DU NORD	Schloß Glücksburg	Schloss Glücksburg	Château Glücksburg
	Maasholm	Maasholm	Maasholm
	38/39 Westerland/Sylt	38/39 Westerland/Sylt	38/39 Westerland/Sylt
	Kampen/Sylt	Kampen/Sylt	Kampen/Sylt
	Schleswig	Schleswig	Schleswig
	Flensburg	Flensburg	Flensburg
	Kappeln/Schlei	Kappeln on the Schlei	Kappeln sur Schlei
	40/41 Lübeck	40/41 Lübeck	40/41 Lübeck
	Travemünde	Travemünde	Travemünde
	Heiligenhafen	Heiligenhafen	Heiligenhafen
	Kiel	Kiel	Kiel
	42/43 Kiel	42/43 Kiel	42/43 Kiel
	44/45 Eidersperrwerk	44/45 The Eider Bulwark	44/45 Eidersperrwerk
	46/47 Greetsiel	46/47 Greetsiel	46/47 Greetsiel
	Meldorf	Meldorf	Meldorf
	Pilsum	Pilsum	Pilsum
	Friedrichstadt	Friedrichstadt	Friedrichstadt
	48/49 Hamburg	48/49 Hamburg	48/49 Hambourg
	50/51 Hamburg	50/51 Hamburg	50/51 Hambourg
	Curslack/Vierlande	Curslack/Vierlande	Curslack/Vierlanden
	52/53 Hamburger Hafen	52/53 Port of Hamburg	52/53 Port de Hambourg
	54/55 Hamburg	54/55 Hamburg	54/55 Hambourg
	56/57 Berlin (West)	56/57 Berlin (West)	56/57 Berlin (Ouest)
	58/59 Berlin (West)	58/59 Berlin (West)	58/59 Berlin (Ouest)
	60/61 Berlin (West)	60/61 Berlin (West)	60/61 Berlin (Ouest)
	62/63 Berlin (West)	62/63 Berlin (West)	62/63 Berlin (Ouest)
	64/65 Pferdezucht	64/65 Horse breeding	64/65 Elevage de chevaux
	Worpswede	Worpswede	Worpswede
	Torfabbau	Peat harvesting	Tourbage
	Wattwanderung	North Sea sandbanks	Excursion dans la bas-fond
	Krabbenkutter	Shrimpboat	Bateau de pêche en cherchant des crevettes
	66/67 Greetsiel	66/67 Greetsiel	66/67 Greetsiel
	Bremerhaven	Bremerhaven	Bremerhaven
	68/69 Bremen	68/69 Bremen	68/69 Brême
	70/71 Bremen	70/71 Bremen	70/71 Brême
	72/73 Wilhelmshaven	72/73 Wilhelmshaven	72/73 Wilhelmshaven
	Oldenburg	Oldenburg	Oldenburg
	Bad Zwischenahn	Bad Zwischenahn	Bad Zwischenahn
	74/75 Emden	74/75 Emden	74/75 Emden
	Pilsum	Pilsum	Pilsum
	76/77 Moor bei Friesoythe/Ammerland	76/77 Moor near Friesoythe/Ammerland	76/77 Marécage dans les environs de Friesoythe/Ammerland
	Jagdschloß Clemenswerth	Clemenswerth, lodge	Clemenswerth, château de chasse
	Leer	Leer	Leer
	78/79 Osnabrück	78/79 Osnabrück	78/79 Osnabrück
	80/81 Lüneburg	80/81 Lüneburg	80/81 Lunebourg
	Lüneburger Heide	Lüneburg Heath	Les Landes de Lunebourg
	82/83 Lüneburger Heide	82/83 Lüneburg Heath	82/83 Les Landes de Lunebourg
	Celle	Celle	Celle
	84/85 Hannover	84/85 Hanover	84/85 Hanovre
	86/87 Hannover	86/87 Hanover	86/87 Hanovre
	88/89 Hannover	88/89 Hanover	88/89 Hanovre

	90/91 Göttingen Braunschweig 92/93 Wolfsburg 94/95 Harz 96 Kalibergwerk	90/91 Göttingen Braunschweig 92/93 Wolfsburg 94/95 Harz Mountains 96 Potash deposit	90/91 Göttingen Brunswick 92/93 Wolfsburg 94/95 La montagne de Harz 96 Mine de potasse
DIE MITTE **THE CENTRAL AREA** **ALLEMAGNE MOYENNE**	105 Xanten 106/107 Schwalenberg Externsteine 108/109 Hameln Wasserschloß Lembeck Rheda 110/111 Paderborn Bodenwerder Hann. Münden 112/113 Merfelder Bruch, Wildpferdherde 114/115 Münster Burgsteinfurt 116/117 Biggetalsperre 118/119 Essen 120/121 Recklinghausen, Int. Ruhrfestspiele Franz Uecker in seinem Atelier Schloß Homburg, Konzert Düsseldorfer Oper, Ballett 122/123 Galopprennen in Düsseldorf- Grafenberg Wettsportfreunde Schützenfest 124/125 Radioteleskop Effelsberg/Eifel, Wasserschloß Anholt Rurtalsperre Kraftwerk Walsum 126/127 Bergbau 128/129 Bergbau 130/131 Duisburg 132/133 Duisburg 134/135 Kahler Asten/Sauerland Möhnesee/Sauerland Sauerlandlinie 136/137 Wuppertal Schloß Homburg Aggertalsperre Wipperauer Kotten an der Wupper 138/139 Rheinhausen 140/141 Duisburg 142/143 Zons Ausflugsverkehr auf dem Rhein bei Kaiserswerth Schloß Benrath in Düsseldorf-Benrath 144/145 Düsseldorf 146/147 Düsseldorf 148/149 Leverkusen 150/151 Karneval 152/153 Köln 154/155 Köln 156/157 Braunkohlenabbau 158/159 Aachen 160/161 Bonn 162/163 Bonn	105 Xanten 106/107 Schwalenberg Extern Stones 108/109 Hamelin Lembeck, Moated Castle Rheda 110/111 Paderborn Bodenwerder Hann. Münden 112/113 "Merfeld Bruch", herd of wild horses 114/115 Münster Burgsteinfurt 116/117 Biggetal Reservoir 118/119 Essen 120/121 Recklinghausen, Int. Ruhr Festival Plays Franz Uecker in his studio music in Homburg Schloss Düsseldorf Opera House 122/123 Horse racing at Düsseldorf-Grafenberg Punters Marksmanship festival 124/125 Effelsberg/Eifel, radio telescope Anholt moated castle Rur Valley reservoir Walsum power station 126/127 Mining 128/129 Mining 130/131 Duisburg 132/133 Duisburg 134/135 "Kahler Asten"/Sauerland Lake Möhne/Sauerland „Sauerland Line" 136/137 Wuppertal Homburg Schloss Aggertal Reservoir Wipperauer Kotten on the River Wupper 138/139 Rheinhausen 140/141 Duisburg 142/143 Zons Excursion traffic on the Rhein near Kaiserswerth Benrath Schloss in Düsseldorf-Benrath 144/145 Düsseldorf 146/147 Düsseldorf 148/149 Leverkusen 150/151 Carnival 152/153 Cologne 154/155 Cologne 156/157 Lignite workings 158/159 Aachen (Aix la chapelle) 160/161 Bonn 162/163 Bonn	105 Xanten 106/107 Schwalenberg Les rochers Externsteine 108/109 Hameln Lembeck, castel d'eau Rheda 110/111 Paderborn Bodenwerder Hannoversch Münden 112/113 Merfelder Bruch, un trou- peau de chevaux sau- vages 114/115 Münster Burgsteinfurt 116/117 Barrage de la vallée Big- ge 118/119 Essen 120/121 Recklinghausen, festival international Franz Uecker dans son atelier Château Homburg, concert Opera de Düsseldorf, ballet 122/123 Course de chevaux à Düsseldorf-Grafenberg Amis du pari tir 124/125 Effelsberg/Eifel, radio-té- lescope Castel d'eau Anholt Réservoir de la Rur Usine de force motrice Walsum 126/127 Mine 128/129 Mine 130/131 Duisburg 132/133 Duisburg 134/135 le mont Kahler Asten/ Sauerland Lac Möhnesee/ Sauerland « Sauerlandlinie » (auto- strade) 136/137 Wuppertal Homburg, château Aggertalsperre « Wipperauer Kotten » au bord de la Wupper 138/139 Rheinhausen 140/141 Duisburg 142/143 Zons Excursions sur le Rhin auprès de Kaiserswerth Château Benrath à Düsseldorf-Benrath 144/145 Düsseldorf 146/147 Düsseldorf 148/149 Leverkusen 150/151 Carnival 152/153 Cologne 154/155 Cologne 156/157 Exploitation de lignite 158/159 Aix-la-Chapelle 160/161 Bonn 162/163 Bonn

	164/165 Kassel Fritzlar	164/165 Kassel Fritzlar	164/165 Kassel Fritzlar
	166/167 Butzbach Wiesbaden Fulda Wasserkuppe in der Rhön	166/167 Butzbach Wiesbaden Fulda Wasserkuppe in the Rhön	166/167 Butzbach Wiesbaden Fulda Le mont Wasserkuppe, Rhön
	168/169 Frankfurt am Main	168/169 Frankfurt am Main	168/169 Francfort-sur-le-Main
	170/171 Frankfurt am Main	170/171 Frankfurt am Main	170/171 Francfort-sur-le-Main
	172/173 Flughafen Frankfurt Main	172/173 Frankfurt Airport	172/173 Aéroport de Francfort
	174/175 Frankfurt-Höchst	174/175 Frankfurt-Höchst	174/175 Francfort-Höchst
	176/177 Pfalzgrafenstein bei Kaub am Rhein Bacharach Rüdesheim	176/177 Pfalzgrafenstein near Kaub am Rhein Bacharach Rüdesheim	176/177 Forteresse de douane Pfalzgrafenstein près Kaub Bacharach Rüdesheim
	178/179 Mainz, Dom Speyer, Dom Worms, Dom	178/179 Mainz, Cathedral Speyer, Cathedral Worms, Cathedral	178/179 Mayence, cathédrale Spire, cathédrale Worms, cathédrale
	180/181 Mainz Koblenz Bad Kreuznach Loreley	180/181 Mainz Koblenz Bad Kreuznach Loreley	180/181 Mayence Coblence Bad Kreuznach Loreley
	182/183 Ludwigshafen	182/183 Ludwigshafen	182/183 Ludwigshafen
	184/185 Trier Wehlen/Mosel Bernkastel	184/185 Trier Wehlen on the Mosel Bernkastel	184/185 Trèves Wehlen sur la Moselle Bernkastel
	186/187 Moselschleife bei Eller und Ediger	186/187 A bend in the Mosel near Eller and Ediger	186/187 Une boucle de la Moselle
	188/189 Moselschleuse bei Zeltingen Cochem/Mosel	188/189 Mosel sluice near Zeltingen Cochem on the Mosel	188/189 Ecluse de la Moselle près de Zeltingen Cochem sur la Moselle
	190/191 Völklingen Saarbrücken	190/191 Völklingen Saarbrücken	190/191 Völklingen Saarbrücken (Sarrebruck)
	192 Ludwigshafen	192 Ludwigshafen	192 Ludwigshafen
DER SÜDEN **THE SOUTH** **ALLEMAGNE DU SUD**	201 Stuttgart	201 Stuttgart	201 Stuttgart
	202/203 Stuttgart	202/203 Stuttgart	202/203 Stuttgart
	204/205 Stuttgart-Untertürkheim	204/205 Stuttgart-Untertürkheim	204/205 Stuttgart-Untertürkheim
	206/207 Heidelberg Neckar	206/207 Heidelberg Neckar	206/207 Heidelberg Neckar
	208/209 Bad Wimpfen Schwäbisch Hall	208/209 Bad Wimpfen Schwäbisch Hall	208/209 Bad Wimpfen Schwäbisch Hall
	210/211 Marbach Ludwigsburg	210/211 Marbach Ludwigsburg	210/211 Marbach Ludwigsburg
	212/213 Remstal Markgröningen Besigheim/Enz	212/213 Rems Valley Markgröningen Besigheim/Enz	212/213 Vallée de la Rems Markgröningen Besigheim/Enz
	214/215 Biberach a.d.Riß Tübingen Ulm Schwäbisch Gmünd	214/215 Biberach on the Riß Tübingen Ulm Schwäbisch Gmünd	214/215 Biberach sur la Riss Tübingen Ulm Schwäbisch Gmünd
	216/217 Donaueschingen Titisee	216/217 Donaueschingen Lake Titi	216/217 Donaueschingen Lac Titisee
	218/219 Hohenzollernburg Rottweil Balingen	218/219 Hohenzollern Castle Rottweil Balingen	218/219 Château Hohenzollern Rottweil Balingen
	220/221 Baden-Baden Schwetzingen Karlsruhe Iffezheim, Rennbahn	220/221 Baden-Baden Schwetzingen Karlsruhe Iffezheim, Racecourse	220/221 Baden-Baden Schwetzingen Karlsruhe Iffezheim, turf
	222/223 Hinterzarten/ Schwarzwald Schwarzwaldhaus im Gutachtal Trachten aus dem Gutachtal	222/223 Hinterzarten Black Forest Black Forest House in the Gutach Valley Tracht garments from the Gutach Valley	222/223 Hinterzarten Fôret-Noire Ferme dans la vallée de Gutach Costumes de la vallée de Gutach
	224/225 Freiburg im Breisgau	224/225 Freiburg im Breisgau	224/225 Freiburg im Breisgau
	226/227 Insel Mainau Lindau Unteruhldingen	226/227 Mainau Island Lindau Unteruhldingen	226/227 Ile Mainau Lindau Unteruhldingen
	228/229 Wasserschloß Mespelbrunn	228/229 Mespelbrunn, castle	228/229 Mespelbrunn, castel d'eau

230/231 Michelstadt Aschaffenburg Miltenberg	230/231 Michelstadt Aschaffenburg Miltenberg	230/231 Michelstadt Aschaffenburg Miltenberg
232/233 Bamberg Veste Coburg	232/233 Bamberg Coburg "Veste"	232/233 Bamberg Coburg, château fort
234/235 Bamberg Selb	234/235 Bamberg Selb	234/235 Bamberg Selb
236/237 Wallfahrtskirche Vierzehnheiligen Weikersheim Würzburg	236/237 "Wallfahrtskirche" of the Fourteen Saints Weikersheim Würzburg	236/237 Eglise de pèlerinage Vierzehnheiligen Weikersheim Würzburg
238/239 Dinkelsbühl Rothenburg o.d. Tauber Nördlingen	238/239 Dinkelsbühl Rothenburg o. d. Tauber Nördlingen	238/239 Dinkelsbühl Rothenburg o.d. Tauber Nördlingen
240/241 Nürnberg	240/241 Nuremberg	240/241 Nuremberg
242/243 Regensburg Kloster Weltenburg	242/243 Regensburg Weltenburg Monastery	242/243 Ratisbonne Weltenburg, abbaye
244/245 Burghausen/Salzach Passau	244/245 Burghausen on the Salzach Passau	244/245 Burghausen sur la Salzach Passau
246/247 Augsburg	246/247 Augsburg	246/247 Augsbourg
248/249 Ravensburg Schloß Linderhof Memmingen Kempten	248/249 Ravensburg Linderhof Schloss Memmingen Kempten	248/249 Ravensburg Linderhof, château Memmingen Kempten
250/251 Allgäuer Land St. Koloman bei Füssen Sylvensteinspeicher Wieskirche	250/251 Allgäu Region St. Koloman near Füssen Sylvanite store "Wieskirche"	250/251 Allgäu St. Koloman, église Sylvensteinspeicher « Wies », église
252/253 Schloß Neuschwanstein Forggensee	252/253 Neuschwanstein Schloss Lake Forggen	252/253 Château Neuschwanstein Lac Forggensee
254/255 München	254/255 Munich	254/255 Munich
256/257 Schleißheim bei München, Neues Schloß München	256/257 Schleissheim near Munich, New Schloss Munich	256/257 Schleissheim près de Munich, château Munich
258/259 Ottobrunn	258/259 Ottobrunn	258/259 Ottobrunn
260/261 Marquartstein Landshut	260/261 Marquartstein Landshut	260/261 Marquartstein Landshut
262/263 Raisting, Erdefunkstelle Ruhpolding	262/263 Raisting, ground communications station Ruhpolding	262/263 Raisting, grand poste radio-télégraphique Ruhpolding
264/265 Frauenchiemsee Wasserburg am Inn Wettersteingebirge	264/265 Frauenchiemsee Wasserburg on the Inn Wetterstein Mountains	264/265 Frauenchiemsee Wasserburg sur l'Inn Panorama de la montagne Wetterstein
266/267 Wallgau	266/267 Wallgau	266/267 Wallgau
268/269 Zauberwald am Hintersee Reiteralpe über Ramsau Ramsau	268/269 "Bewitched Forest" on the Hintersee Reiteralpe above Ramsau Ramsau	268/269 « Zauberwald » près du lac Hintersee « Reiteralpe » dominant Ramsau Ramsau
270/271 St. Bartholomä am Königsee Rießersee bei Garmisch-Partenkirchen	270/271 St. Bartholomew's on Lake König Lake Riesser near Garmisch-Partenkirchen	270/271 Chapelle St. Bartholomä au lac Königsee Lac Riessersee près de Garmisch-Partenkirchen
272/273 Karwendelgebirge Auf dem Königssee Schliersee Mittenwald	272/273 Karwendel Mountains Boat on Lake König Schliersee Mittenwald	272/273 Karwendel, chaîne de montagnes Sur le lac Königssee Schliersee Mittenwald
274/275 Wetterstation auf dem Wendelstein Zugspitze	274/275 Meteorological station on the Wendelstein Zugspitze	274/275 Station météorologique sur le sommet du Wendelstein Zugspitze
276 Raisting, Erdefunkstelle	276 Raisting, ground communications station	276 Raisting, grand poste radio-télégraphique

DER NORDEN
THE NORTH
ALLEMAGNE DU NORD

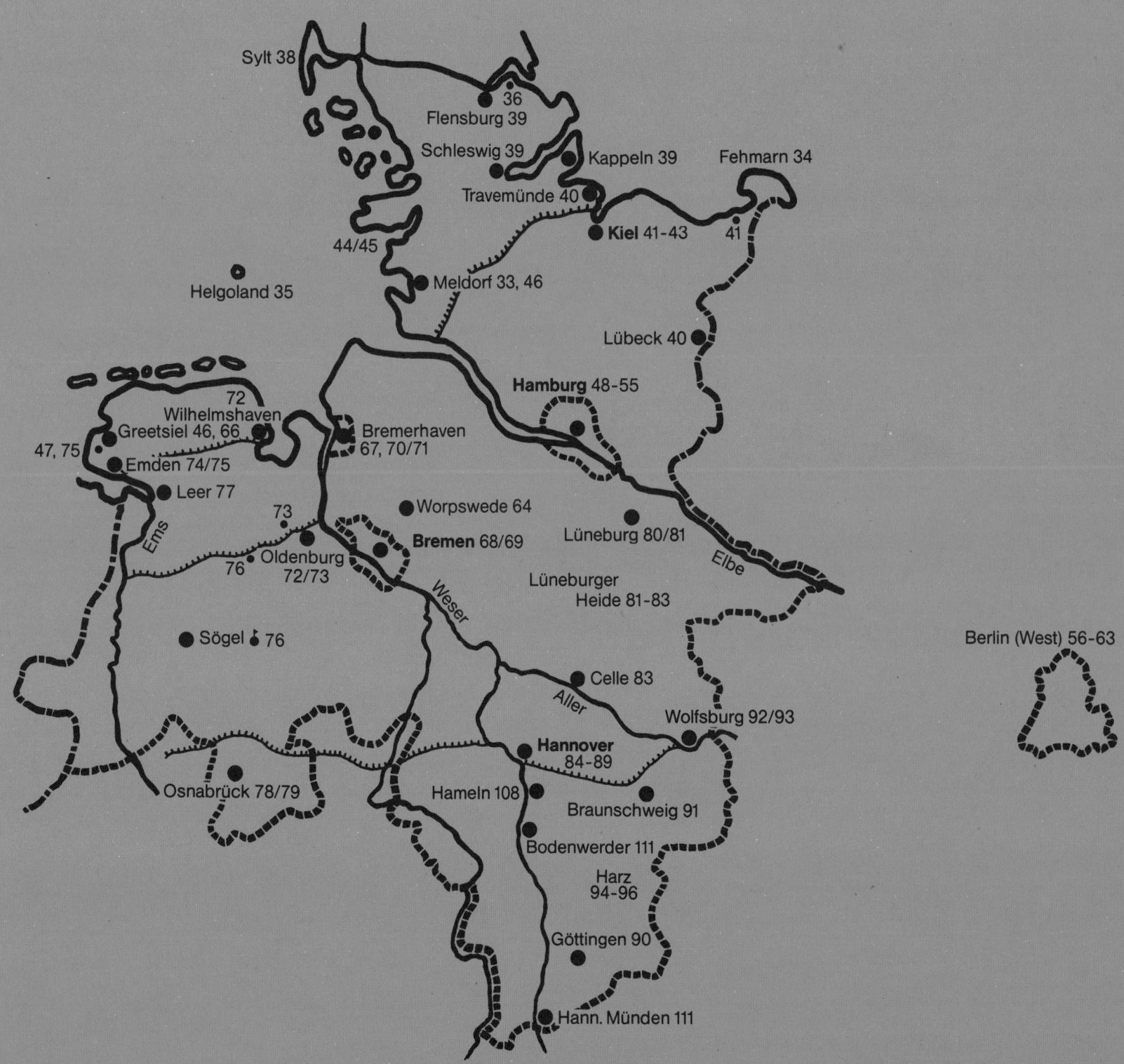

DER NORDEN

THE NORTH

DU NORD

Schleswig-Holstein, das Land zwischen Nordsee und Ostsee, ist, was die Ausdehnung und die Zahl der Bewohner angeht, eines der kleineren Länder der Bundesrepublik Deutschland. Seine geographischen und geologischen Gegebenheiten wie auch seine Kultur und Geschichte verleihen ihm indessen einen besonderen Rang.
Schleswig-Holstein umfaßt den südlichen Teil der Jütischen Halbinsel und die vorgelagerten Inseln — Fehmarn in der Ostsee, die Nordfriesischen Inseln und Helgoland in der Nordsee. Zwischen den Inseln und Halligen vor der Westküste bedeckt das Wattenmeer große Teile ehemals sicheren Landes, das in wiederholten Sturmfluten unterging. Die schlimmsten Fluten unseres Jahrtausends tobten 1362 und 1634. Fettes Marschland im Westen geht in der Landesmitte in weniger ertragreiche Geest über. Im Osten hebt sich das Land bis zu 160 m. Fruchtbare Äcker, Wiesen und Wälder charakterisieren dieses Gebiet an der fjordartig tiefgegliederten Ostseeküste. Zwischen Kiel und Lübeck, den beiden bedeutendsten Städten des Landes, dehnt sich die Holsteinische Schweiz mit ihren schönen Seen und Wäldern.
Die Hauptstadt Kiel im inneren Winkel der Kieler Förde ist die größte Stadt des Landes mit Industrie, Hafen und Werften, mit Universität und Forschungsinstituten, Museen und Schulen, Gerichten und Behörden. Bereits im 13. Jh. gegründet, gewann Kiel seine eigentliche maritime Bedeutung erst im 19. Jh. Vom 100 m hohen Rathausturm bietet sich ein schöner Blick auf Stadt und Förde. Am Nordrand der Stadt, in Holtenau, mündet der Nordostseekanal, der über eine Distanz von 99 km Ostsee und Nordsee verbindet und dessen Frequenz bei 85 000 Schiffen jährlich liegt. Weiter draußen liegt der Olympia-Segelhafen Schilksee, der seit 1972 weithin bekannt ist. Höhepunkt des Kieler Sportjahres ist die Kieler Woche.
Lübeck, die alte Hansestadt an der Trave, gehört seit je zu den bedeutendsten Plätzen an der Ostsee. Die vieltürmige Silhouette bezaubert heute wieder den Besucher. Er bewundert das Holstentor von 1477, das Rathaus aus schwarzglasierten Ziegeln und andere herrliche Bauten der spezifisch norddeutschen Backsteingotik. Lübecks Bedeutung als Handelsplatz, aber auch als Stadt der Kunst kann schwerlich überschätzt werden.

Schleswig-Holstein, the State between the North Sea and the Western Baltic, is, both in terms of area and population, the smallest of the German Federal States. Nevertheless, its geographical and geological characteristics as well as its culture and its history accord it a special status.
Schleswig-Holstein comprises the southern part of the Jutland Peninsular and the outlying islands, Fehmarn in the baltic and the East Friesian Islands and Heligoland in the North Sea. Between the islands and Halligen on the west coast, the "Wattenmeer" (Watten Shallows) now covers what was formerly dry land which became submerged as a result of successive tidal waves. The worst floods of our millenium raged here in the years 1362 and 1634. Rich marsh country in the west becomes transformed into less fruitful sandy uplands in the central area. In the east the level rises to 500 feet. Rich tillage, meadowland and forests are the characteristics of this region bordering the fjordlike, deeply engraved Baltic coast. Between Kiel and Lübeck, the state's two most important cities, there is the Holstein Lake District (Holsteinische Schweiz) with its enchanting lakes and forests.
The State Capital Kiel, at the innermost corner of the "Kiel Fjord," is also the State's largest town, with industries, a port and shipyards, a university and research institutes, museums, schools, courts of justice and administrative authorities. Kiel, founded in the 13th century, first gained maritime prominence six hundred years later. There is a beautiful view of the town and the fjord from the 330 ft. high Town Hall spire. At the northern boundary of the town the canal linking the North Sea with the Baltic ends its 60 mile course across the peninsular. 85,000 ships a year pass through it. Beyond it is the Schilksee Yachting Harbour which gained prominence as a result of the 1972 Olympic Games. The "Kieler Woche" is the week that crowns Kiel's sporting year.
Lübeck, the old Hanseatic City on the River Trave, has for ages been among the most important places on the Baltic. The visitor cannot fail to be enchanted by the skyline with its many spires. Other sights are the Holstein Gateway, built in 1477, the Town Hall, faced with black-glazed tiles, and other attractive buildings of the typical North German brickwork Gothic era. It would be difficult to overestimate the significance of Lübeck, not only as a commercial, but also as an art centre.

Slesvig-Holstein, sépare la mer du Nord et la Baltique. La densité de population du pays n'est pas très forte. C'est un pays de départ des navigateurs à partir de l'antiquité, ce qui était la cause de sa grandeur historique.
Slesvig-Holstein comprend la partie méridionale de la presqu'île de Jutland et les îles voisines ainsi qu'une partie du littoral de la Baltique (y compris Fehmarn dans la Baltique et Helgoland dans la mer du Nord). La côte ouest est inhospitalière inondée réitérément par les hautes marées poussées par les tempêtes dont les plus pires étaient celles de 1362 et de 1634). Dans l'ouest le pays de cultures maraîchères est d'une étonnante richesse agricole, au milieu du pays on trouve un territoire d'élévages et de cultures pauvres (Geest). Dans l'est le pays est formé de plateaux et de collines tertiaires (hauteur maximum 160 m) avec de riches cultures et des régions d'élévage perfectionné, qui entourent la côte entaillée de la Baltique. Entre Kiel et Lübeck, les plus importantes villes de la région, s'étale la « Suisse du Holstein » avec ses forêts pittoresques parsemées de débris glacières et trouées de jolis lacs.
La capitale Kiel auprès de l'affaissement Kieler Förde est la plus grande ville de la région, un centre industriel assidu (constructions navales) et le principal port. A l'essor industriel correspond l'élan culturel : on y trouve l'université, des instituts de recherches scientifiques, des musées renommées et des bureaux.
Fondé au 13e siècle, l'époque d'épanouissement de Kiel était le 19e siècle. De la tour de l'hôtel de ville (100 m de hauteur) on a une merveilleuse vue panoramique sur la ville et ses environs. Au nord à Holtenau, nous voyons le canal de Kiel unissant la Baltique a la mer du Nord (99 km) fréquenté chaque année par 85 000 navires. Dans la banlieue de Kiel se trouve le port olympique de Schilksee, bien renommé depuis 1972. Un événement sportif de première importance est la « semaine de Kiel ».
Lübeck est une ancienne ville hanséatique à l'embouchure de la Trave vivant traditionellement du commerce. La pittoresque ville moyenâgeuse a conservé son atmosphère charmante, à retenir parmi ses nombreux monuments : la porte Holstentor (1477), l'hôtel

An die beiden großen Städte reihen sich zahlreiche mittlere und kleinere Städte zwischen Flensburg und Lauenburg an, die, wie es dem Charakter des Landes entspricht, ihre Bedeutung aus ihrer geographischen Lage an der Küste oder inmitten der bäuerlichen Landschaften im Inneren ableiten. Schleswig-Holstein ist vorwiegend ein Agrarland, vor allem wird Viehzucht und Milchwirtschaft betrieben, Getreide-, Kartoffel- und Gemüseanbau ist ebenfalls verbreitet.

Auch der Fremdenverkehr in Schleswig-Holstein spielt eine wichtige Rolle. Die Küste ist im Westen wie im Osten von einer langen Kette großer und kleiner Seebäder gesäumt. Auch die Holsteinische Schweiz hat viele Liebhaber. Solquellen gibt es in Bramstedt und Segeberg.

Ein Blick ist noch zu werfen auf die zahlreichen kunstvollen Zeugnisse der langen Geschichte des Landes. Da gibt es Feldsteinkirchen aus der Zeit der Christianisierung, prächtige Altäre, Kanzeln und Taufsteine in den früh protestantisch gewordenen Kirchen, die großen Schlösser etwa in Glücksburg und Schleswig, die barocken ländlichen Adelssitze und Bauerngehöfte.

Die Geschichte der Freien und Hansestadt *Hamburg*, die heute ein Land der Bundesrepublik Deutschland ist, beginnt im frühen 9. Jh. mit einer Kirchenburg. 1189 verlieh Barbarossa der Stadt Handels-, Zoll- und Schiffahrtsprivilegien. Im gleichen Jahr beginnt auch die Geschichte des Hafens. Über 300 Jahre lang gehörte Hamburg der Hanse an. Hansischer Geist prägt bis heute die Bürger der Stadt. Die Organisationsform des heutigen Hamburg ist eine Schöpfung unseres Jahrhunderts: 1937 wurden Altona, Wandsbek, Harburg-Wilhelmsburg und 27 Landgemeinden in die Stadt einbezogen.

Hamburg ist die größte Stadt der Bundesrepublik. Seine Lage 110 km landeinwärts an der Norderelbe begünstigte das stetige Wachsen des Hafens; ein Drittel des deutschen Güterverkehrs über See läuft über den Hamburger Hafen. Er hat entscheidenden Einfluß auf die Wirtschaft des Stadtstaates. Daraus resultiert, daß hier die erste deutsche Börse (1558) und die erste deutsche Handelskammer (1665) entstanden. Bis 1918 war die HAPAG die größte Schiffahrtsgesellschaft der Welt.

Vom kulturellen Leben, das sich parallel zu Wirtschaft und Verkehr entwickelte, legen zahlreiche Institutionen Zeugnis ab. Die Oper entstand bereits 1678, viele Museen und Sammlungen haben Weltrang. Die 1919 gegründete Universität gehört zu den größten und bedeutendsten der Bundesrepublik.

Das Gesicht der Innenstadt wird durch die zum See gestaute Alster bestimmt. Von der Lombardsbrücke genießt man den Blick auf die Uferstraßen und Promenaden, über denen die Türme der Stadt aufragen. Von besonderer Schönheit sind die großen Parks, darunter „Planten un Blomen" mit dem neuen Con-

In addition to these two large towns there are also numerous medium-sized and small towns between Flensburg and Lauenburg which, as befits the character of the region, gain their significance either from their geographic location on the coast or from the agricultural interior. Schleswig-Holstein is primarily agricultural, predominantly fat cattle and dairying, but grain, potatoes and vegetables are also widely grown.

Tourism is also important to Schleswig-Holstein. Both the east and west coasts are strewn with long chains of large and small seaside resorts. The Holstein Lake District also has a great many devotees. There are mineral water spas in Bramstedt and Segeberg. Also worthy of note are the numerous artworks that bear witness to the State's long history. There is the Feldstein Church, dating back to the introduction of christianity, magnificent altars, pulpits and baptismal founts in churches that early on turned to protestantism, the huge castles in Glücksburg and Schleswig and the baroque rural seats of the aristocracy and their farmyards.

The history of the Free and Hanseatic City of *Hamburg,* today a State of the Federal Republic of Germany, began in the early ninth century with a fortified church. In 1189 Barbarossa granted the town trading, customs and shipping privileges. The history of the port began in the same year. Hamburg was a member of the Hanseatic League for over 300 years and still today its citizens are imbued with the Hanseatic spirit. Hamburg's organisational structure belongs to this century; in 1937 the urban areas Altona, Wandsbek, Harburg-Wilhelmsburg and 27 outlying communities were absorbed into the city.

Hamburg is West Germany's biggest city. Its location, some 70 miles upstream on the Northern Elbe, favoured the steady growth of the port, which handles a third of German overseas trade. This has had a decisive influence on the economy of the city-state. The first German stock exchange (1558) and the first German chamber of commerce (1665) were set up there. Until 1918 the HAPAG was the world's biggest shipping line.

A large number of worthy cultural institutions give evidence of the cultural life that runs parallel with the city's commerce. The Opera was founded way back in 1678. Many of its museums and collections are world-renowned. The university, founded in 1919, is one of the biggest and most important in the German Federal Republic.

The picture of the centre of the City is dominated by the Alster Lake, which is dammed at its seaward end. There is a fine view of the terraces and promenades along its banks from the Lombard Bridge with the City's spires rising in the background. Its large parks are enchanting, among them "Planten un Blomen" with the new Congress Centre.

de ville (construction en briques noires) et beaucoup de maisons patriciennes et d'hôtels particuliers anciens. Lübeck est aussi un centre culturel et artistique traditionel.

Nous trouvons beaucoup de petites villes dans la région entre Flensburg et Lauenburg, qui ont pris naissance à l'intersection de routes de circulation anciennes reliant la côte et le pays rural. Les ressources sont essentiellement agricoles : orge, avoine, pommes te terre, légumes et surtout prairies. L'élevage est intensif ; Slesvig-Holstein est aussi un territoire touristique. On y trouve des stations climatiques à la côte de la Baltique et de la mer du Nord. Partout on est charmé du sable blanc lumineux. La « Suisse du Holstein » vivant également du tourisme est très fréquentée. On trouve des sources salines à Bramstedt et à Segeberg.

Le pays regorge de nombreux témoins de toutes époques culturelles et de richesses artistiques. On y trouve de très anciennes églises avec des stalles, des panneaux peints, des pierres tombales gravées et des vitraux ainsi que des châteaux somptueux (par exemple à Glücksburg et à Slesvig), des palais baroques et des fermes pittoresques.

La ville libre et hanséatique *Hambourg* a pris naissance à partir du 9e siècle sur l'emplacement d'un castel épiscopal. En 1189 l'empereur Frédéric Barberousse concéda à la ville des privilèges de commerce maritime et de douane. En même temps commence l'histoire du port de Hambourg. Plus de 300 années Hambourg était une ville hanséatique, une métropole commerciale. La cité médiévale ayant été brûlée en 1842, Hambourg est aujourd'hui une ville moderne. En 1937 les communes Altona, Wandsbek, Harburg-Wilhelmsburg et beaucoup d'autres fusionnent. Hambourg est la plus grande ville de la R. F. A., un centre industriel et commercial. Son port se trouve 110 km en amont de l'embouchure de l'Elbe, il est le premier port de l'Allemagne quant à l'importance et prend un tiers du trafic des marchandises. A cause de l'importance traditionelle du commerce on y trouve la plus ancienne Bourse (1558) et la plus ancienne chambre de commerce (1665) de l'Allemagne. Jusqu'à 1918 la HAPAG était la compagnie maritime la plus importante du monde.

A l'essor commercial correspond l'élan culturel : il y a des théâtres renommés, l'opéra (inaugurée 1678) et les musées célèbres. L'université fondée en 1919 est une des plus grandes de la R. F. A.

Au milieu de Hambourg se trouve le petit fleuve Alster, refoulé qui forme un lac. Du pont Lombardsbrücke nous voyons les monuments les plus importants de la ville et les belles promenades. Un très bel échantillon des parcs de Hambourg est nommé « Planten un Blomen », où se trouve le nouveau

gress-Centrum. Erwähnung verdient auch Hagenbecks Tierpark in Stellingen. Wahrzeichen der Stadt Hamburg ist der 132 m hohe Turm der Michaeliskirche, der „Michel".

Knapp 75 Jahre lang war *Berlin* die Hauptstadt des Deutschen Reiches. Davor liegen sechs Jahrhunderte einer wechselvollen Geschichte, danach liegt — vor unser aller Augen — eine Entwicklung, die schwer begreifbar ist.
Die Stadt entstand in der ersten Hälfte des 13. Jh. aus der Vereinigung der beiden rechts und links der Spree an ihrer Mündung in die Havel gelegenen Städte Cölln und Berlin. 1415 wurde Friedrich I. als erster Hohenzoller mit dem Kurfürstentum Brandenburg belehnt. Seit damals begann Berlin sich zu einer kunst- und geistreichen Stadt zu entwickeln, die auch wirtschaftlich immer mehr an Bedeutung gewann. Der Große Kurfürst verlieh ihr den Glanz einer reichen barocken Residenz; die Könige des 18. Jh. fügten der blühenden Stadt eine gewisse Strenge hinzu. Am Ende des Jahrhunderts ist Berlin Mittelpunkt des geistigen Deutschland. Man trifft sich in den Salons bedeutender Frauen — es ist die Zeit der Schleiermacher, Fichte und Hegel, der Humboldt, Schlegel und Tieck. Man liebt Charme und Esprit, die seinerzeit die französischen Hugenotten in die Stadt eingebracht hatten, und vereinigt sie mit dem Witz der Urberliner: eine Mischung, die sich bis heute erhalten hat und den Berlinern viel Zuneigung in aller Welt sichert. Inzwischen wuchs und wuchs die Stadt immer weiter. 1870 hatte sie 800 000 Einwohner, 1920 nach Eingemeindung einer Reihe von Vororten an die vier Millionen. 1945 ein einziges riesiges Trümmerfeld, ist dreieinhalb Jahrzehnte später eine neue moderne Stadt entstanden, die nach wie vor die größte Industriestadt der Bundesrepublik ist. Eine Mauer trennt sie in zwei in jeder Hinsicht ungleiche Hälften, die allerdings trotz aller gewollten und ungewollten Einflüsse von jenseits der Grenzen doch eines nicht vergessen machen kann: Berlin bleibt Berlin, westlich und östlich der Mauer.

Das Land *Bremen* umfaßt die Hansestadt Bremen und den Stadtkreis Bremerhaven.
Bremen liegt 70 km landeinwärts an der Unterweser und ist die älteste Seestadt Deutschlands. Im Jahr 787 erhob Karl der Große die damals schon alte Siedlung zum Bischofssitz. Bremen gedieh zu einer mächtigen Stadt mit Handels- und Schiffahrtsbeziehungen zu allen Ländern der damals bekannten Welt. Es wurde Hansestadt und Freie Reichsstadt. Die Unabhängigkeitserklärung der Vereinigten Staaten von Amerika im Jahr 1776 eröffnete für Bremen neue Möglichkeiten der Handelserweiterung. In neuer Zeit dehnte die Stadt ihre Kapazitäten auf große Industrieunternehmungen der verschiedensten Branchen aus.
In der Mitte des von Wall und Graben umgebenen Altstadtkerns liegt der Marktplatz mit dem Roland, dem mächtigen Sinnbild des

Hagenbeck's Animal Park in Stellingen must also be mentioned. The symbol of Hamburg is the 430 feet high spire of the Michaelis Church, the "Michel."

Berlin was the capital of the German Reich for a bare 75 years. Before that it had undergone a varied history lasting six hundred years, followed by a development which is scarcely comprehensible — although we have witnessed it happening.
The town arose in the first half of the 13th century as a result of the fusion of the two towns Cölln and Berlin on the right and left banks of the River Spree at its point of confluence with the Havel. In 1415 Friedrich I became the first member of the House of Hohenzollern to be a Prince Elector of Brandenburg. Since that time Berlin has developed as a centre of the arts and of human thought, and has also gained more and more in economic significance. The powerful Prince Elector gave it all the pomp of a richly endowed baroque residence, while the Kings of the 18th century brought a degree of severity into the flourishing city. At the close of that century Berlin was the spiritual centre of Germany. The social meeting points were the salons of influential women — it was a period of artificiality, of Fichte and Hegel, of Humboldt, Schlegel and Tieck. Charm and esprit were the qualities sought, qualities introduced by the Huguenots and enriched by the wit of the original Berliners. This is a blend that has persisted up to the present day, and which has made the Berliner a figure appreciated throughout the world.
In the meantime the city continued to grow and grow. In 1870 it had 800,000 inhabitants; in 1920, after the incorporation of several suburbs, they approached four million. In 1945 it was a city of ruins, and three-and-a-half decades later it has risen again to become a new, modern city, still the biggest industrial city in Western Germany. A wall divides it into two parts, in every respect distinct from each other, which however, in spite of all desired and undesired influences from across the frontier, still fail to erase one simple fact: Berlin remains Berlin, west and east of the Wall.

The State of *Bremen* comprises the Hanseatic City of Bremen and the urban area of Bremerhaven.
Bremen is just over 40 miles inland on the Lower Weser and is Germany's oldest maritime city. In the year 787 Charles the Great elevated the already old community to the status of a bishop's see. Bremen thrived and became a powerful city with trading and maritime links with all the countries of the then known world. It became a Hanseatic and Free City of the Reich. The United States' declaration of independence in 1776 opened up new possibilities for Bremen to extend its trading activities. In recent times the city has extended its capacities to include big industrial undertakings of the most varied types.

centre des congrès. Digne d'être visité : le jardin zoologique de Hagenbeck à Stellingen. Une marque distinctive de Hambourg est la tour de l'église St-Michel (132 m de hauteur).

Berlin était la capitale de l'Empire allemand qui existait durant 75 années. Nous connaissons six siecles du passé de la ville, son sort reste incertain et difficile à comprendre. Dans le noyau historique de la ville existaient depuis le troisième tiers du 12e siècle deux villes : Cölln et Berlin, qui ont pris naissance à l'intersection de voies de circulation importantes sur les deux rives de la Spree. En 1415 Frédéric Ier de la maison Hohenzollern devint le premier électeur de Brandenbourg. Protestants ils obtinrent aux traités de Westphalie de vastes territoires. De ces fragments le grand électeur Frédéric-Guillaume (1640 – 1688), fondateur d'une résidence baroque fit un seul et solide Etat. Il attira les réfugiés (20 000 protestants français par exemple) a Berlin. Berlin devint au 18e siècle un centre culturel et artistique. Frédéric Ier (1688 – 1713) se fit couronner roi de Prusse (1700). L'Humour des Berlinois est parent de l'esprit français. Les idées nouvelles furent propagées par les salons, où se coudoyaient les belles femmes et les philosophes (Schleiermacher, Fichte, Hegel, les Humboldt, Schlegel et Tieck).
L'unité allemande et les applications des sciences ont entrainé l'apogée économique et politique de Berlin, qui avait 800 000 habitants en 1870 et à peu près quatre millions en 1920 après la réunion de beaucoup de communes. Très endommagé au cours de la dernière guerre, Berlin est aujourd'hui une ville moderne et toujours la plus grande ville industrielle de la R. F. A. En dépit de la menace des communistes Berlin reste Berlin aux deux côtés du « mur ».

L'ancienne ville hanséatique *Brême* avec son avant-port Bremerhaven est le plus petit Etat fédéral de la R. F. A. Brême se trouve 70 km en amont de l'embouchure de la Weser.
En 787 Charlemagne fonda l'évêché de Brême dans un site ancien. L'ancienne ville hanséatique et ville libre est une ville commerçante et un port important de navigation. Dans la période contemporaine Brême profitait surtout du commerce avec les Etats-Unis. La ville hanséatique vivant traditionellement du commerce est aujourd'hui aussi un centre industriel.

Selbstbewußtseins der Bremer Bürger. Er entstand 1404 und ist mit Sockel und Baldachin an die 10 m hoch. Sein Gesicht ist dem mächtigen Dom zugewandt, der sein frühgotisches Gepräge im 13. Jh. erhielt. Die steilen Turmhelme freilich stammen aus dem späten 19. Jh. Links vom Dom das Rathaus. Es wurde zur gleichen Zeit errichtet, in der auch der Roland entstand. Die weltberühmte Fassade ist jedoch 200 Jahre jünger. Dem Rathaus gegenüber das Haus der Bürgerschaft aus den 60er Jahren, das sich mit modernen Konturen glücklich in die alte gewachsene Umgebung einfügt.

Bremen bietet dem Besucher viele Stätten an, die nicht nur von unternehmerischem Handelsgeist und bedächtiger Tüchtigkeit zeugen, sondern auch von alteingesessener Kultur. In jüngster Zeit ist draußen in Horn die Universität entstanden, die zu ihrem Teil dazu beiträgt, den Ruf Bremens als einer Stadt lebendigen Geistes in alle Welt zu tragen.

Natürlich gehören zum Bild der Stadt ihre Häfen, darunter Überseehafen, Europahafen, Neustädter Hafen mit Container-Terminal und ein Dutzend andere.

Von ihren Häfen geprägt ist auch die Stadt Bremerhaven, die Bürgermeister Johann Smidt 1827 45 km weiter nördlich an der Wesermündung errichtete. Sie ist ein bedeutender Passagier- und Auswandererhafen und besitzt den größten Fischereihafen Europas, wo auch regelmäßige Fischauktionen abgehalten werden. Vor dem Columbus-Bahnhof erstreckt sich 1250 m lang die Columbus-Kaje, wenig weiter die Nordschleuse und der Container-Terminal. Nahe dem Alten Hafen befinden sich das vielbesuchte Schiffahrtsmuseum und der 116 m hohe Radarturm.

Niedersachsen, das der Fläche nach zweitgrößte Land der Bundesrepublik Deutschland, dehnt sich zwischen Harz und Emsland, zwischen Nordseeküste und den Bergen und Hügeln in den südlichen Landesteilen. Niedersachsen ist vorwiegend ein Bauernland, seine Bevölkerung ist im wesentlichen niederdeutsch, nur in Oldenburg gibt es eine friesische Sprachinsel.

Die agrarische Struktur des Landes bringt es mit sich, daß die niedersächsischen Städte, abgesehen von Hannover, allesamt nicht gerade Weltstadtformat haben. Die Landeshauptstadt allerdings läßt zumindest während der alljährlich im April stattfindenden Messe alle Alltagsmaßstäbe hinter sich. Die Hannover-Messe ist *die* große Industrie-Schau, ein internationaler Treffpunkt für alle, die Industriegüter kaufen oder verkaufen wollen. Außerhalb der Messe ist Hannover eine ebenso geschäftige wie gepflegte und kulturell aktive norddeutsche Großstadt. Auch die anderen größeren Städte des Landes — Braunschweig etwa oder Hildesheim, Lüneburg und Osnabrück, auch Oldenburg oder

In the middle of the area surrounded by the city wall and moat is the market place with the Roland Statue, the mighty symbol of the self-assurance of the Bremen citizens. Roland was erected in 1404 and stands some 33 feet high, including plinth and canopy. His face is directed towards the mighty Cathedral, dating back to the early Gothic thirteenth century, although its spire cupolas belong to the late nineteenth century. To the left of the Cathedral is the Town Hall, built at the time Roland was erected. The world-famous façade was put up 200 years later. Opposite the Town Hall is the House of the Citizens, built during the sixties, whose modern contours blend neatly into their old-time surroundings.

Bremen offers the visitor any number of places which not only bear witness to the enterprising trading spirit and workmanlike endeavour, but also to a tradition of culture. More recently the University was inaugurated in outlying Horn, which now also contributes to spreading the fame of Bremen to all parts of the world as a place of spiritual activity.

Naturally a part of the picture of Bremen are its port, including its facilities for ocean-going vessels, its "Euro-Port," the Neustadt Docks and container terminal, and a dozen others.

The town of Bremerhaven, brought into being by the then Bürgermeister Johann Smidt in 1827, some 30 miles to the north at the estuary of the Weser, also gravitates around the port. It is a port for passenger vessels, through which many emigrants pass, and also contains Europe's biggest fishing port with regular fish auctions. In front of the Columbus Railway Station stretches the 1,500 yards long Columbus Quay; a little further is the northern lock and the container terminal. Near the old docks is the world-famous Maritime Museum and the 380 feet high radar tower.

Lower Saxony, in terms of area the second largest state in the Federal Republic of Germany, extends from the Harz Mountains to the Ems and from the North Sea coast to the hill country in the south. Lower Saxony is primarily agricultural, its population is essentially Low German, although there is a pocket of Fresian speech in Oldenburg.

The agrarian structure of the area means that inherently the towns of Lower Saxony, apart from Hanover, are not what might be described as cosmopolitan. The state capital, Hanover, at least, sheds this aspect every year in April at the time of the big Fair. The Hanover Fair is THE big industrial show and an international meeting point for all those who buy or sell industrial products. Outside of the Fair, Hanover is both a busy commercial and a culturally active North German metropolis. The other larger towns of Lower Saxony too, as for example Braunschweig or Hil-

Au milieu de la cité sur la place du Marché se trouve la statue de Roland, symbole de la liberté des bourgeois de Brême, qui y est installée en 1404 sur l'emplacement d'une statue sculptée sur bois (10 m de hauteur) regardant la puissante cathédrale gothique St-Pierre (fondée 1042, édifée jusqu'au 13e siècle). A gauche de la cathédrale l'hôtel de ville gothique, de la même époque, sa façade mondialement célèbre est installée 200 années plus tard. Les statues sont des maîtres d'œuvre de l'école de Parler. Vis-à-vis de l'hôtel de ville se trouve la nouvelle maison de la bourgeoisie, adaptée aux anciennes maisons voisines. Brême n'est pas seulement une ville assidue du commerce mais aussi un centre culturel et artistique traditionel. La ville est aujourd'hui aussi siège d'une université à Horn.

La ville a ses ports célèbres : Überseehafen, Europahafen et Neustädter Hafen avec son Container-Terminal, qui sont complémentaires de l'avant-port Bremerhaven.

Bremerhaven, fondé en 1827 par le maire Johann Smidt — 45 km en aval, est un port important de paquebots et un des plus grands ports de pêche de l'Europe, où des enchères aux poissons ont lieu. Devant la gare de Chr. Colomb s'étend le quai Columbus-Kaje. Plus au Nord se trouvent l'écluse nord et le Container-Terminal. Non loin de l'ancien port on arrive au musée de navigation (très fréquenté) et à la tour de radar (116 mètres de hauteur).

La Basse-Saxe, le deuxième Etat quant à la superficie, comprend avec le littoral de la mer du Nord, avec les îles de la Frise, la région de l'Ems, les Landes de Lunebourg et le Harz beaucoup d'attractions touristiques. La Basse-Saxe est surtout un pays rural. Les habitants parlent le plat-allemand et à la côte et autour de la ville Oldenbourg la langue des Frisons.

Les villes de la Basse-Saxe ne sont pas des grandes capitales cosmopolites, à l'exception de Hanovre. La foire de Hanovre, qui a lieu chaque avril est bien renommée dans tout le monde : une exposition internationale, qui étale la capacité productive de l'industrie, une place à l'ambiance internationale — les acheteurs et les vendeurs des marchandises industrielles s'y donnent rendez-vous. Hanovre est une grande ville moderne, à son essor industriel correspond l'élan culturel. Les anciennes villes Brunswick, Hildesheim,

Stade, Göttingen, Goslar, Wolfenbüttel — atmen diese traditionsbewußte typische Atmosphäre. Andere Städte wirken mehr von ihrer Industrie durchdrungen, allen voran Wolfsburg, aber auch Wilhelmshaven oder Salzgitter.

Zwischen all diesen Städten breiten sich Felder, Wiesen, Wälder aus. Drei Fünftel der Gesamtfläche werden landwirtschaftlich genutzt, ein Fünftel ist Wald. Im flachen Norden des Landes hat die Viehzucht den Vorrang vor dem Anbau von Roggen, Hafer und Kartoffeln. Im höher gelegenen Süden überwiegen Weizen und Zuckerrüben, im Braunschweigischen findet sich auch Gemüse. Die wichtigsten Industriezweige sind Fahrzeug- und Maschinenbau, auch Elektrotechnik und Nahrungsmittelproduktion. In Osnabrück spielt auch die Textilindustrie eine Rolle. Von erheblicher Bedeutung ist die Erdöl- und Erdgasgewinnung im Emsland. Hier ist in den Jahrzehnten nach dem Krieg ein Industriezentrum von beachtlichen Ausmaßen gewachsen. Bohrtürme und Schornsteine, Bunker und Kessel, Fabriken und Verwaltungsbauten bilden eine völlig neue Kulisse für das ansonsten agrarische Land. Ebenfalls im Nordwesten bilden die Torflager eine nicht unwesentliche Komponente der Wirtschaftskraft des Landes.

Wenn von der niedersächsischen Wirtschaftsleistung die Rede ist, muß auch von den großen und kleinen Häfen gesprochen werden. Von Cuxhaven bis Emden zieht sich die Küste. Ihre Häfen sind eng mit dem Hinterland verbunden, sie haben Import- und Exportaufgaben und sind weitgehend spezialisiert. Als Beispiel mag der Ölhafen von Wilhelmshaven gelten, der zugleich die Kopfstation der Rohölfernleitungen beheimatet. Heute können Tanker bis zu 250 000 t vollbeladen den Ölhafen anlaufen. Neben den großen Handelshäfen haben liebenswerte kleine Häfen wie Neuharlingersiel und Greetsiel mehr lokale Bedeutung für Fischfang und Fremdenverkehr.

Alle industrielle und landwirtschaftliche Geschäftigkeit ist nicht denkbar ohne die geistigen Grundlagen, die in einer nicht geringen Zahl von Bildungs- und Forschungsstätten erarbeitet werden: neben der altehrwürdigen Landesuniversität in Göttingen und den Neugründungen in Oldenburg und Osnabrück gibt es drei Technische Universitäten in Hannover, Braunschweig und Clausthal (Bergakademie), ferner eine Reihe von Fachhochschulen. Erhebliche Bedeutung haben auch viele Museen, Sammlungen und Bibliotheken. Zum Bild des Landes gehören neben Städten und Dörfern, neben Äckern und Wiesen, Fabriken und Schornsteinen auch die Oasen, die der Regeneration vorbehalten sind. Die zahlreichen Seebäder an der Küste, aber auch die großen Heilbäder im Land, Pyrmont etwa, daneben die zahlreichen Erholungsorte in der Lüneburger Heide und im Harz.

desheim, Lüneburg and Osnabrück, or even Oldenburg, Göttingen, Goslar or Wolfenbüttel, exude this consciously typical atmosphere. Other towns are stamped more by their local industry, above all Wolfsburg, and also Wilhelmshaven, Emden or Salzgitter.

Between all these towns there are wide expanses of fields, grassland, forests. Three fifths of the total area is agricultural, one fifth is forestland. In the northern flatlands cattle raising predominates, with the cultivation of rye, oats and potatoes secondary. In the more elevated southern regions wheat and sugar beet are to the fore, and in the Braunschweig area vegetables are grown. The most important industrial production of the state are motor vehicles and machinery, as well as electrical apparatus and foodstuffs. Textiles come into the picture in Osnabrück. In the Ems region petroleum and natural gas production play an important part. In the period following the war an industrial centre of considerable dimensions has grown up here. Oil rigs and chimneys, bunkers and boilers, factories and administrative buildings now create a completely new background for this otherwise agricultural country. In the north-western area the peat deposits form an essential part of the economic strength of the state.

Within the framework of the industrial and economic activity of Lower Saxony, both the small and large ports must not be overlooked. The coastline stretches from Cuxhaven to Emden, and the ports are closely linked to the hinterland. They handle both exports and imports and are for the greater part specialised, one example being Wilhelmshaven, a port of entry for oil and also the terminal point of long-distance crude oil pipelines. Today fully-laden tankers of up to 250,000 tons can enter the oil port. In addition to the big commercial ports there are charming small harbours, such as Neuharlingersiel and Greetsiel, which are of local importance for fishery and tourism.

All this industrial and agricultural activity would be unthinkable without the necessary intellectual foundations, and these are most adequately provided by the number of educational and research establishments at hand. In addition to the venerable State University in Göttingen and the new seats of learning in Oldenburg and Osnabrück, there are technical universities in Hanover, Braunschweig and Clausthal, as well as a number of specialised technical high schools. A great number of museums, art collections and libraries also play a significant part.

New townships and villages, nestling among tilled fields and grassland, factories and chimneys, as well as oases for recuperation, are all a part of the landscape. On the coast there are numerous seaside resorts, inland there are noteworthy spas such as Pyrmont, as well as countless recuperative resorts on the Lüneburg Heath and in the Harz.

Lunebourg, Osnabrück, Stade, Göttingen, Goslar et Wolfenbüttel sont les centres culturels traditionels, produits pittoresques de l'antique terroir culturel. On y trouve aussi des villes modernes assidues comme Lingen, Salzgitter, Wolfsburg, Emden et Wilhelmshaven.

Et dans l'entourage de ces villes vous trouvez des champs fertiles et un pâturage gras traversé de ruisseaux et de canaux. La Basse-Saxe est un pays de riches cultures (blé, orge, avoine, betteraves et pommes de terre), d'élevage perfectionné. L'industrie alimentaire transforme les produits du sol. Outre les industries mécaniques (machines), l'industrie électrique et les industries textiles (à Osnabrück) nous y trouvons des tours de sondage (dans la région de l'Ems), des raffineries et des usines. Dans le nord-ouest les tourbières sont des ressources du pays.

Les voies de communication sont très denses. On y trouve surtout beaucoup de voies navigables et de ports entre Cuxhaven et Emden. Le commerce extérieur est actif. Un échantillon des ports modernes spécialisés est Wilhelmshaven (dont l'histoire commence en 1856). Aujourd'hui Wilhelmshaven est surtout un port de petrole ; des navires-citernes (jusqu'à 250 000 t.) y peuvent décharger. Les petits ports (villages des pêcheurs) Neuharlingersiel et Greetsiel comptent parmi les buts d'excursions et de visite les plus fréquentés des touristes.

Les recherches scientifiques sont la base de l'essor économique. La plus vieille ville universitaire est Göttingen. Aujourd'hui Oldenbourg et Osnabrück sont aussi des villes universitaires. La tradition intellectuelle se fait voir aussi par les universités techniques à Hanovre, Brunswick et Clausthal (école des mines) ainsi que par les écoles polytechnique et par beaucoup de musées et de bibliothèques.

Le touriste y trouve beaucoup de bains de mer et de stations climatique à la côte de la mer du Nord et sur les îles. Pensez aux Landes de Lunebourg — c'est une paysage pittoresque couvert de pins et de bouleaux, de bruyères et de genêts. La montagne romantique Harz est aussi un territoire touristique.

Geschichte und Kultur des Landes sind dokumentiert in Domen und Palästen, nicht weniger aber auch in den bürgerlichen Bauten vergangener Epochen und in den technischen Bauwerken unserer Tage. Das gewaltige Gotteshaus St. Michael in Hildesheim hat nahezu ein Jahrtausend überdauert, das liebenswürdige Jagdschloß Clemenswerth, der Park von Herrenhausen charakterisieren eine andere Zeit. Ein köstliches Beispiel bürgerlicher Repräsentation im ausgehenden Mittelalter ist der sog. Huldigungssaal im Rathaus der tausendjährigen Kaiserstadt Goslar. Symbol für die Baukunst in der zweiten Hälfte des 20. Jh. sind Fernsehtürme und Staudämme, Kernkraftwerke und Hafenanlagen, Industrie- und Verwaltungsbauten. Die Verbindung nach rückwärts halten die großartigen Rekonstruktionen im Krieg zerstörter wertvoller Bauten. Das Stadthaus von Emden zum Beispiel demonstriert vorzüglich diese einfühlsame Kunst, indem es die Grundgedanken des alten Baues in die Formensprache des 20. Jh. übersetzt.

The State's history and culture are reflected in cathedrals and palaces and no less in the bourgeois structures of past eras and in contemporary architecture. The magnificent ecclisiastical structure in Hildesheim, St. Michael, has survived for almost a thousand years, the enchanting Clemenswerth Hunting Lodge and the Herrenhausen Park (Hanover) are characteristic of other epochs. A magnificent example of bourgeoise representation through the middle ages is the so-called "Huldigungssaal" (Hall of Homage) in the thousand-year-old Imperial City of Goslar. Television masts and huge dams, nuclear power plants and port installations, industrial and administrative buildings symbolise the 20th century. Magnificent reconstructions of almost irreplaceable buildings destroyed during the war retain a link with the past. The Emden Municipal Hall is a superb example of the way in which the basic thought behind the architecture of former times can be translated into the formal language of the twentieth century.

Enfin il y a des villes d'eaux, des stations de bains renommées comme Bad Pyrmont, joliment situées dans un paysage charmant. On y trouve maintes localités intéressantes sur le plan historico-artistique en Basse-Saxe : La puissante église St-Michel à Hildesheim existe depuis à peu près mille ans. L'hôtel de ville de Goslar avec sa célèbre salle gothique richement ornée nous montre la puissance de la bourgeoisie médiévale. Nous admirons le château de plaisance baroque Herrenhausen avec ses gracieux motifs de jardin et le château de chasse Clemenswerth. L'ancien hôtel de ville de la ville Emden, très endommagé au cours de la dernière guerre mondiale, a été fort bien restauré. Dans beaucoup de cités médiévales des édifices anciens ont été reconstruits. Autres villes ont été amenagées en centres industriels avec des usines et des bâtiments d'administration, accentuant le dynamisme de la vie moderne.

Orientierungspunkte im weiten, ebenen Land der norddeutschen Tiefebene — Windmühlen. Hier die Mühle in Meldorf/Dithmarschen.

Landmarks in the sprawling North German flatlands — windmills. Shown is the mill in Meldorf/Dithmarschen.

Dans la vaste plaine de 'Allemagne du Nord on peut s'orienter grâce aux moulins à vent ; voilà le moulin de Meldorf/Dithmarschen.

Fehmarn, die Ostseeinsel, besitzt fruchtbaren Boden / The rich land of the Baltic Island Fehmarn / Fehmarn dans la Baltique a un sol fertile.

Brücke über den Fehmarnsund / Bridge over the Fehmarn Sound / Pont traversant le Fehmarnsund.

Helgoland · Die „weiße" Flotte auf der Reede / Heligoland · The "White Fleet" at anchor / Helgoland · Rade avec la « flottille blanche ».

Helgoland · Nordwestspitze mit „Hengst" / Heligoland · North West headland and the "Stallion" / Helgoland · Le « cheval entier » au nordouest de l'île.

35

Vierzig Kilometer tief dringt der breite Wasserarm der Schlei an der Ostseeküste Schleswig-Holsteins in das Land ein. Beliebte Wassersportorte — für „Gäste" jeglicher Art — sind die Städtchen Arnis (links oben) und Maasholm (rechte Seite).

The wide arm of the Schlei penetrates 25 miles inland on the Schleswig-Holstein Baltic coast. The small townships Arnis (above left) and Maasholm (right) are favourite water sports venues for all types of visitors.

La côte de la Baltique est coupée par la Schlei. Les barques à voiles sont dans leur élément auprès des stations climatiques et de plaisance Arnis (à gauche et Maasholm (à droite).

Schloß Glücksburg · In einem kleinen aufgestauten Teich dicht neben der Flensburger Förde liegt das Stammschloß der Herzöge von Holstein und Könige von Dänemark, eines der Hauptwerke der Renaissance im Norden (1582 — 1587).

Schloss Glücksburg · The family castle of the Dukes of Holstein and the Kings of Denmark lies surrounded by a small artificial pool close to the Flensburg Fjord. One of the North's major examples of Renaissance (1582 — 1587).

Le château Glücksburg (un castel d'eau) non loin de la Flensburger Förde (édifié 1582/87) était la résidence estivale des rois du Danemark et des ducs de Holstein (sommet architectural de la Renaissance).

Westerland auf Sylt.
Kampen · Mondäner Badeort auf der Nordseeinsel Sylt.

Westerland on the Island of Sylt.
Kampen · Bathing resort on the North Sea Island.

Westerland/Sylt.
Kampen · Station de plaisance sur l'île Sylt.

RECHTE SEITE

Schleswig · Südhafen
Flensburg · Nordertor
Kappeln an der Schlei

Schleswig · South Harbour
Flensburg · Northern Gate
Kappeln on the Schlei

Schleswig · Port méridional
Flensburg · « Porte du Nord »
Kappeln sur Schlei

Lübeck · Das Holstentor (1477), ein stolzes Monument norddeutscher Backsteingotik.

Travemünde · Ältestes Ostseebad in Schleswig-Holstein. Im Hintergrund die Viermastbark „Passat" (links).

Sommer, Sonne, Wasser — Urlaubsfreuden im Ostseebad Heiligenhafen (oben).

Kiel, die Landeshauptstadt von Schleswig-Holstein. Hier arbeitet die größte Werft des europäischen Festlands, die Howaldswerke Deutsche Werft — HDW.

Lübeck · The Holstein Gate (1477), proud monument in North German brickwork Gothic.

Travemünde · The oldest Baltic resort in Schleswig-Holstein. Background the four-masted "Passat" (left).

Summer, sun, water — holiday enjoyment in Heiligenhafen on the Baltic (above).

Kiel, Capital of Schleswig-Holstein. The largest shipyards on the European continent, the Howaldswerke Deutsche Werft — HDW.

Lübeck · La porte Holstentor (construction en briques, gothique allemande, 1477).

Travemünde · Le plus ancien bain de mer de Slesvig-Holstein (au fond : la barque « Passat »).

Heiligenhafen — plages, canotages, vedettes à moteurs, ski nautique — le plaisir de l'été.

Kiel, la capitale de Slesvig-Holstein, centre industriel et le principal port. Le chantier Howaldswerke Deutsche Werft (HDW) est le plus grand de l'Europe.

Die „Kieler Woche", das Wimbledon der Segler (oben links und rechts). Kiel-Holtenau, Endpunkt des 99 km langen Nordostseekanals.

The "Kiel Week", the yachtsmen's Wimbledon (top left and right). Kiel-Holtenau, end of the 60 miles long North Sea-Baltic Canal.

Un événement sportif de première importance pour ceux, qui font voile c'est la semaine de Kiel. Holtenau est le bout du canal de Kiel (99 km).

43

Das 1973 eingeweihte Eidersperrwerk schützt die Eiderniederung vor Sturmfluten. Fünf Sieltore von je 40 m Breite sorgen für die Regulierung des Wasserstandes (links). Molenhafen am Eidersperrwerk (oben).

The Eider Bulwark protects the Eider lowlands from floodtides. Five sluices each 130 ft. wide regulate the water level (left). The mole of the Eider bulwark (above).

Depuis 1973 la dépression de l'Eider est protégée grâce à la construction de digues à cinq écluses (40 m de largeur) nommée Eidersperrwerk. Voilà le port auprès du barrage.

Greetsiel · Fischerhaus
Meldorf · Windmühle

Greetsiel · Fisherman's house
Meldorf · Windmill

Greetsiel · Maison de pêcheurs
Meldorf · Moulin à vent

Pilsum · Leuchtturm
Friedrichstadt · Haustür
Kräftige Farben an Häusern und Bauten gehören zum Bild Norddeutschlands.

Pilsum · Lighthouse
Friedrichstadt · Housedoor
Strong Colours on houses and buildings are part of the North German picture.

Pilsum · phare
Friedrichstadt · Porte d'une maison
Les ornements des maisons et monuments de l'Allemagne du Nord sont souvent peints.

Hamburg ist mit rund 1,7 Millionen Einwohnern nach Berlin die größte deutsche Stadt. Wie Amsterdam, Stockholm oder Kopenhagen ist sie eine weltoffene Stadt, die aber längst nicht mehr nur allein von ihrem Hafen lebt, sondern sich eine diversifizierte Industriestruktur zugelegt hat.

Hamburg, 1,700,000 inhabitants, is, after Berlin Germany's biggest city. Like Amsterdam, Stockholm or Copenhagen, it is a city whose gates are wide open, but which no longer lives from its port alone, now boasting a diversified industrial structure.

Hambourg (1,7 millions d'habitants) est après Berlin la plus grande ville de la R.F.A. Comme Amsterdam, Stockholm et Copenhague c'est une métropole cosmopolite, un centre industriel et commercial.

Blick über die Stadt (oben); links im Bild die zum See aufgestaute Alster, das Segelrevier mitten im Häusermeer.
A view of the city (above): left is the Alster shored up on its seaward side, sailing ships among a sea of houses.
La vue à vol d'oiseau nous montre les structures de la cité ; à gauche l'Alster refoulée.

Das Nikolaifleet (links außen), Wasserweg durch die Stadt.
The "Nikolaifleet" (extreme left), waterway through the town.
Le canal Nikolaifleet, voie navigable dans la ville.

Insel der Ruhe, 50 Schritte vom Rathausmarkt (links).
A peaceful retreat, 50 paces from the Rathausmarkt (left).
Un repos libre de tout vacarme — non loin du Marché de l'hôtel de ville.

St. Pauli (rechts/right/à droite).

Das Hamburger Rathaus, 1897 errichtet, steht wegen des moorigen Untergrundes auf 4 000 Pfählen.
Der linke Flügel des Baues gehört der Bürgerschaft, der rechte dem Senat.
The Hamburg Rathaus (Town Hall), built in 1897, stands on 4,000 piles on account of its marshland.
The left wing is for the citizenry, the right for the Senate.
L'hôtel de ville de Hambourg (1897), bâti sur 4000 pilotis à cause du terrain marécageux. L'aile gauche appartient à la bourgeoisie, l'aile droite au sénat.

Blick auf die Howaldtswerke — Deutsche Werft (unten Mitte).
View of the Howaldtswerke — Deutsche Werft (below centre).
Vue à vol d'oiseau sur le chantier Howaldtswerke — Deutsche Werft.

Die neue Köhlbrandbrücke im Hamburger Hafen strahlt den ästhetischen Reiz funktionaler Technik aus.
The new Köhlbrand Bridge in the Port of Hamburg radiates all the aesthetic excitement of functional technology.
Le nouvel pont Köhlbrandbrücke dans le port de Hambourg est un sommet de l'architecture technique.

Das Freilichtmuseum Curslack in den Vierlanden, dem größten zusammenhängenden Gemüseanbaugebiet Deutschlands (oben Mitte).
The Open Air Museum in Curslack in the Vierlanden, the largest compact vegetable growing area in Germany (above centre).
Le musée de Curslack (Vierlanden), la région de cultures de légumes la plus grande de l'Allemagne.

Der Hamburger Hafen bietet auf einer Gesamtfläche von 89 qkm (52 qkm Landfläche und 37 qkm Wasserfläche) Faszilitäten für jede nur denkbare Funktion im Zusammenhang mit dem Umschlag, der Zwischenlagerung, der Verarbeitung und Verteilung von Waren und Produkten des Welthandels. Mit etwa 1100 Häfen in der Welt gibt es ständig Verbindungen, etwa 55 000 Menschen üben hier Funktionen aus, die unmittelbar mit dem Hafen zu tun haben.

The Port of Hamburg, with a total area of 34 sq. miles (20 sq. m dockland, 14 sq. m of water), offers facilities for every conceivable operation in terms of cargo transfer, transit storage and the handling and distribution of goods and products involved in world trade. It is constantly linked with some 1,100 ports all over the world. Some 55,000 people are directly involved in the functioning of the Port.

Le port de Hambourg avec 52 km² de quais et 37 km² de voies navigables est un des plus grands ports de l'Europe, un labyrinthe de bassins, de hangars et de rampes de chargement. La prospérité de Hambourg tient en grande partie de la communication avec plus de 1100 ports dans le monde entier. A peu près 55 000 hommes travaillent dans le port et les bénéfices réalisés sont considérables.

Ausrüstungskai / Fitting-out quay / Quai d'équipement.

Schiffsmaschinenbau bei M.A.N. / Marine engine building at M.A.N. / Construction des machines de vaisseaux chez M.A.N.

Montagehalle für den BO-105-Helikopter bei MBB/HFB / BO-105 helicopter assembly shop / Hangar de montage chez MBB/HFB.

Endmontage des Airbus 300 bei MBB/HFB / Final assembly of the "Airbus 300" at MBB/HFB / Montage de l'airbus 300 chez MBB/HFB.

Pulsierendes Leben auf dem Kurfürstendamm, West-Berlins Flanier- und Shoppingstraße. / Pulsating life on the Kurfürstendamm, West Berlin's promenading and shopping boulevard. /

Le Kurfürstendamm à Berlin (-Ouest), le « grand-monde » s'y donne rendez-vous.

58

Berlin (West) · Blick auf Europa-Center und Kaiser-Wilhelm-Gedächtniskirche. Kongreßhalle am Tiergarten (oben). Der Funkturm (rechts). Blick auf das ICC-Internationales Congress Centrum. Stadtautobahn mit Avus-Verteiler.

Berlin (West) · View of the Europa Center and the Kaiser Wilhelm Memorial Church. Congress Hall at the Zoo (above). The Radio Tower (right). View of the ICC — International Congress Centre. Urban Motorway and Avus intersection.

Vue à vol d'oiseau : le « centre européen » et l'église commémorative de l'empereur Guillaume. Le hall des congrès dans le parc Tiergarten (en haut). L'ancien radiophare de Berlin (à droite). L'autostrade métropolitaine et Avus.

Badefreuden am Wannsee / Bathing on the Wannsee / une plage au bord du Wannsee.

Englischer Briefkasten an der Greenwich-Promenade in Berlin-Tegel.
A Londoner letter-box on the Greenwich-promenade, Berlin-Tegel.
Une boîte aux lettres anglaise sur la promenade de Greenwich, Berlin-Tegel.

Der neue Flughafen Berlin-Tegel / The new Berlin-Tegel Airport / le nouvel aéroport Berlin-Tegel.

Schleuse Spandau an der Zitadelle / The sluice of Spandau near the citadel. / L'écluse de Spandau auprès de la citadelle.

Seit 1695 wurde am Schloß Charlottenburg (oben links) in West-Berlin gebaut. Joh. Arn. Nering hatte damals begonnen, 1698 folgt eine Erweiterung, um 1712 wurde auf den Mitteltrakt der Kuppelbau gesetzt und der Orangeriewestflügel gebaut, dem 1740—43 der Ostflügel durch C. G. von Knobelsdorff hinzugefügt wurde, Langhaus baute 1788—1791 ein Theater.
Von Paul Wallot (1884—94) stammt das Reichtagsgebäude (links unten); nach den Zerstörungen im letzten Krieg wurde der Bau in etwas schlichterer Fassung renoviert.
Die „Kaiser-Wilhelm-Gedächtniskirche" (oben rechts), ein von Prof. Eiermann entworfenes Gotteshaus, wurde neben der Ruine des alten Baus errichtet.
Links im Bild das „Europa-Center"

Building on the Charlottenburg Schloss (above left) in West Berlin was begun by Joh. Arn. Nering in 1695. An extension followed in 1698 and in 1712 a dome was set above the centre and the "Orange" west wing erected, to which the east wing was added by von Knobelsdorff (1740—43), followed by a theatre by Langhans in 1788—1791
The Reichstag building (1884—94) is the work of Paul Wallot (below left). After the destruction of the last war it was renovated in a somewhat simpler style
The "Kaiser Wilhelm Memorial Church" (top right), a place of worship designed by Professor Eiermann, was built alongside the ruins of the old edifice. On the left is the "Europa Center"

Le château Charlottenburg à Berlin(-Ouest) fondé 1695/99 (dessins de J. A. Nering), extensions considérables (1701/07) par 'larchitecte Eosander v. Goethe et (1740/43) par Knobelsdorff. L'orangerie fut édifié 1709/12, le théâtre (G. G. Langhans) 1788/91. La coupole fut ajoutée vers 1712.
Le bâtiment de la Diète (1884/94) est un édifice impressionnant (dessins de Paul Wallot), restauré jusqu'à 1966 après les destructions de la guerre.
La nouvelle église commémorative de l'empereur Guilleaume à côté de l'ancien clocher (E. Eiermann 1961/63) est surnommé la »cathédrale bleue«.
A gauche le »centre européen«.

Pferdezucht / Horse breeding / élevage de chevaux

Worpswede · Rodeliuspark / parc de Rodelius

Torfabbau / Peat harvesting / Tourbage

Wattwanderung an der Nordseeküste / Rambling on the North Sea sandbanks / Excursion dans la plaine maritime marécageuse de la mer du Nord

Krabbenkutter auf „kleiner Fahrt" und bei Ebbe im Schlick / Shrimpboat in coastal waters and at ebbtide in the Schlick / Bateaux de pêche en cherchant des crevettes

Gegensätze an der Nordseeküste: Der verträumte Fischereihafen Greetsiel in Ostfriesland und „Große Pötte" in Bremerhaven.

Contrasts on the North Sea coast: the romantic fishing harbour Greetsiel in East Friesland and the "Grosse Pötte" in Bremerhaven.

Des contrastes à la côte de la mer du Nord : le petit port de pêcheurs Greetsiel (Frise orientale) et les vaisseaux gigantesques à Bremerhaven.

Bremen, das kleinste Bundesland, besitzt den nach Hamburg größten Hafen der Bundesrepublik. Das Bild zeigt das Rathaus, dessen Bau 1409 begonnen wurde. Der Roland (oben rechts), Symbol bürgerlicher Freiheit, wurde 1404 errichtet; daneben die Böttchergasse, ein Kulturzentrum en miniature in Bremen. Unten historische Häuser am Bremer Rathausmarkt

Bremen, the smallest Federal State, has, after Hamburg, the biggest West German port. Shown is the Town Hall, begun in the year 1409. "Roland" (above right), symbol of free citizens, came into being in 1404; adjacent is the Böttchergasse, a Bremen cultural centre in miniature, and below historic houses on the Rathausmarkt

Brême, le plus petit land de la R.F.A., est le deuxième port de commerce de la R.F.A. Voilà l'hôtel de ville édifié en 1405/10. La statue de Roland (à droite) est le symbole de la liberté des bourgeois. La rue Böttcher est un centre artistique traditionel. En bas : anciennes maisons patriciennes bordant la place du Marché.

Als in der ersten Hälfte des vorigen Jahrhunderts die Weser versandete, kaufte der Bremer Bürgermeister Johann Smidt 45 km flußaufwärts vom Königreich Hannover einen Küstenstreifen an der Wesermündung. Hier wurde Bremerhaven gegründet, heute einer der bedeutendsten deutschen Seehäfen, der größte Fischereihafen Deutschlands dazu. Da es später doch noch gelang, die 70 km lange Unterweser zu vertiefen, besitzt Bremen jetzt zwei Seehäfen. Die Zahl der Liniendienste in den bremischen Häfen erhöhte sich z. B. von 1950 bis 1978 von 120 auf 459; mit etwa 1000 Häfen in aller Welt werden Verbindungen gehalten.

When the River Weser began to silt up in the first half of the last century, Bremen Bürgermeister Johann Smidt purchased a strip of coast some 28 miles seawards at the mouth of the Weser from the Kingdom of Hanover. This became Bremerhaven, today one of Germany's most

important seaports and her biggest fishing port. Later it became possible to dredge 45 miles of the Lower Weser, so that Bremen now has two ports. The number of regular shipping lines in these ports rose from 120 to 459 between 1950 and 1978. There are links with some 1,000 ports throughout the world

Quand le port de Brême, s'ensablait, le maire de Brême J. Smidt a fondé en 1827 l'avant-port de Bremerhaven au milieu d'un territoire auprès de l'embouchure de la Weser acheté du royaume de Hanovre. Bremerhaven est le plus grand port de pêche de L'Allemagne, où les enchères aux poissons ont lieu. Aujourd'hui les ports de Brême et de Bremerhaven sont complémentaires. Le trafic des deux ports est considérable (augmentation des lignes de 1950 à 1976 : de 120 à 459), communication avec à peu près 1000 ports dans le monde entier

Wilhelmshaven

Oldenburg · Hafen/Port/port

Oldenburg · Schloß / Schloss / le château

Bad Zwischenahn · Bauernhaus / Farmhouse / ferme

Emden an der Emsmündung gehört mit zur Spitzengruppe der deutschen Häfen, in erster Linie durch Kohle- und Erzverladung aus dem Ruhrgebiet

Emden, at the mouth of the Ems, is among the leading ports in Germany, primarily as a transit port for coal and ore from the Ruhr area

La ville Emden auprès de l'embouchure de l'Ems est le troisième port de la R.F.A. (après Hambourg et Brême), débouche principal de la Ruhr

Emden · Rathaus am Delft (links)
Emden · Hafentor am Delft (rechts außen)
Emden · Rathausdetail (links unten)

Emden · Town Hall on the Delft (left)
Emden · Port gateway on the Delft (extreme right)
Emden · Town Hall, detail (extreme left)

Emden · l'ancien hôtel de ville (à gauche)

Emden, » Porte du Port «
(à droite à l'extérieur)
Emden, détail de l'hôtel
de ville (à gauche à
l'extérieur)

Emden · Bruchstraße
(links)

Emden · Rückseite
des Rathauses (rechts)

Pilsum · Leuchtturm
(oben)

Emden · Bruchstrasse
(left)

Emden · Rear view
of the Town Hall (right)

Pilsum · Lighthouse
(above)

Emden · rue Bruch
(à gauche)

Emden, partie derrière
de l'ancien hôtel de
ville (à droite)

Pilsum · phare (en haut)

Das Jagdschloß Clemenswerth am Hümmling (links) wurde 1736–50 von Johann Conrad Schlaun für den Wittelsbacher Clemens August, Kurfürst von Köln, erbaut.

Clemenswerth hunting lodge on the Hümmling (left) was built between 1736 and 1750 by Johann Conrad Schlaun for Clemens August Wittelsbach, Prince Elector of Cologne

Le château de chasse Clemenswerth bâti sous l'impulsion de l'électeur de Cologne Clemence Auguste (de la famille Wittelsbach) par J. C. Schlaun (1736–50) auprès de la colline Hümmling (à gauche)

Moor bei Friesoythe im Ammerland (links)

Moor near Friesoythe in the Ammerland (left)

Marécage dans les environs de Friesoythe, Ammerland (à gauche)

Leer. Die Alte Waage, ein Barockbau aus dem Jahr 1714, und Rathaus (rechts)

Leer. The old Baroque weighbridge dating from 1714 and the Town Hall (right)

Leer : la maison de la balance ancienne, édifice baroque de 1714 et l'hôtel de ville (à droite)

Leer · Die Sonnenuhr an der Alten Waage

Leer. The sundial on the old weighbridge

Leer : Cadran solaire ornement de la façade de la maison de L'ancienne balance

77

Osnabrück · Rathaus; Bischöfliches Palais; Dom St. Peter / Town Hall; Bishop's Palace; St. Peter's Cathedral / l'hôtel de ville ; résidence des évêques ; cathédrale St-Pierre

Osnabrück · Blick auf die Stadt; Schnitzereien am Willmannschen Haus / View of the town; Carvings on the "Willmann House" / vue à vol d'oiseau ; la maison Willmann, détail

Lüneburg · Rathaus und Markt (links)
Lüneburger Heide (oben)
Lüneburg · Bürgerhäuser an der Ilmenau

Lüneburg · Town Hall and market (left)
Lüneburg Heath (above)
Lüneburg · Dwelling houses on the Ilmenau

Lunebourg · hôtel de ville et marché (à gauche)
Les Landes de Lunebourg (en haut)
Lunebourg · maisons patriciennes auprès de l'Ilmenau

Im Totengrund am Wilseder Berg mitten im Naturschutzgebiet Lüneburger Heide
In the burial place on the Wilsed Rise in the middle of the Lüneburg Heath Natural Park
Les Landes de Lunebourg : territoire de protection de la nature » Totengrund « auprès du mont Wilseder Berg

Celle · Schloß (1533—1558) der Herzöge von Braunschweig-Lüneburg
The Schloss (1533—1558) of the Dukes of Brunswick-Lüneburg
Château, résidence des ducs de Brunswick-Lunebourg (1533—58)

Heidschnucken, eine für die Lüneburger Heide charakteristische Schafrasse
Heidschnucken, a characteristic sheep breed on the Lüneburg Heath
Troupeau des Moutons » Heidschnucken «

Hannover ist die Hauptstadt des Landes Niedersachsen. Nach den schweren Zerstörungen des 2. Weltkrieges wurde die Stadt großzügig und modern wiederaufgebaut, manches zerstörte Bauwerk konnte wiederhergestellt werden, so das Alte Rathaus, die gotische Marktkirche, das Opernhaus oder das Leineschloß, in dem heute der niedersächsische Landtag residiert.

Das Bild links zeigt die Festhalle. Die „Herrenhäuser Gärten" (oben), angelegt im 17. Jahrhundert, gehören zu den schönsten Gartenanlagen Deutschlands. Streng geometrisch, wohl geordnet und gepflegt, bedeckt der Große Garten ein weites Areal mit Blumen und Bäumen, mit Skulpturen und Wasserkünsten. Allein die Hainbuchenhecken sind 21 km lang

Hanover is the capital of the State of Lower Saxony. The town was rebuilt on modern, sweeping lines following the devastation of World War II, and many an almost destroyed building was restored, among these the old Town Hall, the Gothic "Marktkirche," the Opera House and the Leineschloss, today the seat of the State Parliament

The picture right shows the Festival Hall. The "Herrenhaus Gardens" (above), laid out in the 17th century, are among the modt beautiful in Germany. Severely geometrical, superbly ordered and cared for, the gardens cover a vast area with flowers and trees, sculptures and aquatic artworks. The Hainbuchen Basins alone extend over 12 miles

Hanovre est la capitale politique de la Basse-Saxe. Très endommagé au cours de la dernière guerre mondiale, Hanovre a été fort bien restauré ; à signaler particulièrement : l'ancien hôtel de ville, l'église gothique du Marché, l'opéra et le château Leineschloß, aujourd'hui établissement de la diète

A gauche : le hall des fêtes. Un très bel échantillon des parcs est le célèbre et charmant grand parc du château Herrenhausen, établi au 17e siècle selon l'ordonnance sévère géométrique des parcs classiques ; gracieux motifs de jardin et nombreuses fontaines (longeur de haies : 21 km !)

Hannover · Historisches Museum am Hohen Ufer mit Beginenturm (links oben)
Hannover · Rathaus am Maschsee (links außen)
Hannover · Die Marktkirche aus der Mitte des 14. Jh. (links)
Hannover · Hauptbahnhof mit Fußgängerzone

Hanover · Historic Museum on the Hohes Ufer with the "Beginenturm" (above left)
Hanover · Town Hall on the Maschsee (extreme left)
Hanover · The Marktkirche dating from the middle of the 14th century (left)
Hanover · Main Station with pedestrian area

Hanovre · Musée historique et » Tour des Béguines « (à gauche en haut)
Hanovre · hôtel de ville auprès du lac Maschsee (à gauche à l'extérieur)
Hanovre · l'église du Marché (14e siècle)
Hanovre · gare centrale et la zone réservée aux piétons

Alljährlich im April sprengt Hannover alle Maßstäbe. Zur Hannover-Messe, der größten Industrieschau der Welt, kommen mehr als eine Million Besucher und annähernd 5000 Aussteller.

Each year in April Hanover bursts at the seams. More than a million visitors and almost 5,000 exhibitors come to the Hanover Fair, the world's biggest industrial show.

La foire de Hanovre, qui a lieu chaque avril, est une exposition internationale bien renommée. Une million de visiteurs et à peu près 5000 exposants s'y donnent rendez-vous

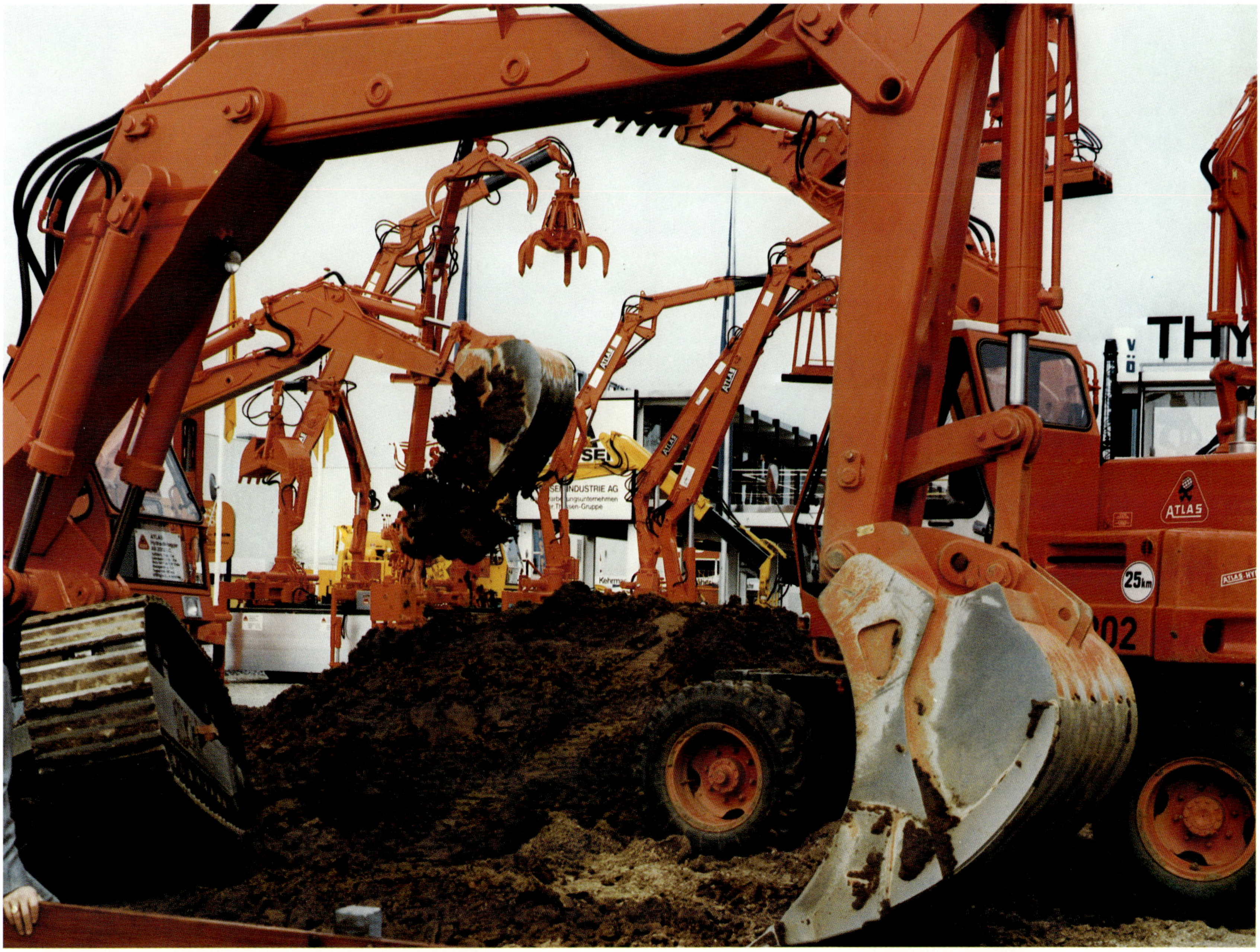
ATLAS
25km

aerospatiale
SNECMA
D-EGGI
F-ZWRX
alpha jet 04

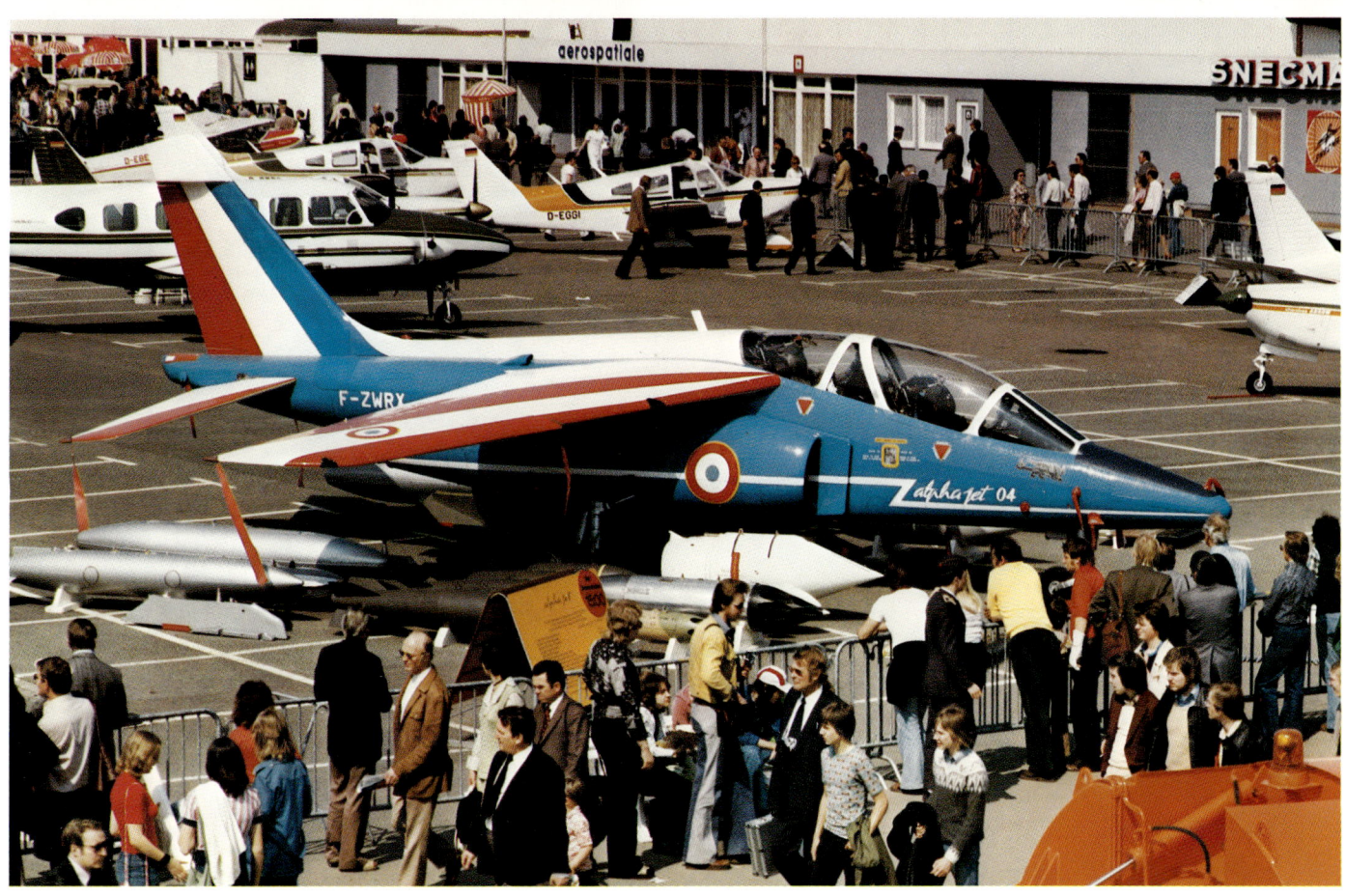

Göttingen · Gänselieselbrunnen
Göttingen · Gänseliesel Fountain
Göttingen · la Fontaine de la Lisette aux oies

Jugend
Young people
Jeunesse

Braunschweig · Rathauslauben (oben)

Braunschweig · Town Hall passage (above)

Brunswick · arcades de l'hôtel de ville (en haut)

Braunschweig · Burgplatz mit Burg Dankwarderode, Dom und Löwenmonument

Braunschweig · Burgplatz with Dankwarderode Castle, Cathedral and "Lions Monument"

Brunswick · la Place du Château, le château fort Dankwarderode, la cathédrale St-Blaise et le lion de bronze

Das Volkswagenwerk in Wolfsburg, eines der größten und modernsten Industrieunternehmen Deutschlands

The Volkswagen Factory in Wolfsburg, one of Germany's largest and most modern industrial undertakings

Volkswagen (à Wolfsburg) est une des entriprises industrielles les plus grandes de l'Allemagne

93

Die Okertalsperre im Harz hat ein Fassungsvermögen von 47,5 Millionen m³, gestaut von einer Sperrmauer, die 260 m lang und 75 m hoch ist. Auf der rechten Bildseite der Harz, wie ihn die Natur formt, unten das unberührte Tal der Oker

The Okertal Reservoir in the Harz Mountains has a capacity of 47.5 million cubic meters contained by a dam 850 feet long and 290 feet high. To the right of the picture are the Harz Mountains, a natural wonderland, below the natural Oker Valley

Le bassin du barrage » Okertalsperre « dans la montagne Harz refoule l'eau de l'Oker (47,5 millions m³). Le barrage a 260 m de longueur et 75 m de hauteur. A droite : la forêt, en bas : la vallée pittoresque de l'Oker

Kalibergwerk der Wintershall AG im Harz
The Wintershall AG potash deposits in the Harz
Mine de potasse de la Wintershall AG dans le Harz

DIE MITTE
THE CENTRAL AREA
ALLEMAGNE MOYENNE

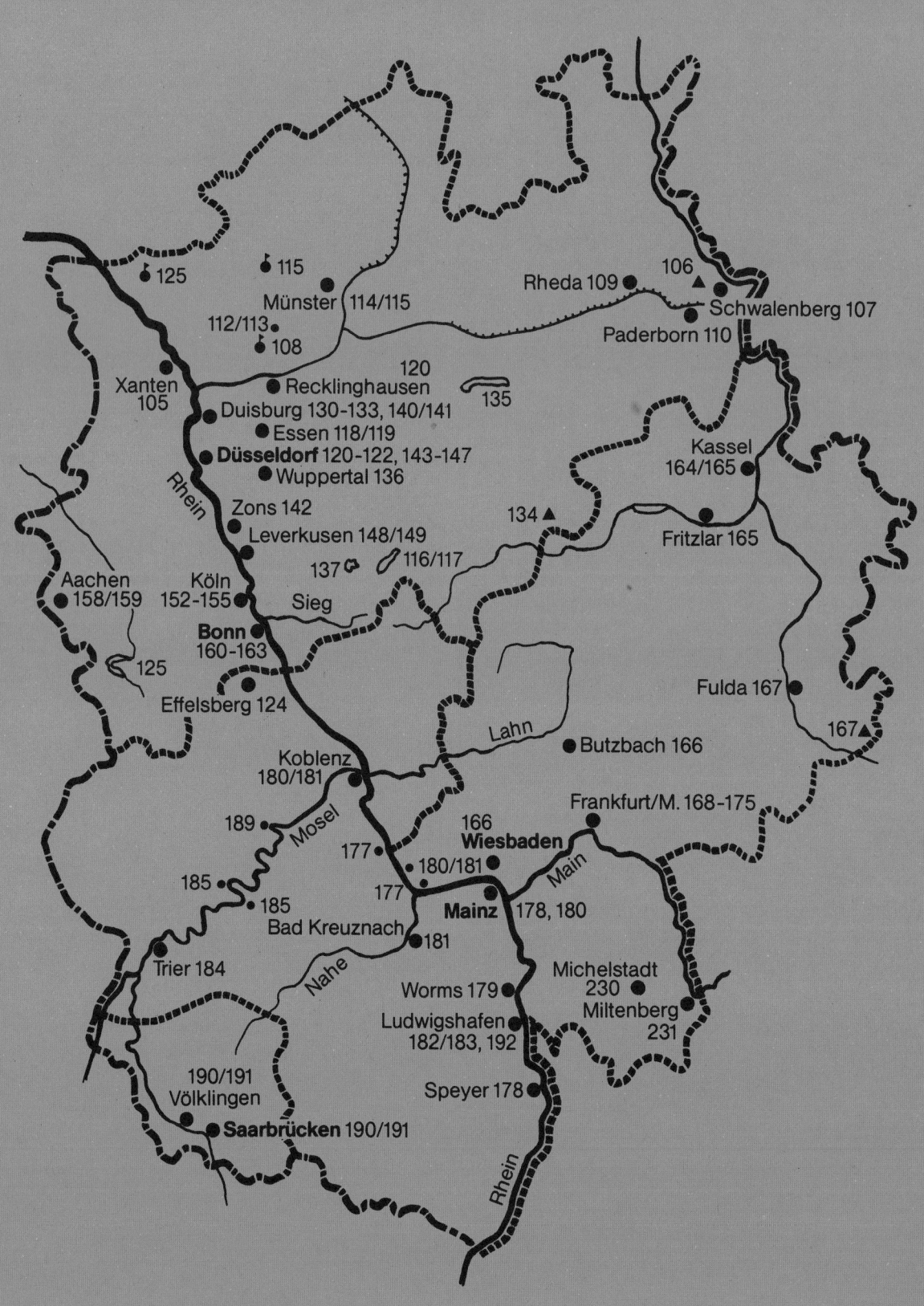

DIE MITTE

THE CENTRAL AREA

L'ALLEMAGNE MOYENNE

Nordrhein-Westfalen, mit rund 17 Millionen Einwohnern das bevölkerungsreichste Land der Bundesrepublik Deutschland ist ein Land der Gegensätze. Der ungeheuren Konzentration von Menschen und Maschinen im Gebiet um Rhein und Ruhr stehen weite Landstriche gegenüber, in denen die Agrarwirtschaft dominiert. Das Gebirgsland im Süden kontrastiert mit dem breit hingelagerten Flachland in den nördlichen Landesteilen. Unterschiedlich sind auch die Menschen: Während man im Rheinland auf aufgeschlossene, fröhliche Herzlichkeit trifft — in tausenderlei Abstufungen wohlgemerkt —, lassen die Westfalen eine mehr in sich gekehrte Mentalität erkennen. Zwei Zahlen sollte man in diesem Zusammenhang auch festhalten: Etwa die Hälfte der Bevölkerung wohnt in Städten mit mehr als 100 000 Einwohnern; und fast ein Viertel der Menschen in Nordrhein-Westfalen sind Heimatvertriebene und Zugewanderte. Diese Tatsachen beeinflussen das Leben des Landes in besonderem Maß.

Während das Tiefland des Niederrheins und der Westfälischen Bucht etwa zwei Drittel des Landes einnimmt, besteht das restliche Drittel aus verschiedenen Zügen des Rheinischen Schiefergebirges. Links des Rheins liegen die nördliche Eifel und Hohes Venn, die vulkanischen Ursprungs sind, rechts finden wir das Bergische Land, Sauerland und Siegerland. Im Nordosten des Landes liegen Teutoburger Wald und Wiehengebirge. Neben den natürlichen Wasserstraßen (an der Spitze Rhein und Ruhr, an deren Zusammenfluß in Duisburg der größte Binnenhafen der Welt liegt) durchqueren zahlreiche Kanäle das Land. In vielen Gebieten wurden darüber hinaus Flüsse zu großen künstlichen Seen gestaut, die in erster Linie der Versorgung mit Wasser und Energie dienen, die außerdem aber auch unschätzbaren Wert als Erholungsgebiete rings um die großen Städte haben.

Die Hauptstadt des Landes ist Düsseldorf. Reiche Bodenschätze sind die wichtigste Grundlage der massierten Industrien im Zentrum des Bundeslandes. Das stärkste wirtschaftliche Kraftfeld Deutschlands bildet das Ruhrgebiet mit Schwerpunkt in Essen, mit Kohlenbergbau, Eisen- und Stahlerzeugung, Maschinenindustrie. Der Düsseldorfer Raum beherbergt eine Vielzahl von Industrien und ist zugleich Sitz der bedeutendsten Industrieverwaltungen. Leverkusen ist durch die chemische Industrie groß geworden. Solingen hat sich einen Namen gemacht als Fabri-

Northrhein-Westphalia, this state, with some 17 million inhabitants, is the most heavily populated state in the Federal Republic of Germany and also a region of contrasts. The vast concentration of people and machinery in the Rhein and Ruhr area are contrasted by areas of sprawling country in which agriculture dominates. The mountainous country in the south is offset by broad stretches of flat country in the northern parts of the state. The people too display marked differences: In the Rheinland one is greeted by frank and open, cheerful heartiness — albeit in a thousand-and-one different shades — while the Westphalians display a far more introverted mentality.

Here, two statistical facts are noteworthy: around half of the inhabitants live in towns with over 100 000 inhabitants, and almost a quarter of all residents in Northrhein-Westphalia are either refugees from the former Central and East German provinces or immigrants from other areas. These facts have a very powerful influence on the life of the State. While the lowlands of the Lower Rhein and the Westphalian Bight make up some two-thirds of the State, the remaining third consists of various sectors of the schist uplands of the Rhein. Left of the Rhein are the Northern Eifel and the "Hohes Venn," both of volcanic origin, and to the right lie the Bergisches Land, the Sauerland and the Siegerland. To the north-east of the state are the Teutoburg Forest and the uplands of the Wiehengebirge. In addition to the natural waterways (the most important being the Rhein and the Ruhr with the world's biggest inland port, Duisburg, at their confluence), numerous canals criss-cross the State. In many regions rivers have been dammed to form artificial lakes, aimed primarily at producing power and water, but which are also of inestimable value as spots for recuperation around the large towns. The state capital is Düsseldorf. Rich mineral deposits are the vital basis of the concentrated industries in the centre of the State. The Ruhr area with its axis Essen is Germany's most powerful industrial and economic motor, with coal mining, iron and steel production and machine building industries. The Düsseldorf area contains a multiplicity of industries and is also the administrative centre of the big industrial firms. The chemical industry has transformed Leverkusen into a vital centre, Solingen has become renowned as the centre of the world famous

La densité de *Nordrhein-Westfalen* (17 millions d'habitants) est la plus élevée de la R.F.A., c'est une région caractérisée par sa diversité, qui comprend la vaste agglomération dans le bassin de la Ruhr, le pays des riches cultures dans la grande plaine et sur les collines tertiaires recouvertes d'un épais manteau de limons fertiles et le sol pauvre des montagnes méridionales. Aussi la mentalité des gens des bords du Rhin et celle des Westphaliens est différente : les uns sont gais et de bonne humeur et les autres peu communicatifs.

Deux tiers du pays sont formés de la plaine de Cologne et de celle de la Westphalie, très morcelé il comprend aussi des fragments du Massif schisteux rhénan et les petits massifs volcaniques (Eifel septentrionale et Hohes Venn) et sur l'autre rive du Rhin les montagnes couvertes de forêts (Bergisches Land, Sauerland et Siegerland), plus au nord-est la Forêt de Teutobourg et la montagne Wiehengebirge. La densité des voies navigables et la présence de riches bassin houillers ont favorisé l'essor industriel dans le bassin de la Ruhr. Duisburg-Ruhrort, au confluent de la Ruhr et du Rhin est le premier port fluvial du monde. Les barrages et réservoirs pourvoient les grandes villes d'eau et d'électricité et ils sont des terroirs de récréation populaires. La capitale est Düsseldorf.

La métallurgie allemande est surtout groupée dans le bassin de la Ruhr (Essen, Dortmund, Bochum). Düsseldorf, la métropole de Nordrhein-Westfalen est un centre industriel, et commercial, siège de beaucoup d'associations et de sociétes. Beaucoup d'entreprises industrielles (surtout des fabriques de produits chimiques sont domiciliés dans la ville Leverkusen sur le Rhin. Solingen est un centre métallurgique ancien. Les ciseaux et les

kationsort der weltberühmten Solinger Scheren und Messer, Wipperfürth durch seine Textilindustrie. Im sauerländisch-siegerländischen Bereich spielt die Kleineisenindustrie eine wichtige Rolle. Köln ist Sitz großer Bank- und Versicherungszentralen. Linksrheinisch dehnt sich das Braunkohlengebiet bis hinüber nach Aachen. Nordrhein-Westfalen liefert 90% der deutschen Steinkohle und 85% der Braunkohle; 70% der Rohstahlerzeugung entfallen auf das Land. Zu erwähnen sind die Schwerpunkte der Textil- und Bekleidungsindustrie in Aachen und Krefeld, aber auch in Bielefeld. Von Bedeutung sind auch die Produktionsstätten für Feinmechanik und Optik sowie für Nahrungs- und Genußmittel. Dortmund, die Stadt im Schnittpunkt der nordsüdlichen und ostwestlichen Verkehrswege, ist eine berühmte Bierbrauerstadt.

Im flacher werdenden Norden des Landes spielt die Landwirtschaft eine größere Rolle: Mehr als die Hälfte der Gesamtfläche ist Bauernland. Sowohl Getreide- und Zuckerrüben- als auch Futtermittel- und Hackfruchtanbau sind verbreitet. Überall finden sich Viehzucht- und Milchwirtschaftsbetriebe, im Nordosten auch Schweinezucht. Dülmen und Warendorf im Westfälischen zeichnen sich durch ihre Pferdezucht aus.

Die industriellen wie die landwirtschaftlichen Kapazitäten könnten ihren Rang nicht erreicht haben ohne ein umfassendes Bildungsangebot. Nicht weniger als sieben Universitäten und eine Technische Universität bilden die Spitze mit ihren Hörsälen und Forschungsstätten. Einige von ihnen haben lange Traditionen, andere sind erst in unserer Zeit entstanden und rasch gewachsen. An ihre Seite treten Fachhochschulen und Akademien für die verschiedensten Bildungszweige.

Den Hintergrund für alle wirtschaftlichen und wissenschaftlichen Erfolge des Landes bildet die ungewöhnlich vielschichtige politische Vergangenheit. Hier ist nicht Raum, alle die verschlungenen Wege nachzuzeichnen, die die vielen Dutzend kleinen und großen Territorien durch die Jahrhunderte genommen haben, die seit dem Zweiten Weltkrieg das heutige Land Nordrhein-Westfalen bilden. Geistliche und weltliche Fürsten haben Macht und Einfluß gewonnen und wieder verloren, die Städte haben mit Ehrgeiz und Energie Machtpositionen aufgebaut, die ihnen auf kürzere oder längere Zeit einen beachtlichen Rang sicherten. Glaubenskriege haben zu schweren Auseinandersetzungen geführt, der 30jährige Krieg hat Spuren hinterlassen, desgleichen die Ära des großen Korsen, nicht zu sprechen von den beiden großen Kriegen unseres Jahrhunderts.

Zeugnisse all dieser Entwicklungen sind in unglaublicher Fülle über das Land verstreut. Am Rhein entlang finden sich allenthalben Reminiszenzen an die römische Besetzung. Mittelalterliche Dome und Münster stehen heute noch in herrlicher Kette von Aachen über Köln und Bonn, Altenberg und Essen, Münster, Paderborn und Freckenhorst bis hinüber nach Herford, Minden und Corvey.

Solingen cutlery, Wipperfürth on account of its textiles. In the Sauerland-Siegerland region the small ironware industry plays an important part. Cologne is the seat of big banking and insurance undertakings. To the left of the Rhein the lignite area extends across as far as Aachen. Northrhein-Westphalia supplies 90 per cent of German hard coal and 85 per cent of the lignite; 70 per cent of basic steel production is supplied by this State. The textile and garment industry centres Krefeld, Bielefeld and Aachen should also be mentioned. There are a number of important centres of production for fine mechanics and optics as well as for foodstuffs and beverages. Dortmund, at the intersection of the north-south and east-west traffic routes, is a world-renowned brewing centre.

In the northern parts, which become ever flatter, agriculture plays a vital role; more than half of the total area is agricultural land. Grain, sugar beet, fodder crops and silage are widespread. Cattle raising and dairying farms are to be found everywhere, with pig production in the north-east. Dülmen and Warendorf in Westphalia are renowned for horse breeding.

Neither the industrial nor the agricultural capacities could ever have achieved their present status without adequate educational facilities. No fewer than seven universities plus one technical university, with research facilities and auditoriums, lead the field. Some of these have long traditions, others emerged in our time and have grown rapidly. Alongside these are technical high schools and academies for all branches of training.

The background for all the economic and scientific successes of this area was set by the unusually diversified political past. There is no room here to go into all the tortuous paths taken in the past by many dozens of small and large territories throughout the centuries and which together, following the second World War, form present-day Northrhein-Westphalia. Both spiritually-minded and material Princes gained and lost their power, the cities built up positions of power through ambition and energy and ensured for themselves a respected status on the long or short-term. Religious wars led to grave conflicts. The Thirty Years' War has left its scars, just as has also the era of the "Mighty Corsican," not to mention the two World Wars.

Evidences of all these historic events are scattered all over the region in unimaginable abundance. All along the Rhein there are reminders of the Roman occupation. Cathedrals and minsters from the middle ages form a magnificent chain from Aachen through Cologne and Bonn and on to Altenberg and Essen, Münster, Paderborn and Freckenhorst as far as Herford, Minden and Corvey. Out-

couteaux de Solingen sont connus dans le monde entier. Wipperfürth est une ville industrielle assidue (industrie textile, des appareils électriques et de la papeterie). Cologne est siège de maintes banques et compagnies d'assurances. Les industries mécaniques et textiles sont dispersées (Aix-la-Chapelle, Wuppertal, Krefeld et Bielefeld). Les industries alimentaires sont très actives. Dortmund n'est pas seulement un foyer industriel mais aussi un lieu des brasseries renommées. L'houille et l'acier ont depuis longtemps dominé la vie économique de la région industrielle aux bords du Rhin et de la Ruhr (90 % de l'houille allemande, 85 % du lignite, 70 % de l'acier).

Le nord est surtout un pays rural. Les principales cultures sont le seigle, le blé, la betterave à sucre et la pomme de terre. L'élevage est très important (vaches à lait renommées), bovins et porcs. L'élevage des chevaux est traditionel dans la Westphalie (par exemple à Warendorf et à Dülmen, dans le nord-est vous trouvez l'élevage des porcs.

Sept universités et une université technique, des écoles polytechniques et beaucoup de musées, produits de l'antique terroir culturel, sont des témoins de la tradition intellectuelle du pays et la base de l'essor industriel et rural.

Nordrhein-Westfalen faisait autrefois partie de plusieurs Etats, au cours de son histoire politique et culturelle il y avait de continuelles variations de son territoire. Le territoire de Nordrhein-Westalen s'émiettait en une multitude d'Etats de toutes les dimensions (pensez aux électeurs de Cologne, dont la résidence se trouvait à Bonn). Les frontières de la Westphalie changeaient à plusieurs reprises (conséquences des guerres de Trente Ans et de Sept Ans) et des victoires de Napoléon. Beaucoup de villes ont été endommagées au cours des guerres perpétuelles — très graves les destructions des guerres mondiales. Nordrhein-Westfalen est riche en témoins de toutes époques culturelles. Auprès du Rhin des monuments artistique surgissent avec la présence romaine. Vous trouvez des cathédrales sublimes à Aix-la-Chapelle, à Cologne, à Bonn, à Altenberg, à Essen, à Münster, à Paderborn et à Minden. A retenir parmi les nombreux monuments : l'église de l'ancien collège à Freckenhorst, le couvent des chanoinesses à Herford et l'abbaye bénédictine Corvey. Bel échantillon des édifices profa-

Unter den Profanbauten jener Zeit ragt das gotische Rathaus von Köln (1360) hervor. Schlösser aus der Zeit von Renaissance und Barock, die einst höfischer Repräsentation dienten oder fürstliche Launen widerspiegeln, haben heute Universitäten aufgenommen wie Bonn und Münster, vielfach dienen sie auch als Sitz von Museen und Behörden; so das Poppelsdorfer Schloß in Bonn, die Hohe Burg in Homburg, das Schlößchen von Krefeld.

Schloß Augustusburg bei Brühl ist Repräsentationsstätte der deutschen Bundesregierung geworden. Ein eigenes Kapitel würden die Wasserschlösser verdienen, über hundert an der Zahl, die überall in Westfalen an vergangene Zeiten und große Namen erinnern, wenngleich sie in unserer Zeit meistens die Herren gewechselt haben und nun Behörden Raum bieten.

Bürgerliche Baukunst alter Zeit zeigt sich in wunderschönen alten Fachwerkbauten, besonders in der Eifel und im Sauerland. Auch unser Jahrhundert hat Baudenkmäler hervorgebracht, die jedoch allzu häufig nicht als solche erkannt werden, einfach weil sie zu unserem Alltag gehören, seien es nun die kühnen Rheinbrücken oder die riesigen Fernsehtürme, Fabriken oder moderne Theaterbauten. Auch viele Museen sind in neue Häuser gezogen. Eines der überzeugendsten Beispiele ist das Römisch-Germanische Museum in Köln, das der ältesten Geschichte des Landes Platz bietet und gerade durch den Kontrast zwischen Inhalt und Präsentation der Objekte förmlich eine Wiedergeburt herbeiführt. Zahlreiche andere Museen überall im Land haben die Aufgabe, künstlerische, wissenschaftliche und wirtschaftliche Entwicklungen aufzuzeigen. Erinnert sei an das Folkwang-Museum in Essen, das Klingenmuseum in Solingen, das Röntgenmuseum in Lennep (das heute ein Stadtteil von Remscheid ist).

Die Bevölkerung Nordrhein-Westfalens ist überall an harte Arbeit gewöhnt. Gerade der Zwang zur Selbstbehauptung in der heutigen Arbeitswelt begünstigt aber die Lust zu leidenschaftlich betriebenen Hobbys: vielerlei Basteleien und jede Art von Sport — wem wären nicht die berühmten Fußball-Clubs des Landes ein Begriff. Nicht gerade dem Sport, aber auch dem Ausgleich dient eine andere Art von Körperpflege: Man ißt gern bodenständig und trinkt nicht weniger gern, was das Land zu bieten hat. Schinken und Pumpernickel, Bier und Korn gehören auch zum Image des Landes.

Hessen ist, abgesehen von den Stadtstaaten, das einzige Land Deutschlands, dessen Grenzen keine nichtdeutschen Länder berühren, es ist wirklich ein Land der Mitte, reich an Wald und Gebirgen, vom breiten Main, von Lahn und Fulda und manchem anderen Fluß durchzogen. Der Taunus erreicht fast 900 m Höhe, der Vogelsberg 774 m, der Hohe Meissner 750 m.

Fremde von irgendwo in der Welt, die auf dem Luftweg anreisen und auf dem Rhein-

standing among the secular structures of that period is the Gothic Town Hall in Cologne (1360). Renaissance and Baroque castles, once serving to express courtly pomp or the whims of Princes, today serve to house universities, as in Bonn and Münster. They also serve for museums and local authorities — Poppelsdorfer Schloss in Bonn, the Hohe Burg in Homburg, the "Schlösschen" in Krefeld. Schloss Augustusburg, near Brühl, is now the big reception place of the Federal Government. The moated castles, over a hundred of them, which everywhere in Westphalia remind us of bygone times and impressive names, would fill a chapter — even though in our day they have mostly changed ownership and serve as administrative buildings. Ancient civic architecture is evidenced in beautiful half-timbered structures, particularly in the Eifel and the Sauerland. Even our present century has produced structural monuments which, however, are often not recognised as such, simply because they are a part of everyday life. These are the architecturally daring Rhein bridges, the gigantic television masts or modern factories and theatres. Many museums too have moved into new homes. One of the most outstanding examples is the Roman-Germanic Museum in Cologne which provides a home for the most ancient German history and which, by means of the daring contrast between content and presentation, appears to give new birth to the objects on view. Almost countless other museums throughout the State show artistic, scientific and economic developments over the years. Noteworthy are the Folkwang-Museum in Essen, the Klingenmuseum (Blade Museum) in Solingen and the Roentgen-Museum (X-Ray Museum) in Lennep (now a suburb of Remscheid).

Everywhere in Northrhein-Westphalia the inhabitants are used to hard work. In fact the compulsion to hold one's own in the working world of today enhances the desire for hobbies, which are pursued with passion: all sorts of handiworks and sports — almost everybody knows the names of the famous football clubs. Another way of supplying the needs of the body — which can scarcely be described as sport — is the art of eating, a leisure time pursuit which, with the attendant drinks, is eagerly pursued, taking advantage of all that the area has to offer. Ham and "Pumpernickel," beer and grain spirits are also a part of the image of Northrhein-Westphalia.

Apart from the City States, *Hessen* is the only German State whose frontiers fail to border on to a non-German State — it can really be described as a Central State. It is rich in forests and mountains and traversed by the wide River Main, the Lahn and the Fulda as well as many others. The Taunus range attains a height of almost 2,950 ft., the Vogelsberg 2,540 ft, and the Hohe Meissner 2,460 ft. Strangers from all over the world arriving by air either to land or change machines at

nes : l'ancien Hôtel de ville de Cologne, un bâtiment gothique (1360). Beaucoup de châteaux (constructions des périodes Renaissance et baroque) sont des sièges d'universités (à Bonn et à Münster), des musées et des offices. Dans le château Augustusburg près de Brühl les accueils du gouvernement de la R.F.A. ont lieu. Vous pouvez faire l'inspection de plus de cent castels d'eau en Westphalie, qui reflètent une évolution de beaucoup de siècles. Dans les villes pittoresques vous trouvez de magnifiques constructions à pans de bois et beaucoup de rangées de belles maisons anciennes (par exemple dans les régions Eifel et Sauerland) mais aussi des échantillons de l'architecture moderne et des constructions techniques imposantes (par exemple les ponts du Rhin, des tours de télévision, des usines et des théâtres). A retenir parmi les nombreux musées célèbres : le musée Romain-Germanique à Cologne remarquablement amenagé, qui abrite l'héritage romain ainsi que des collections préhistoriques, le musée Folkwang à Essen, le musée Deutsches Klingenmuseum à Solingen et le musée Röntgen à Lennep (aujourd'hui un quartier de Remscheid).

Les habitants de Nordrhein-Westfalen sont habitués au travail pénible. Autrefois les pigeons voyageurs étaient le plaisir de beaucoup de mineurs. On connaît les footballeurs clubistes de Schalke. Des spécialités alimentaires de la région sont le jambon et le pain « Pumpernickel ». La bière de la Westphalie est renommée et un petit verre se trouve partout.

La Hesse est un pays pittoresque au milieu de la R.F.A. qui n'a pas des frontières communes avec des Etats étrangers. La dépression de Hesse est obstruée par de petits massifs volcaniques (Rhön 950 m, et Vogelsberg 774 m) et par les montagnes Taunus (à peu près 900 m) et Hoher Meissner (750 m). Des forêts couvrent les montagnes ; les vallées sinueuses des fleuves Main, Lahn et Fulda fascilitent la circulation.

Main-Flughafen, der großen Drehscheibe im europäischen Luftverkehr, landen oder umsteigen, lernen vor allem Frankfurt kennen, die Metropole am Main, die größte Stadt des Landes, Sitz von Banken und Versicherungen, der wichtigsten deutschen Börse. Die ehem. Freie Reichsstadt zieht ihre Bedeutung aber nicht allein aus ihrer zentralen Verkehrslage, die sie seit den Tagen des Mittelalters zur weithin bekannten Messestadt werden ließ, sondern auch aus ihrer Geschichte. Im Frankfurter Dom wurden die deutschen Kaiser gekrönt, in der Paulskirche tagte 1848/49 die Frankfurter Nationalversammlung. Die große Handels- und Industriestadt Frankfurt ist stolz auf Vergangenheit und Gegenwart. Die Hauptstadt aber ist Wiesbaden, die alte Kurstadt zwischen Taunus und Rhein. Die Stadt, die ihre Geschichte bis ins erste christliche Jahrundert zurückführt, bietet heute neben ihren vorbildlichen Kuranlagen zahlreichen Bildungsstätten und Behörden eine Heimat. Neben Wiesbaden haben Darmstadt und Kassel Bedeutung als regionale Verwaltungsstätten. Sie waren einst, seit der Teilung von 1567, Hauptstädte der Länder Hessen-Darmstadt und Kurhessen. In der Produktion dominieren heute in Kassel Maschinen- und Fahrzeugbau, in Darmstadt die pharmazeutische Industrie. Neben den Verwaltungszentren spielen aber auch zahlreiche andere Städte eine Rolle im Wirtschaftsleben des Landes. So finden wir die optische Industrie mit Schwerpunkt in Wetzlar, Gold- und Silberwaren in Hanau, Leder in Offenbach, chemische Industrie in Frankfurt-Höchst, Automobilindustrie in Rüsselsheim, um nur einige der wichtigsten zu nennen. Neben diesen industriellen Aktivitäten gibt es auch viel bäuerliche Arbeit im Land: 45 % der Gesamtfläche sind landwirtschaftlich genutzt.

Im Bergland werden Roggen, Hafer, Gerste und Kartoffeln angebaut, im Flachland vor allem Weizen und Zuckerrüben, am Rhein und an der Bergstraße vorzugsweise Wein und Obst.

Das Erwerbsleben des Landes wird begleitet durch ein vielfältiges Angebot von Bildungsmöglichkeiten. Schulen und Universitäten, Bibliotheken und Museen sind breit über das Land verteilt. Neben den Universitäten in Frankfurt, Marburg und Gießen gibt es die Gesamthochschule in Kassel und die Technische Universität in Darmstadt und eine ganze Reihe von Fachhochschulen.

Eine wichtige Rolle im Leben des Landes spielen zahlreiche Kur- und Erholungsorte. Dank der Heilquellen, die überall im Taunus, aber auch anderwärts zu Tage treten, konnten sich Badeorte entwickeln, deren Ruf weit über die hessischen Grenzen hinausreicht: Wiesbaden und Schlangenbad, Schwalbach und Soden, Homburg und Nauheim, aber auch Orb, Wildungen, Salzschlirf und viele andere.

Das heutige Land *Rheinland-Pfalz* ist eine Konstruktion der Zeit nach dem Zweiten Weltkrieg. Es umfaßt die bayerische Pfalz und Rheinhessen sowie Teile der preußischen

Rhein-Main Airport, the vital European air traffic junction point, get a glimpse of the Main metropolis Frankfurt, the State's biggest city, seat of banking and insurance houses and the vital German Stock Exchange. But the former Free Imperial City is not solely important as a communications centre, which has made it a renowned venue for fairs ever since the middle ages, but also by virtue of its history. The German Kaisers were crowned in the Frankfurt Cathedral, in 1848/49 the Frankfurt National Assembly met in the Paulskirche. Frankfurt, the big trading and industrial city can be proud both of its past and its present. Nevertheless, the State Capital is Wiesbaden, the ancient watering place between the Taunus and the Rhein, a town whose history goes back to the first century a.d. Today, in addition to its exellent spa facilities and its numerous places of learning, it is the seat of administrative authorities. In addition to Wiesbaden, Darmstadt and Kassel are also important administrative centres. Formerly, following the partition of 1567, they were the capitals of the States of Hessen-Darmstadt and Kurhessen. In Kassel the dominant industries are machine-building and transport vehicles, in Darmstadt the pharmaceutical industry. But a great many other towns play a part in the economic life of the State. The optical industry is centered in Wetzlar, the gold and silver centre is Hanau, leather in Offenbach, the chemical industry in Höchst, near Frankfurt, and the automotive industry in Rüsselsheim, to name only a few of the most important. In addition to industry, agriculture has a prominent role in the State: 45 per cent of the total area is arable.

In the uplands rye, oats, barley and potatoes are grown, wheat and sugar beet dominate in the flat lowlands. On the Rhein and along the "Bergstraße" vineyards and fruit-growing are widespread.

The productive life of the State is complemented by an abundance of seats of learning. Hessen boasts large numbers of schools and universities, libraries and museums everywhere. In addition to the universities in Frankfurt, Marburg and Giessen there is the Comprehensive High School in Kassel and the Technical University in Darmstadt, as well as a great number of specialised High Schools. A great number of curative and recuperative spas are also of great importance. Thanks to the curative waters, found in abundance in the Taunus as well as other regions, spas have emerged whose renown has spread far beyond the frontiers of the State of Hessen: Wiesbaden and Schlangenbad, Schwalbach and Soden, Homburg and Nauheim, as well as Orb, Wildungen, Salzschlirf and a great many others.

The present-day *Rheinland-Palatinate* emerged in the period following World War II. It comprises parts of the Bavarian Palatinate and Rheinhessen as well as parts of the

Beaucoup d'étrangers du monde entier arrivent à Francfort (aéroport intercontinental Rhein-Main). Francfort, l'ancienne ville libre impériale, est la plus grande ville du pays, un centre culturel et artistique. Dans la cathédrale gothique St-Barthélemy les empereurs furent couronnés. L'église St-Paul était le siège du Parlement, qui se réunit à Francfort (1848/49). Francfort conscient de son histoire est aussi une ville commerciale et industrielle avec la bourse la plus importante de la R.F.A. Mais la capitale politique c'est Wiesbaden, une station climatérique entre Taunus et Rhin, fondation de la période antique finissante, qui a pris naissance au carrefour de voies très anciennes. A retenir parmi ses nombreux monuments : le château Biebrich, la résidence et l'ancien hôtel de ville (1609). Autres centres de l'administration sont Darmstadt et Kassel, les anciennes capitales des Etats Hessen-Darmstadt et Kurhessen. Les deux villes sont aussi des villes industrielles (machines, pharmacie). Des foyers industriels traditionels sont : Wetzlar (appareils optiques), Hanau (orfèvrerie), Offenbach (peausserie) et Rüsselsheim (construction des automobiles). L'agriculture occupe 45 % du sol (seigle, blé, pomme de terre, betterave à sucre, arbres fruitiers et vignes).

Les universités, bibliothèques et musées sont dispersées : universités à Francfort, Marburg, Giessen et Kassel, l'université technique à Darmstadt et beaucoup d'écoles polytechniques.

Dans ce pays vous trouvez beaucoup de stations climatiques et de villes d'eaux (par exemple dans la montagne Taunus). Les sources thermales de Wiesbaden, Schlangenbad, Orb, Wildungen et Salzschlirf sont renommées.

Rheinland-Pfalz fut crée après la seconde guerre mondiale et comprend des territoires prussiens aux bord du Rhin, le Palatinat bavarois et province rhénane de Hesse. Le Rhin

Rheinprovinz und der Provinz Hessen-Nassau. Die Lebensader des Landes ist der Rhein, der hier Mosel, Nahe und Ahr aufnimmt. Hauptstadt ist Mainz, das früher auch dem geistlichen Kurfürstentum Mainz in gleicher Funktion diente. Mainz ist kulturell und wirtschaftlich Mittelpunkt des Landes am Rhein. Als Universitätsstadt und Sitz des Römisch-Germanischen Zentralmuseums wie des Gutenberg-Museum und anderer Institutionen strahlt die Stadt wichtige Impulse aus.
Mainz, Speyer und Worms setzen mit ihren Kaiserdomen Akzente in der Geschichte des Abendlandes, und geschichtsträchtiger Boden ist das ganze Land. Das Gebiet um Mosel und Rhein ist seit der Antike besiedelt. Man denke nur an Trier, die älteste Stadt Deutschlands, mit ihrem Wahrzeichen, der Porta Nigra. Bad Kreuznach und Bad Ems werden seit Römertagen zu Badekuren aufgesucht. Das Mittelalter wird nicht nur durch herrliche Kirchen repräsentiert — darunter Maria Laach in der Eifel, eine der vollkommensten Schöpfungen romanischer Baukunst —, sondern auch durch eine große Zahl historisch bedeutsamer Wehrbauten. Einer der berühmtesten ist Burg Trifels über der alten Reichsstadt Annweiler, in der lange Zeit hindurch die Reichskleinodien verwahrt wurden.

Obwohl sich in den größeren Städten eine erhebliche industrielle Konzentration zeigt — Chemie in Ludwigshafen, Maschinenindustrie in Frankenthal und Zweibrücken, Schuhfabrikation in Pirmasens, Schmuckindustrie in Idar-Oberstein —, ist das Land vor allem von Land- und Forstwirtschaft geprägt. Wälder bedecken mehr als ein Drittel des Landes. Um Kaiserslautern dehnt sich im Naturpark Pfälzer Wald das größte geschlossene Waldgebiet Deutschlands.

Neben anderen landwirtschaftlichen Kulturen spielt in Rheinland-Pfalz der Weinbau eine dominierende Rolle. In der Pfalz wie in Rheinhessen, am Rhein und an der Mosel, an der Nahe und an der Ahr liegen ergiebige Weinbaugebiete. Die Deutsche Weinstraße verbindet die bekannten Weinorte am Ostabfall des Pfälzer Waldes. Überall begegnen zwischen Rebengelände und Obstgärten freundliche Fachwerkdörfer und -städte, deren Namen man von den Etiketten der Weinflaschen kennt. Nicht anders ist es an der Mosel, die sich in unzähligen engen Windungen zwischen Hunsrück und Eifel dahinschlängelt. Und vom Rhein weiß ohnehin jedermann, daß an seinen Hängen die köstlichsten Reben gedeihen. Die steil über dem Strom aufragende Loreley an der engsten und tiefsten Strecke des Flusses ist Inbegriff aller Rheinromantik. Am Zusammenfluß von Mosel und Rhein liegt Koblenz, die wichtige, große Stadt mit vielen architektonischen Erinnerungen an ihre lange Vergangenheit. Nördlich von Bingen und Rüdesheim greift das Land auf das östliche Rheinufer über und schließt Teile des Westerwalds und das untere Lahntal ein. Westlich dehnt sich die Eifel, die vulkanischen Ursprungs ist. An Basaltkuppen und Kraterseen, den sog. Maaren, ist dies noch heute

Prussian Rhein Province and the Province of Hessen-Nassau. The State's major artery is the Rhein, into which the rivers Mosel, Nahe and Ahr here converge. The capital is Mainz which earlier served the same function for the spiritual Prince Electors of Mainz. It is the cultural and economic centre of this State on the Rhein. As a university city and the seat of the Roman-Germanic cultural inheritance embodied in the Gutenberg Museum and other institutions, Mainz emits many vital impulses.
With their imperial cathedrals, Mainz, Speyer and Worms played a big part in western history, in which the whole area is rich. The region around the Mosel and the Rhein has been settled since ancient times. One need think only of Trier, Germany's oldest city, with its historic "Porta Negra." Since Roman times Bad Kreuznach and Bad Ems have been watering places of renown. The middle ages are not alone represented by many fine churches (among them Maria Laach in the Eifel, one of the finest examples of Romanesque architecture), but also by a great number of historically significant fortified buildings. One of the most famous is Burg Trifels above the old Imperial Town Annweiler, in which the imperial jewels were housed for a long period.
Although there are big concentrations of industry in the big towns — chemicals in Ludwigshafen, machinery in Frankenthal and Zweibrücken, footwear in Pirmasens, jewellery in Idar-Oberstein — agriculture and forestry are the State's prime occupations. Over a third of the State is forestland. The Pfälzer Wald natural park around Kaiserslautern is Germany's biggest enclosed forest area.
As well as general agriculture, wine-growing plays a dominant role in the Rheinland-Palatinate. Rich vineyards are to be found in the Palatinate, in Rheinhessen and on the Rhein, Mosel, Nahe and Ahr. The German "Weinstrasse" links the well-known wine areas at the eastern outcrop of the Palatinate Forest. Amongst vineyards and orchards, friendly towns and villages with half-timbered houses, whose names are to be found on the labels of wine bottles, are to be encountered everywhere. The same applies to the Mosel, which meanders in countless narrow loops between Hunsrück and Eifel. All the world knows that the most cherished vines flourish on the slopes of the Rhein. The Loreley, perched on top of a steep precipice, and the deepest and most narrow stretches of the river, embody the romance of the region. The largest and most important town, Koblenz, at the confluence of Rhein and Mosel, has many architectural reminders of its lengthy past. North of Bingen and Rüdesheim the State takes in a part of the east bank, encompassing parts of the Westerwald and the lower Lahn Valley. To the west stretches the Eifel, of volcanic origin. Still today this is evidenced by basalt peaks and crater lakes, the so-called "Maaren." The

s'écoule au milieu d'une région d'un attrait irrésistible. Les vallées du Rhin et de ses affluents (Moselle, Nahe et Ahr) étaient des terroirs préférés depuis longtemps. Mayence, la capitale de Rheinland-Pfalz, ancienne capitale de l'électorat Mayence, est un centre culturel et artistique important, foyer commercial et siège d'une université et de maintes musées (musée central romain-germanique et le musée Gutenberg).
Trèves, est la plus ancienne ville de l'Allemagne. Une marque distinctive de la ville c'est la « Porta Nigra ».
Déjà les Romains profitaient des sources minérales chaudes à Bad Kreuznach et à Bad Ems. Les puissantes églises étaient les marques distinctives des villes médiévales. Les villes Mayence, Spire et Worms sont dominées par des cathédrales illustrant l'histoire de l'occident. Le Rhin est entouré de châteaux forts, de palais majestueux et de ruines romantiques. Les insignes de l'empire furent gardées dans la forteresse impériale Trifels, dominant l'ancienne ville impériale Annweiler. Les fascilités de circulation fluviale ont favorisé l'essor des villes aux bords du Rhin. L'entreprise BASF était très importante pour le développement de la ville Ludwigshafen. L'industrie mécanique est importante à Frankenthal et à Zweibrücken. La ville Pirmasens est le centre de l'industrie des chaussures. Idar-Oberstein est un centre bien renommé de la bijouterie. Des forêts couvrent deux tiers du pays ; la Forêt du Palatinat aux environs de Kaiserslautern est un territoire de protection de la nature. Les Romains ont initié la culture du vin aux bords du Rhin et de la Moselle, qui est aujourd'hui très importante.
Joliment situés au carrefour de la route du vin dans des sites charmants les villages pittoresques enthousiasment les voyageurs. Les nombreuses maisons à pans de bois des villes et des villages reflètent la vie confortable de la bourgeoisie aisée. La Moselle passe sinueusement par les villages de vignobles au milieu de coteaux plantés de vignes. Les villes séduisent par l'atmosphère médiévale. Le rocher Loreley jaillit au-dessus de la vallée du Rhin resserré dans ce site romantique. Au confluent du Rhin et de la Moselle vous trouvez Coblence, qui renferme beaucoup de témoins de l'histoire culturelle et des monuments importants.
En aval de Bingen et de Rüdesheim Rheinland-Pfalz comprend aussi la rive droite jusqu'à la vallée de la Lahn et le massif du Westerwald. La montagne Eifel accompagne la rive gauche de la Moselle. Dans les cratères

auszumachen. Für unsere eigene Zeit kennzeichnend ist der Nürburgring, Deutschlands Automobilrennstrecke Nummer eins, mit seinen 172 Kurven. Er liegt mitten in der Eifel in Nähe des Städtchens Adenau.

Das *Saarland* ist das jüngste Land der Bundesrepublik Deutschland. Nach Ende des Zweiten Weltkrieges war das Land zunächst einem zwölfjährigen Interregnum unterworfen, ehe es am 1. Januar 1957 definitiv in die Bundesrepublik eingegliedert wurde. Das Saarland umfaßt das Hügelland südlich des Hunsrück mit ausgedehnten Steinkohlenlagern. Hauptstadt ist Saarbrücken. Die Stadt ist Sitz bedeutender Industrieunternehmungen, zugleich aber auch Heimat der Landesuniversität und kultureller Mittelpunkt des Landes. Die geologische Beschaffenheit des Landes prädestiniert es zu einem Land des Bergbaus und der Schwerindustrie, die sich besonders im Raum zwischen Neunkirchen und Völklingen konzentriert. Das Saarland wird durchflossen von der namengebenden Saar, die weiter nördlich in der Mosel mündet. Der Fluß berührt eine Reihe von industriereichen Städten und Städtchen. Im Norden des Landes windet er sich in der berühmten engen Schleife bei Mettlach durch ausgedehnte Wälder. Mettlach besitzt übrigens auch eine kulturgeschichtliche Besonderheit: das monumentale Gebäude der Benediktinerabtei, die in der Zeit des Barocks errichtet wurde und zu den Meisterleistungen jener Zeit gehört.

hallmark of our present age is the Nürburgring, Germany's premier racing circuit with 172 curves. It is in the centre of the Eifel, near the township Adenau.

The *Saarland* is the youngest state of the Federal Republic of Germany. After the end of the Second World War it was subject to a twelve-year interim period before being finally integrated into the Federal Republic on 1st January 1957. The Saarland comprises the hilly area south of the Hunsrück and has extensive coal deposits. The capital is Saarbrücken, the seat of important industrial concerns and also of the State University. It is also the State's cultural centre. The State's geological structure makes it predestined as an area of mining and heavy industry, which is particularly concentrated between Neunkirchen und Völklingen. The Saarland is traversed by the Saar, the river which gives it its name, which further north enters the Mosel after passing by a great many industrial towns and townships. In the north is meanders through extensive forests, the well-known Mettlach "loops." Mettlach, by the way, offers a culturally and historically unique item: the monumental Benedictine Abbey, a Baroque structure which is regarded as one of the masterpieces of the period.

des anciens volcans se trouvent des lacs nommés Maare. L'autodrome Nürburgring avec 172 courbes (non loin du village Adenau) passe par une contrée pittoresque.

La Sarre, attachée économiquement à la France après la dernière guerre mondiale, fut, restituée en 1957. Aux bords de la Sarre vous trouvez beaucoup de grandes et de petites villes industrielles. Le bassin houiller a suscité une puissante industrie métallurgique entre Neunkirchen et Völklingen (centre minier et métallurgique : à partir de 17e siècle la houille y est exploitée). Les villes sont entourées de montagnes couvertes de forêts. Saarbrücken (Sarrebruck) est la capitale de la Sarre, une ville industrielle importante et aussi un centre culturel et artistique. Le pays doit son nom au fleuve Sarre, affluent de la Moselle. C'est un massif boisé avec, dans le sous-sol, un vaste bassin houiller. Aux environs de Mettlach la Sarre tourne deux fois de 180 degrés et traverse les forêts. L'ancienne abbaye de Mettlach, un vaste bâtiment est joliment situé au bord de la Sarre.

Xanten am Niederrhein ist eine der ehrwürdigsten Stätten abendländischer Geschichte. Hier soll der Held des Nibelungenlieds, Siegfried, seinen Geburtsort haben, hatten die Römer einen ihrer wichtigen Stützpunkte an der Grenze zu Germanien, Castra Vetera, und hier ließ Kaiser Augustus um 15 v. Chr. ein Heerlager errichten, von dem aus später Varus in die Schlacht am Teutoburger Wald zog, die er gegen Hermann den Cherusker verlor. Unser Bild zeigt das Klever Tor und den Dom (1190 – 1330).

Xanten on the Lower Rhein is one of the most venerable places of western history. This is presumed to have been the birthplace of Siegfried, hero of the "Song of the Nibelungs." The Romans here had their vital military fortification facing the German Tribes, the Castra Vetera, and it was here that the Emperor Augustus in the year 15 b.c. set up his encampment from which later Varus went into the Battle of the Teutoburg Forest which he lost against Hermann the Cherusker. The picture shows the Gateway of Kleve and the Cathedral (1190 – 1330).

Xanten est un lieu vénérable de l'Occident, une ville chargée d'histoire. Dans la chanson des Nibelungen c'est le lieu natal du héros fameux Siegfried. Les légions des Romains y avaient leur camp « Castra Vetera » au temps de l'empereur Auguste. On dit, que les troupes de Varus se retiraient après la bataille dans la Forêt de Teutobourg à Xanten. Voilà la Porte de Clèves et la cathédrale St.-Victor (1190 – 1330).

Die kleine Stadt Schwalenberg im lippischen Bergland wird wegen ihrer schönen Fachwerkbauten häufig das westfälische Rothenburg genannt. Der schönste Bau ist das im Bild gezeigte Rathaus von 1579.

The small township of Schwalenberg in the Lippe Hill Country is often called "the Westphalian Rothenburg" on account of its fine half-timbered houses. Shown is the most beautiful, the town Hall (1579).

On appelle la petite ville Schwalenberg dans la région montueuse de Lippe souvent le Rothenburg westphalien. Voici le plus beau monument de la ville pittoresque : l'hôtel de ville (1579).

Die Externsteine im Teutoburger Wald waren in vorgeschichtlicher Zeit ein Heiligtum heidnischer Religionen. Ende des 11. Jh. wurden sie vom Paderborner Abdinghof-Kloster in ein christliches Heiligtum umgewandelt.

The Extern Stones in the Teutoburg Forest were a heathen religious shrine in prehistoric times. They were transformed into a Christian Shrine at the end of the 11th century by the Abdinghof Monastery of Paderborn.

Les rochers Externsteine dans la Forêt de Teutobourg étaient avant l'ère chrétienne un sanctuaire germain. En 11e siècle possession du couvent Abdinghof, on a transformé la groupe des rochers en sanctuaire chrétien.

Rheda · Altstadt/Old Town/cité

Links oben: Hameln (Niedersachsen), Ostergasse / Above left: Hamelin (Lower Saxony), Ostergasse /
En haut à gauche : Hameln, Basse-Saxe, rue Ostergasse

Links: Wasserschloß Lembeck / Left: Lembeck, Moated Castle / A gauche : Lembeck, castel d'eau

Das Rathaus von Paderborn, errichtet vom Baumeister Hermann Baumbauer, ist ein typisches Beispiel der Weserrenaissance (oben).

The Paderborn Town Hall, built by architect Hermann Baumbauer, is a typical example of the Renaissance in the Weser region (above).

Paderborn, hôtel de ville (architecte Hermann Baumbauer) un bel échantillon de la Renaissance de la Weser (en haut).

Rechte Seite: Das Denkmal für den 1720 in Bodenwerder geborenen Lügenbaron, daneben das Wappen derer von Münchhausen (oben rechts).

Hann. Münden (rechts unten) am Zusammenfluß von Werra und Fulda gelegen, die sich hier zur Weser vereinigen, bietet in seinem Stadtbild zahlreiche Beispiele für die Weserrenaissance.

Right: Monument to the Master of the Tall Story, von Münchhausen, b. 1720 in Bodenwerder, and the family arms (above right).

Hann. Münden (below right), at the confluence of Werra and Fulda where they become together the Weser, can show countless examples of the Renaissance on the Weser.

A droite : Le monument du « baron menteur » (v. Münchhausen) né en 1720 à Bodenwerder et le blason des Münchhausen (en haut à droite).

Hannoversch Münden est joliment situé au confluent de la Werra et de la Fulda. Dans la cité se trouvent maintes vieilles et pittoresques maisons (Renaiss. de la Weser).

1779

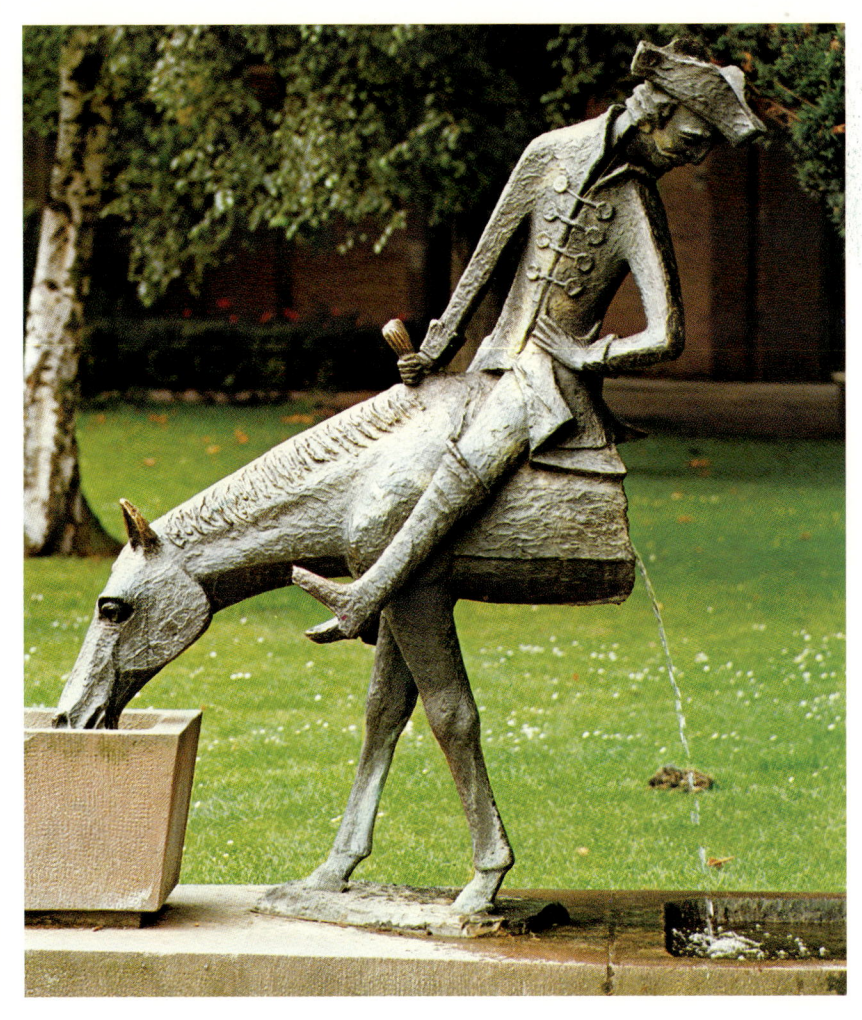

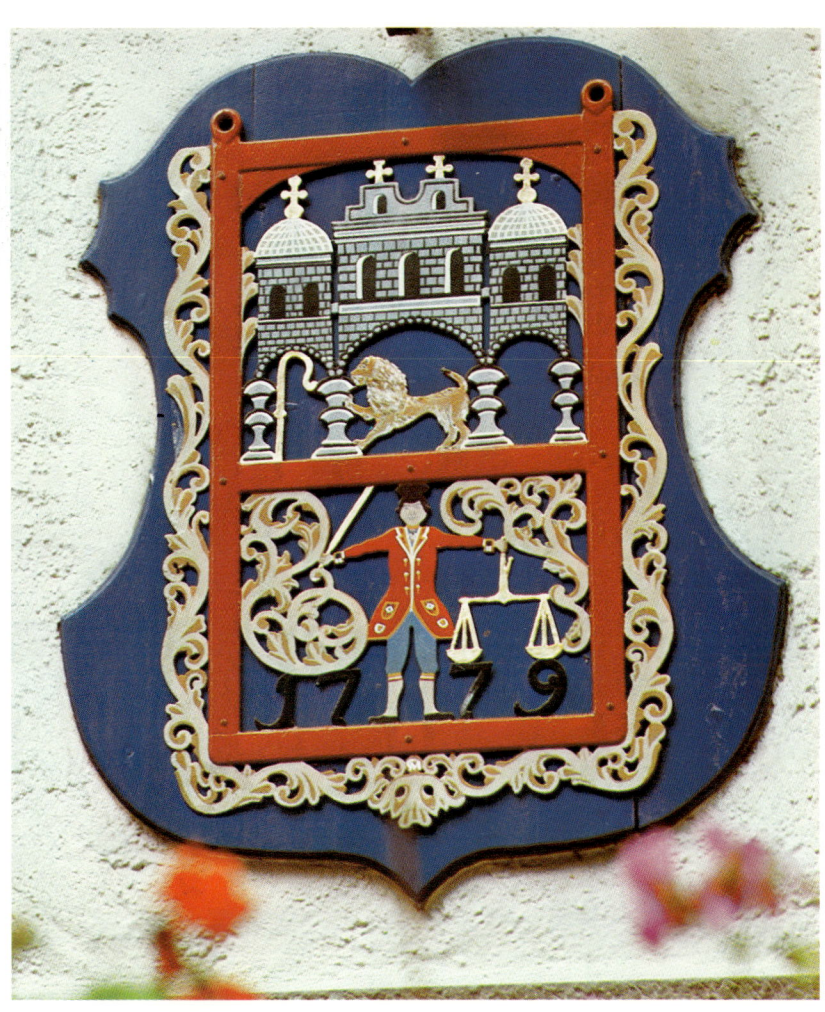

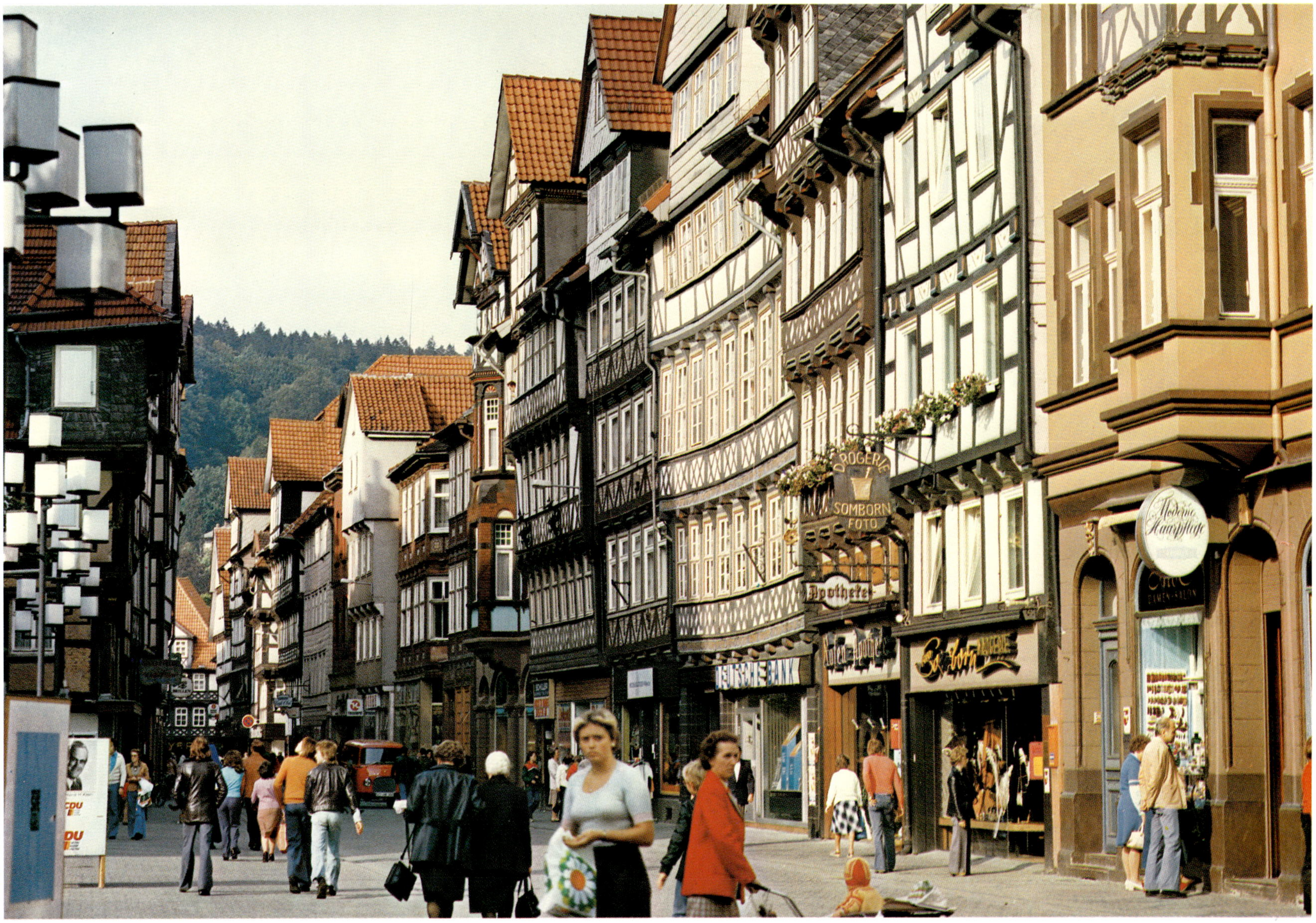
SOMBORN
FOTO
Apotheke

Westlich von Dülmen und nicht weit von Münster lebt im Merfelder Bruch eine Herde Wildpferde. Auf einer rund 200 Hektar großen Wildbahn sind die Tiere nahezu sich selbst überlassen.

A herd of wild horses lives in the "Merfeld Bruch", west of Dülmen, not far from Münster. The animals are more or less left to themselves in a run covering some 500 acres.

Une singularité de la Westphalie est un troupeau de chevaux sauvages galoppant librement dans les terres en friche (200 ha) aux environs de Dülmen non loin de Münster.

Die Universitätsstadt Münster gehört zu den wichtigen Städten Westfalens mit reicher historischer Vergangenheit. Im Friedenssaal (oben rechts) des gotischen Rathauses (oben) wurde 1648 der Westfälische Friede unterzeichnet. Die Lamberti-Kirche im Stadtzentrum ist ein hochgotischer Bau aus dem 14. Jh.; der durchbrochene Turm wurde allerdings erst im 19. Jh. aufgesetzt.

The university town of Münster belongs to the important Westphalian cities rich in history. In the Friedenssaal (Hall of Peace) of the Gothic Town Hall (above right) the Peace Treaty of Westphalia was signed. The Lamberti Church in the town-centre is a high 14th century Gothic building, although the fenestrated spire was added only in the 19th century.

La ville universitaire Münster, riche passé et période constructive au Moyen-Age. Dans la salle de l'hôtel de ville (en haut à droite) les traités de Westphalie ont été signés (1648). L'église St.-Lambert (14e siècle) est une construction gothique (avec une tour du 19e s.).

Burgsteinfurt · Teil des Schlosses
Burgsteinfurt · Part of the Schloss
Burgsteinfurt · partie du château

Neben ihrer Funktion, Wasser und Strom für die Großstädte des Ruhrreviers zu liefern, dienen die zahlreichen Stauseen des Sauerlands auch als Erholungsoasen für den streßgeplagten Großstädter. Die Biggetalsperre hat zusammen mit dem angrenzenden Listersee ein Fassungsvermögen von 165 Millionen Kubikmetern Wasser.

In addition to their function of supplying water and power to the urban areas of the Ruhr, the countless reservoirs in the Sauerland also serve as places of recuperation for the stress-plagued town dwellers. The Biggetal Reservoir has, with the Lister Lake to which it is linked, a capacity of 165 million cubic metres of water.

Les barrages et réservoirs du Sauerland pourvoient les grandes villes industrielles de la région industrielle de la Ruhr d'eau et d'électricité. Le plus grand lac artificiel est celui du barrage de la vallée Bigge ; conjointement avec le lac voisin Lister il comprend en total 165 millions m³ d'eau.

Essen, im Herzen des Ruhrgebiets, ist ein Zentrum der Schwerindustrie. 1979 wurde das neue Rathaus eingeweiht (oben und Bildmitte unten rechts).

Typisch für Essen sind die Bergarbeitersiedlungen (oben rechts).

Essen, in the heart of the Ruhr area, is a heavy industry centre. The new Town Hall (top and centre of picture bottom right) was inaugurated in 1979.

The miners' dwellings (top right) are typical of Essen.

Essen, une grande ville de l'agglomération industrielle de la Ruhr est un centre traditionel de la métallurgie lourde. Le nouveau hôtel de ville (1979) (en haut et en bas à droite).

Typiques les faubourgs des mineurs.

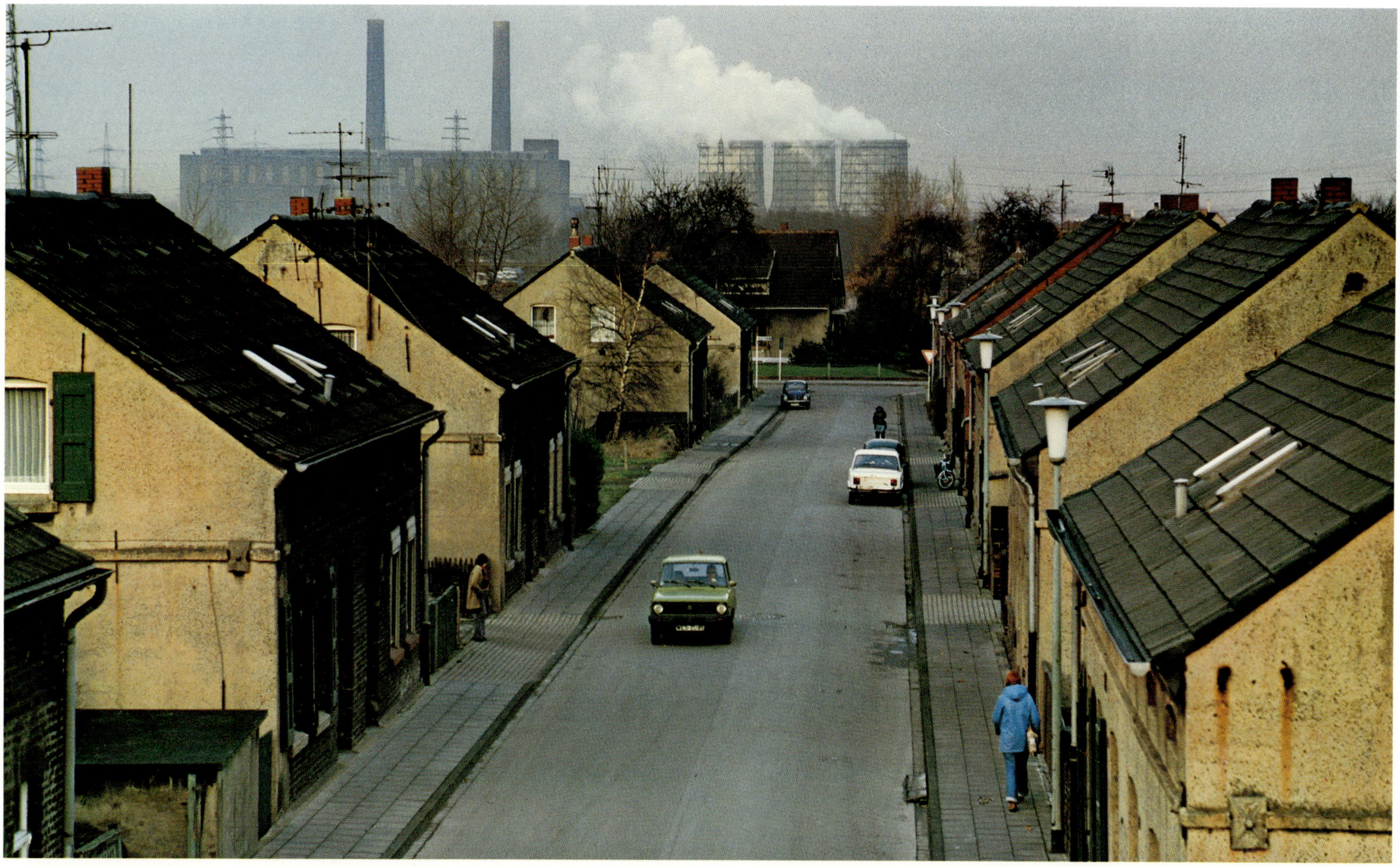

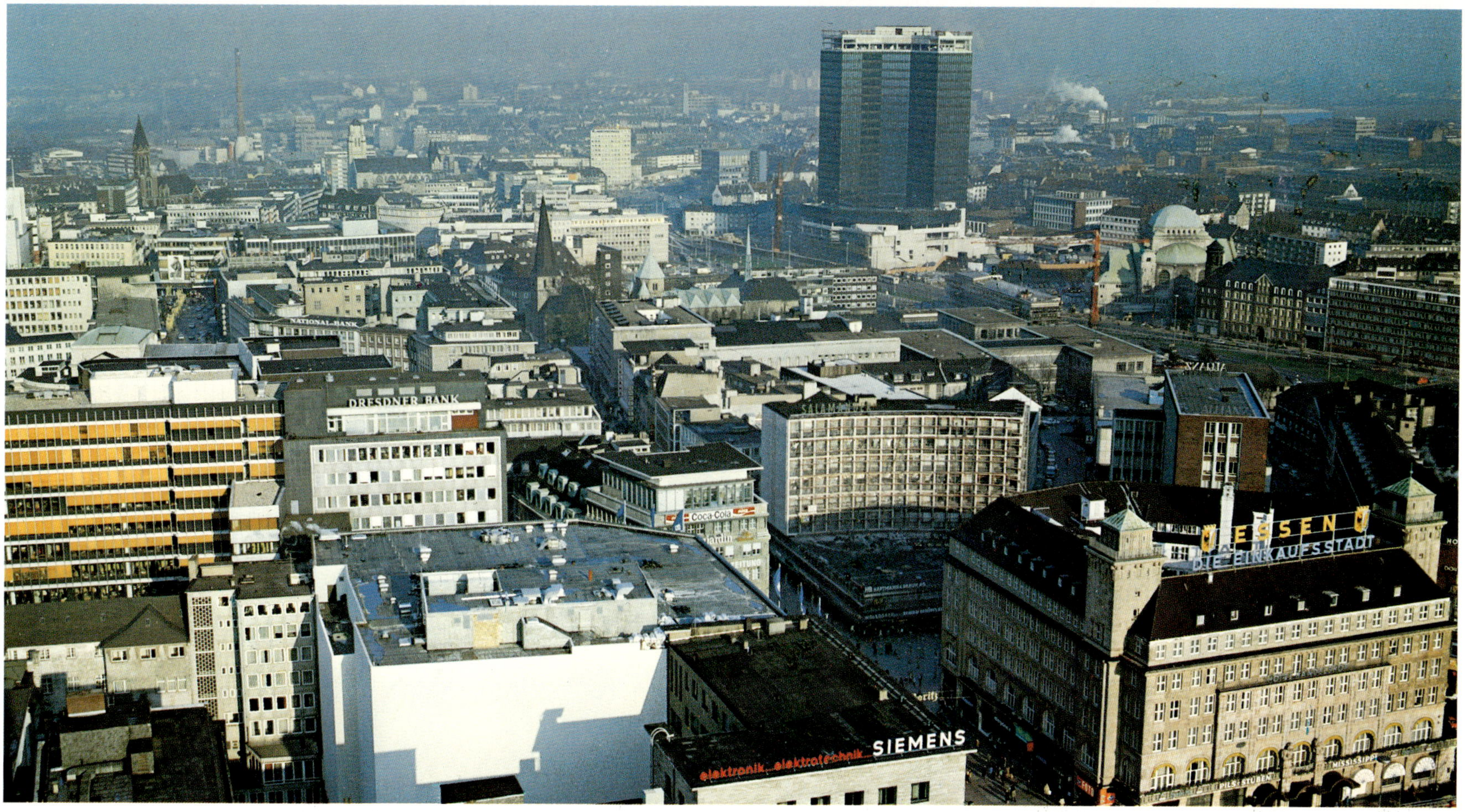
DRESDNER BANK
Coca-Cola
ESSEN
DIE EINKAUFSSTADT
elektronik elektrotechnik
SIEMENS

Recklinghausen · Internationale Ruhrfest-Spiele / International Ruhr Festival Plays / festival international

Prof. Franz Uecker in seinem Düsseldorfer Atelier / Professor Franz Uecker in his Düsseldorf studio / Prof. Franz Uecker dans son atelier à Düsseldorf

Kammerkonzert auf Schloß Homburg / Chamber music in Homburg Schloss / Musique de chambre dans le château Homburg

Ballett in der Düsseldorfer Oper / Ballet in the Düsseldorf Opera House / l'Opera de Düsseldorf, ballet

Galopprennen in Düsseldorf-Grafenberg / Horse racing at Düsseldorf-Grafenberg / Course de chevaux (galop) à Düsseldorf-Grafenberg

Schützenfest / Marksmanship festival / tir

Wettsportfreunde / Punters / Amis du pari

Schützenfest / Marksmanship festival / tir

Das größte vollschwenkbare Radioteleskop der Erde, 100 m Durchmesser, steht in Effelsberg bei Bonn und wird vom Max-Planck-Institut für Radioastronomie betrieben.

The world's biggest fully rotatable radio telescope, 100 metres diameter, is in Effelsberg near Bonn. It is operated by the Max-Planck-Institute for radio-astronomy.

Dans les environs du petit village Effelsberg se trouve le radio-télescope gigantesque de l'institut astronomique Max Planck de Bonn. Le diamètre de la calotte sphérique mesure 100 mètres.

Wasserschloß Anholt im Münsterland
Anholt moated castle in the Münsterland
Castel d'eau Anholt, pays de Münster

Der Mensch formt sich seine Landschaft: oben die Rurtalsperre in der Eifel;

unten das Steinkohle-Bergwerk und Kraftwerk Walsum vor grünen Weiden

Man changes the landscape: above is the Rur Valley reservoir in the Eifel;

below the Walsum coal mine and power station in green pastureland

L'homme a formé le paysage : (en haut :) le réservoir de la Rur (dans la montagne Eifel) ;

(en bas :) la houillière et l'usine de force motrice Walsum

Die Kohle hat wieder Zukunft. Die deutschen Bergbautechnologien gehören zu den modernsten in der Welt — und zu den sichersten.

Once again there is a future for coal. German mining technology is among the most advanced in the world, and the safest.

Le prix élevé du pétrole est une nouvelle chance pour l'extraction de la houille. La technologie minière allemande est très moderne.

Unsere Bilder zeigen
Oben links:
Zeche Walsum, Hängezug unter Tage

Unten links: Kohlenhobel im Haus Aden

Rechts oben: Walzenschrämme im Steinkohlenabbau, Zeche „Westfalen" in Ahlen

Unten rechts: Streckenvortriebsmaschine

The pictures show
Top left:
the Walsum colliery, cage below ground

Bottom left: coal remover in "Haus Aden"

Top right: shearers in hard coal workings; "Westfalen" Colliery in Ahlen

Bottom right: tunneling machine

En haut à gauche : mine Walsum

En bas à gauche : rabot de houille

En haut à droite : machine d'exploitation dans la houillière « Westfalen » à Ahlen

En bas à droite : exploitation des galeries

Kilometerweit erstrecken sich unter Tage die Schächte der Bergwerke. Dieses Bild zeigt einen Förderstreckenabzweig in einem Dortmunder Steinkohlenbergwerk.

The collieries' shafts extend for miles underground. This picture shows a wagon road branch line in a Dortmund pit.

Les galeries d'exploitation des mines ont une longueur de plusieurs kilomètres. Notre illustration montre une partie d'une galerie dans une houillière à Dortmund.

Duisburg ist durch die Schwerindustrie und seinen Hafen, den größten Binnenhafen der Welt, eines der Zentren im Ruhrgebiet.

Duisburg is thanks to its heavy industry and its port, the biggest inland port in the world, one of the big Ruhr centres.

Duisburg est une des plus importantes villes industrielles et commerciales. Son port fluvial est le plus grand du monde.

Duisburg-Ruhrort · Mannesmannwerke
Duisburg-Ruhrort · Mannesmann Works
Duisburg-Ruhrort · Usine Mannesmann

Wintersport auf dem Kahlen Asten im Sauerland / Winter sports on the "Kahler Asten" in the Sauerland / Le sport d'hiver : le mont Kahler Asten, Sauerland

Sommerfreuden auf dem sauerländischen Möhnesee / The joys of summer on Lake Möhne in the Sauerland / La joie de l'été : sur la lac Möhnesee, Sauerland

Die Sauerlandlinie gehört zum großen Autobahnnetz der Bundesrepublik

The "Sauerland Line", a part of the huge German motorway network

L'autostrade « Sauerlandlinie » est une des voies les plus pittoresques de l'Allemagne

Mehr als 1 Million Fahrkilometer hat die Schwebebahn im Wuppertal im engen Tal der Wupper bisher hinter sich. Schon Kaiser Wilhelm II. hatte das erste Teilstück des technischen Unikums eingeweiht, als es Wuppertal noch gar nicht gab, sondern die Orte Elberfeld und Barmen.

The Schwebebahn (overhead tramway) in Wuppertal, in the narrow Wupper Valley, has covered more than a million kilometres. Kaiser Wilhelm II inaugurated the first section of this unique technological structure when what is now Wuppertal consisted of the towns Elberfeld and Barmen.

Le chemin de fer aérien de Wuppertal, inauguré par l'empereur Guillaume II, liant à partir de 1901 les stations Vohwinkel et Oberbarmen (dans les quartiers Barmen et Elberfeld) est la marque distinctive de la ville.

Schloß Homburg
Homburg Schloss
Homburg, château

Die Aggertalsperre im Bergischen Land speichert über 20 Millionen Kubikmeter Wasser.
The Aggertal Reservoir in the Bergisch Country can store over 20 million cubic metres of water.
Le réservoir du barrage Aggertalsperre comprend en total 20 millions m³ d'eau.

Wipperauer Kotten an der Wupper
Wipperauer Kotten on the River Wupper
Ancienne maison « Wipperauer Kotten » au bord de la Wupper

Die Friedrich-Alfred-Hütte (gegründet 1896 von Krupp) beherrscht bei Rheinhausen den Rhein, die meistbefahrene Wasserstraße Europas.

Friedrich-Alfred Steelworks (founded by Krupp in 1896) dominates the Rhein, Europe' most traversed waterway, at Rheinhausen.

La fonderie Friedrich-Alfred-Krupp-Hütte (fondée en 1896 par Krupp) à Rheinhausen. Le Rhin est la voie navigable la plus fréquentée de l'Europe.

DEMAG, Duisburg, Turboverdichter mit einem Läufergewicht von 15,6 Tonnen
DEMAG, Duisburg: turbo-compressor with a rotor weighing 15½ tons
DEMAG, Duisburg, roue de la turbine (15,6 tons)

August-Thyssen-Hütte in Duisburg-Beeckerwerth, Kokillenabguß
August-Thyssen Steel Mill in Duisburg-Beeckerwerth, ingot
L'usine métallurgique August-Thyssen-Hütte à Duisburg-Beeckerwerth, fonderie

Zons am Niederrhein · Rheinstraße / Zons on the Lower Rhein · Rheinstrasse / Zons sur le Rhin inférieur · Rheinstrasse

Rechte Seite:

Ausflugsverkehr auf dem Rhein bei Kaiserswerth

Schloß Benrath in Düsseldorf-Benrath ist eines der schönsten Jagdschlösser Deutschlands. Erbaut wurde es Mitte des 18. Jh. von Nicolas de Pigage.

Right:

Excursion traffic on the Rhein near Kaiserswerth

Benrath Schloss in Düsseldorf-Benrath is one of Germany's most beautiful hunting castles. It was built by Nicolas de Pigage in the middle eighteenth century.

A droite :

Excursions sur le Rhin auprès de Kaiserswerth

Le château Benrath à Düsseldorf-Benrath est un des plus beaux châteaux de chasse de l'Allemagne, édifié 18e siècle, l'architecte en était Nicolas de Pigage.

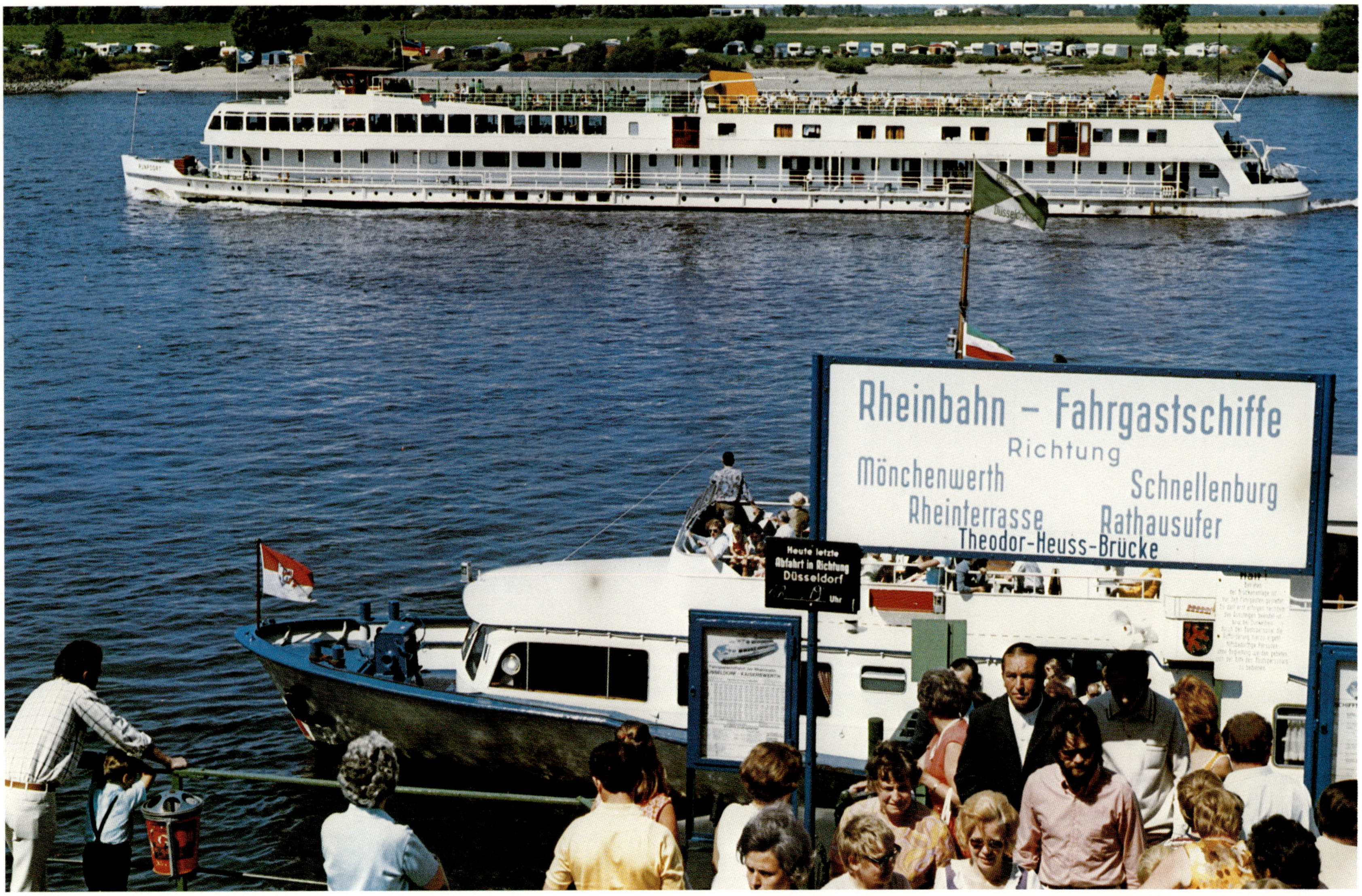
Rheinbahn – Fahrgastschiffe
Richtung
Mönchenwerth
Schnellenburg
Rheinterrasse
Rathausufer
Theodor-Heuss-Brücke
Heute letzte
Abfahrt in Richtung
Düsseldorf
Uhr

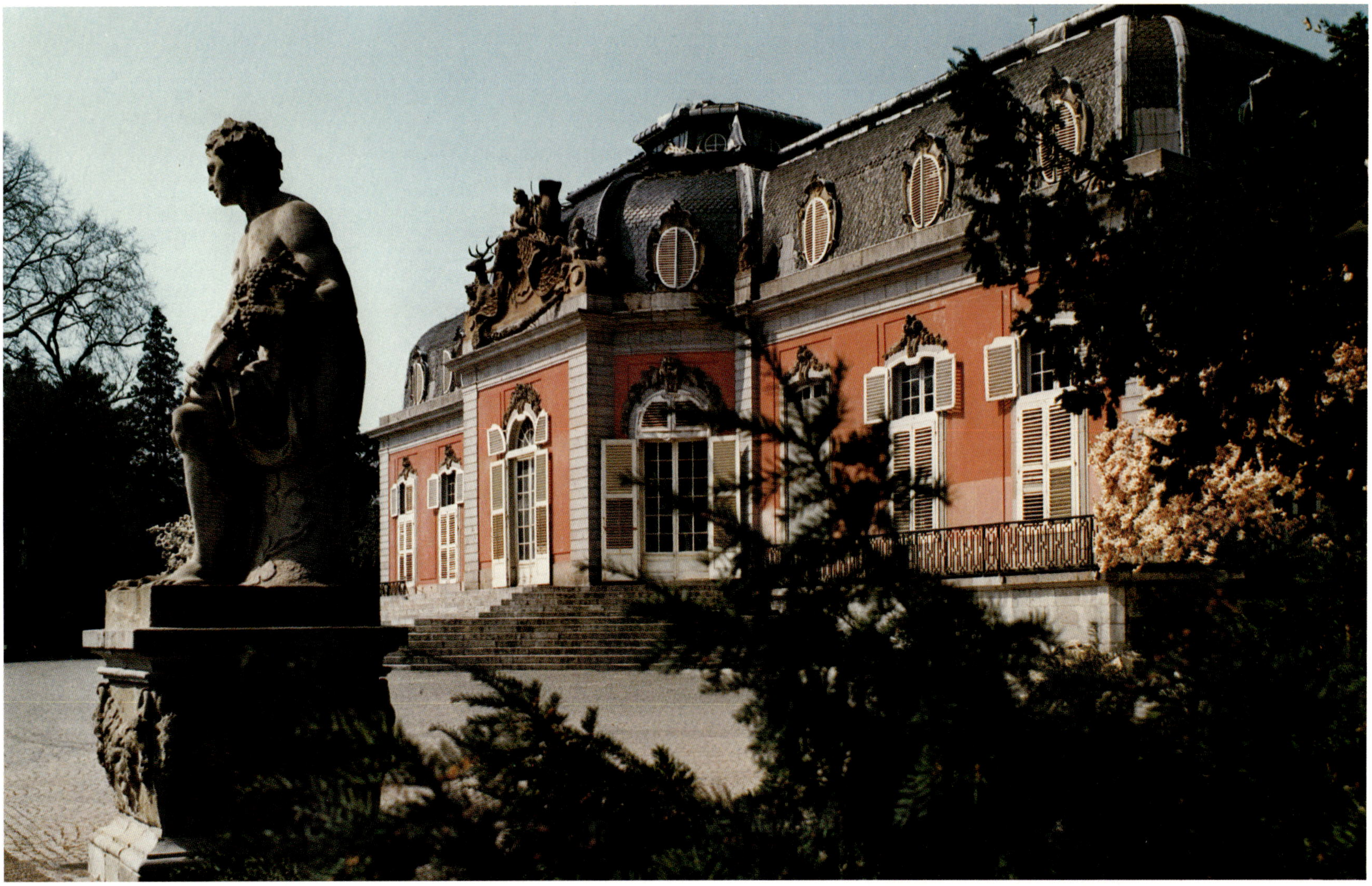

Düsseldorf, die Landeshauptstadt Nordrhein-Westfalens, ist der „Schreibtisch des Ruhrgebiets", denn hier befindet sich der Hauptsitz vieler Konzernzentralen und Banken. Auch als Messestadt — oben rechts das Messegelände — hat sich Düsseldorf profiliert, ebenso als zweitwichtigster Börsenplatz nach Frankfurt (unten rechts). Kunst und Kommerz sind in Düsseldorf eine glückliche Ehe eingegangen: Schauspielhaus und Thyssen-Hochhaus (oben).

Düsseldorf, State Capital of North-Rhein-Westphalia, is the "desk of the Ruhr area" — here are to be found the headquarters of a great many big firms and banks! As a city of fairs too — top right are the fairgrounds — Düsseldorf has won renown. It is also the second most important stock exchange (bottom right), after Frankfurt. There has been a happy marriage of art and commerce in Düsseldorf: Theatre and Thyssen Building (above).

Düsseldorf, la métropole de Nordrhein-Westfalen, est depuis longtemps une ville commerçante. La foire de Düsseldorf est renommée (en haut à droite). La bourse est importante la deuxième à pres Francfort (en bas à droite). Düsseldorf est aussi un centre culturel et artistique. Nous voyons des échantillons de l'architecture moderne : le théâtre et le gratte-ciel de Thyssen (en haut).

145

Rathaus mit Jan-Wellem-Denkmal (oben)

Schützenfest auf den Oberkasseler Rheinwiesen (unten)

Town Hall and Jan Wellem Monument (above)

Marksmanship festival on the Rhein Grasslands at Oberkassel (below)

L'hôtel de ville avec le monument de Jan-Wellem (en haut)

Un tir au bord du Rhin (en bas)

Weltberühmt ist die Altstadt Düsseldorfs als Vergnügungszentrum; Standardgetränk: Düsseldorf Alt.

Oben die Schneider-Wibbel-Gasse.

Nicht minder berühmt ist die Königsallee, kurz „Kö" genannt, Flanier- und Einkaufsstraße.

Düsseldorf's Altstadt (Old Town) is world-renowned as a place of enjoyment. The staple brew is Düsseldorf Alt (beer).

Above is the Schneider-Wibbel-Gasse.

No less famous is the Königsallee, in short the "Kö", for promenading and shopping.

Mondialement célèbre : la cité de Düsseldorf, un centre des plaisirs ; la boisson préférée : la bière Düsseldorf Alt.

En haut : la rue « Schneider-Wibbel-Gasse »

La Königsallee (surnommée « Kö ») une rue élégante bordée de maisons néo-classiques

Einer der großen deutschen Chemie-Konzerne — der Welt überhaupt — ist die Bayer AG in Leverkusen. Etwa 65 000 Menschen arbeiten in den Werken der Bayer AG, weltweit sind es etwa 170 000. Das Produktionsprogramm umfaßt beinahe die gesamte Chemiepalette.

One of the biggest German, and world, chemical concerns, the Bayer AG in Leverkusen. Some 65,000 people work in the Bayer plant; throughout the world there are 170,000 employees. Production encompasses the whole spectrum of chemicals.

L'entreprise Bayer AG à Leverkusen, une des plus grandes du monde, fabrique presque tous les produits chimiques ; à peu près 65 000 hommes y travaillent, dans le monde entier Bayer AG en emploie à peu près 170 000.

Karneval / Carnival / Carneval

Karneval / Carnival / Carneval

Köln und der Rhein, Begriffe, die nicht zu trennen sind. Das Bild oben zeigt den Blick vom Dom auf das Deutzer Ufer.

Hohe Straße (links)

Kölner Dom und Groß St. Martin (rechts)

Cologne and the Rhein are inseparable. The picture above shows the Deutzer Ufer (Deutz Bank) as seen from the Cathedral.

Hohe Strasse (left)

Cologne Cathedral and Gross St. Martin (right)

Cologne et le Rhin, c'est un ensemble traditionel. Vue de la cathédrale St.-Pierre-et-Notre-Dame sur la rive de Deutz

Hohe Strasse (à gauche)

La cathédrale de Cologne et Grand-St.-Martin (à droite)

Köln und der Dom, St. Peter und Maria (links das Hauptportal und rechts außen eine Gesamtansicht). 1248 wurde der Grundstein nach Plänen von Meister Gerhard gelegt, 1322 wird der Chor geweiht, doch dann bleibt er 500 Jahre lang ein Torso, bis im Jahr 1842 ein neuer Anlauf genommen wurde. Nach den wiederaufgefundenen Plänen aus dem Mittelalter ist der Bau 1880 vollendet worden.

Cologne and its Cathedral, St. Peter and Maria (left the main portal, right a general view). The corner stone was laid in 1248 according to plans by architect Gerhard; the choral gallery was dedicated in 1322, but it then remained no more than a torso for 500 years until a new start was made in 1842. The structure was then completed in 1880 in accord with the new-found plans from the middle ages.

Cologne : la cathédrale St.-Pierre-et-Notre-Dame (à gauche le portail principal), à partir d'un édifice de 804 a été fondée en 1248 (dessins du maître Gerhard), le chœur a été consacré en 1322, mais au bâtiment manquait toujours sa façade ouest et la tour du sud restait inachevée jusqu'au 19e siècle. La construction etait achevée en 1880.

Das Römisch-Germanische Museum zeugt nicht nur von der römischen Vergangenheit der Stadt — von Ara Ubiorum, dann später Colonia Claudia Ara Agrippinensis —, sondern besitzt wertvolle Sammlungen zur Vorgeschichte aus ganz Mitteleuropa. Unser Bild zeigt das Denkmal des Lucius Poblicius.

The Roman-Germanic Museum not only bears witness to the City's Roman past — Ara Ubiorum, later Colonia Claudia Ara Agrippinensis — but has in addition valuable collections from early history from all over Central Europe. The picture shows the Lucius Poblicius Monument.

Le musée Romain-Germanique présente entre autres choses des objets trouvés dans la région de Cologne (l'ancien oppidum Ubiorum, Colonia Claudia Ara Agrippina des Romains) ainsi que des collections préhistoriques concernant l'Europe centrale. Voilà le monument funéraire de Lucius Poblicius.

Wie Urwelttiere, Saurier mit riesigen Gliedmaßen, sehen die Kettenbagger für den Braunkohlenabbau aus (hier westlich von Köln Tagebau der Zeche „Fortuna"). Die durch die Ungetüme geschaffenen „Mondlandschaften" werden nach erfolgtem Abbau durch Aufforstung und Überflutung zu Naherholungsgebieten umgestaltet.

Like prehistoric animals with enormous limbs: bucket-wheel excavators for lignite workings (seen here in the "Fortuna" open-cast workings to the west of Cologne). The naked "moon landscapes" laid bare by the giant machines are later turned into places of retreat and recreation after afforestation and flooding.

Voilà la drague puissante de la mine « Fortuna » dans l'ouest de Cologne déblayant le lignite et la terre. Ce qui reste du terrain après l'exploitation à ciel ouvert au moyen de machines gigantesques est semblable aux cratères de la lune et on doit reduire le paysage en terrain forestier (terroir de récréation).

Aachen ist im Bewußtsein des Abendlandes die Metropole Karls des Großen. Hier ließ er das bedeutendste erhaltene Bauwerk der karolingischen Zeit errichten, die Pfalzkapelle. Im Aachener Domschatz befindet sich das Büstenreliquiar Karls des Großen. Kaiser Karl IV. stiftete es 1349. Die Büste nahm die Hirnschale Karls des Großen auf (rechts außen).

Das Rathaus enthält noch immer Teile vom Mauerwerk der karolingischen Pfalz. Im 14. Jh. erhielt es eine gotische Fassade (links). Die Bilder in der Mitte zeigen den Brunnen „Kreislauf des Geldes" und eine Altstadtgasse mit Blick auf den Dom.

Aachen (Aix la Chapelle) is regarded as the Metropolis of Charlemagne. Here he had erected the most important structure of Carolingian times still extant, the Palatinate Chapel. Charlemagne's bust reliquiem is among the treasures of Aachen Cathedral, donated by Emperor Karl IV in 1349. Bust and skull of Charlemagne (above right).

The Town Hall still contains parts of the masonry of the Carolingian Palatinate. In the 14th century it was given a Gothic façade (left). The centre pictures show the "Circulation of Money" fountain and a laneway in the old town with a view of the Cathedral.

Aix-la-Chapelle (né de la fondation romaine Aquae Granni) était la métropole de Charlemagne. Le monument le plus important de la ville est la cathédrale avec la chapelle palatine fondée par Charlemagne. Le buste reliquiaire de Charlemagne fait partie du trésor de la cathédrale, donation pieuse de Charles IV (1349) (à droite).

L'hôtel de ville fut édifié au 14e siècle sur l'emplacement de l'ancien palais de Charlemagne (incorporation de parties anciennes) (à gauche) « Fontaine de la circulation de l'argent » ; une rue de la cité et la cathédrale.

Bonn, die Hauptstadt der Bundesrepublik Deutschland, war bis 1949 eine Stadt, von der man gerade wußte, daß hier die Rheinische Landesuniversität seit 1818 in der ehemaligen Kurfürstlichen Residenz ihren Sitz hatte (rechts unten) und daß es die Geburtsstadt Beethovens war (oben rechts).
Dann folgte 1949 der Umbruch: Aus der „provisorischen Hauptstadt" wurde mehr (siehe folgende Seite), wenn auch der Marktplatz mit dem Rathaus (oben) noch an die Zeit als Residenzstadt erinnert.

Bonn, Capital City of the Federal Republic of Germany, was until 1949 a town known in limited circles as the seat of the Rhein State University in the former Residence of the Prince Electors since 1818 (below right) and, of course, as the birthplace of Beethoven. In 1949 the change came: the "Provisional Capital" emerged to become something more (see next page), even though the Market Place and the Town Hall (above) recall its earlier role as a residential town.

Bonn, édifié sur l'emplacement d'un castel romain (castra Bonnensia), ancienne résidence des électeurs, est à partir du 18e siècle une ville universitaire, berceau de Beethoven (en haut à droite). Monuments intéressants : la cathédrale St.-Martin, le château (ancienne résidence, aujourd'hui université) et l'hôtel de ville (en haut). A partir de 1949 Bonn est la capitale provisoire de la R.F.A.

Staatsempfang in der Villa Hammerschmidt / State reception in the Villa Hammerschmidt / Une réception d'Etat dans la villa Hammerschmidt

Regierungsviertel / Government area / quartier du gouvernement

Wissenschaftszentrum / Science Centre / centre scientifique

Demonstration / Demonstration / démonstration

Schloß Poppelsdorf / Poppelsdorf Schloss / château de Poppelsdorf

Abgeordnetenhochhaus / Parliamentary Deputies' Building / le bureau des députés

Gelegen im Habichtswald findet sich im nordhessischen Kassel einer der kühnsten Bauten barocker Landschaftsgestaltung: Riesen-Schloß und Kaskaden im Park Wilhelmshöhe mit dem 10 m hohen Herkules (links)

Fritzlar · Marktplatz mit Rolandsbrunnen (rechts)

Among the boldest of Baroque landscape architecture: the Riesen-Schloß (Giant Castle) and Cascades with the 33 ft. high Hercules (left) in the Habichtswald (Hawk's Forest) near Kassel, North Hessen

Fritzlar · Market Place and Roland's Fountain (right)

Le célèbre et charmant parc du château Wilhelmshöhe dans la forêt Habichtswald près de Kassel est un des plus coûteux de l'époque baroque : château et cascades, monument d'Hercule (10 m ; à gauche)

Fritzlar · Place du Marché et « Fontaine de Roland » (à droite)

Kassel ist die Stadt der „documenta"; rechts das Museum Fridericianum, in dem diese Ausstellung moderner Kunst stattfindet

The Museum Fridericianum in Kassel, in which the "documenta", the exhibition of modern art takes place each year (right)

Kassel est un centre artistique. A droite : L'exposition « documenta » dans l'édifice Fridericianum

165

Butzbach · Marktplatz / Market Place / place du Marché

Wiesbaden · Kurhaus / The waters / Kurhaus

Fulda · Dom / Cathedral / cathédrale

Wasserkuppe in der Rhön / Wasserkuppe in the Rhön / Le mont Wasserkuppe, Rhön

Frankfurt am Main: Alptraum für den, der es nicht gut genug kennt; pulsierende Großstadt, anregend und gemütlich zugleich für den Kenner.

Der Blick auf die Stadt zeigt von links die Alte Nikolaikirche, Römer und Paulskirche vor dem Hintergrund moderner Hochhäuser.

Links die Bürostadt Niederrad

Frankfurt am Main, pulsating metropolis, a nightmare for those who do not know it well enough, but full of both inspiration and charm for those familiar with it.

View of the town shown, from left, the Old Nikolai Church, the "Römer" and the Paul's Church against modern high-rise buildings.

Left: Niederrad office area

Francfort-sur-le-Main : une grande ville épouvantable pour celui, qui ne la connaît pas justement, mais aussi intéressante et confortable.

Voilà l'église St.-Nicolas, l'hôtel de ville (Römer) et l'église St.-Paul, au loin des gratte-ciels

A gauche : le quartier des administrations : Niederrad

169

Im Dom von Frankfurt (links oben) wurden seit 1356 die deutschen Kaiser und Könige gewählt; seit 1562 auch gekrönt. Davor die Justitia auf dem 1611 errichten Gerechtigkeitsbrunnen auf dem Römerberg

German Emperors and Kings were elected from 1356 on in Frankfurt Cathedral (above left). From 1562 they were crowned there. In front is the "Justitia" on the Fountain of Justice on the "Römerberg" (1611)

Dans la cathédrale de Francfort les empereurs et rois allemands ont été élus depuis 1356 et couronnés depuis 1562. La « Fontaine de la Justice » (1611)

Flohmarkt am Mainufer (links)

Flea market on the Main embankment

Le marché aux puces au bord du Main

Die um 1730 erbaute Hauptwache war einst ein Wachlokal. Nach dem Kriege mußte sie der Verkehrsplanung weichen und wurde Stein für Stein abgebrochen und an anderer Stelle wieder aufgebaut.

The Hauptwache, built in 1730, was once a post for town sentinels. After the war it had to yield to traffic planning and was taken down stone by stone and re-erected at a different spot.

L'ancienne maison baroque « Hauptwache » édifiée en 1730 a été démolie à cause de la construction de la métro de Francfort et restaurée ensuite dans la rue Zeil.

Der Eschenheimer Turm (rechts) gehörte zur alten Stadtbefestigung.

The Eschenheimer Turm (right) was once part of the old town fortifications.

La « Tour d'Eschenheim » (à droite) faisait partie de l'ancienne enceinte.

Der Frankfurter Flughafen ist der größte Verkehrsflughafen auf dem europäischen Kontinent. In Spitzenzeiten landen und starten hier stündlich 55 Flugzeuge; ca. 17,5 Mill. Passagiere benutzten die Einrichtungen des Flughafens, und jährlich werden hier 640 000 Tonnen Luftfracht umgeschlagen; rund 14 500 Menschen — ohne die Angehörigen der Fluggesellschaften — arbeiten auf dem Flughafen.

Frankfurt Airport is the biggest civil airport on the European continent. At peak times 55 aircaft an hour take-off and land. Some 17½ million passengers use the Airport's facilities annually and some 640,000 tons of air freight are handled. Around 14,500 people work at the Airport, not counting employees of the airlines.

L'aéroport de Francfort est un des plus grands de l'Europe. Parfois l'indicateur aérien indique 55 avions d'heure en heure. A peu près 17,5 millions de voyageurs par an profitent des excellentes communications et 640 000 tons de marchandises sont transportées. A peu près 14 500 hommes y traivaillent de plus les employés des compagnies aériennes.

Die Farbwerke Hoechst AG vorm. Meister Lucius & Brüning in Frankfurt-Höchst gehören neben der BASF in Ludwigshafen und Bayer Leverkusen zu den Großen im deutschen und internationalen Chemiegeschäft. Intensive Forschungsarbeiten helfen die Spitzenstellung zu sichern.

Farbwerke Hoechst AG in the suburb Höchst is, along with BASF in Ludwigshafen and Bayer Leverkusen, among the giants in both German and international chemical operations. Its pre-eminent position is supported by constant and intensive research.

La fabrique de couleurs Hoechst AG (autrefois Meister Lucius & Brüning) à Francfort-Höchst est une des grandes entreprises de l'industrie chimique de l'Allemagne comparable à BASF à Ludwigshafen et à Bayer Leverkusen. Des recherches diligents favorisent l'essor économique.

Der Pfalzgrafenstein bei Kaub am Rhein wurde um 1327 mitten im Rhein von Kaiser Ludwig dem Bayern erbaut und diente einst als Zollburg.

The Pfalzgrafenstein near Kaub am Rhein was built in the middle of the Rhein around 1327 by Emperor Ludwig the Bavarian and was once a customs post.

La forteresse de douane Pfalzgrafenstein près de Kaub a été édifiée par l'empereur Louis de Bavière en 1327 sur une île du Rhin.

In aller Welt berühmt sind die Weinorte am Rhein, sei es nun Bacharach mit dem 1568 erbauten Alten Haus oder die Drosselgasse in Rüdesheim.

The vineyards on the Rhein are world renowned, be they in Bacharach with its Old House (1568) or Rüdesheim: "Drosselgasse" (Thrush Laneway).

Mondialement célèbres sont les vieux lieux viticoles aux bords du Rhin : l'« Ancienne Maison » à Bacharach (1568) ; et la rue Drosselgasse à Rüdesheim.

178

Mainz, Speyer, Worms — drei Städte, drei Begriffe, drei Dome, die Kaiserdome. Der Grundstein für den Mainzer Dom (oben links) wurde 975 gelegt, 1036 fand die Weihe im Beisein Kaiser Konrads II. statt. Der Dom von Speyer, wie wir ihn heute kennen (unten links), wurde um 1030 begonnen und 1061 geweiht. Durch seine mächtige Überwölbung des Mittelschiffs wurde er beispielgebend für den abendländischen Kirchenbau. Worms war im Frühmittelalter Hauptstadt des Burgunderreichs. Um das Jahr 1000 begann man mit dem Bau des Kaiserdoms (oben), 1018 wurde er in Anwesenheit Kaiser Heinrichs II. geweiht.

Mainz, Speyer, Worms — three Cathedral Cities, Imperial Cathedrals. The corner stone of the Mainz Cathedral (top left) was laid in 975, in 1036 the Cathedral was dedicated in the presence of Emperor Konrad II. Speyer Cathedral today (below left); it was begun in 1030 and dedicated in 1061. The mighty arch of the nave made it exemplary for western ecclesiastic architecture. In the early middle ages Worms was capital of the Burgundian Empire. The building of the Imperial Cathedral (above) began around the year 1,000. It was dedicated in the presence of Emperor Heinrich II in 1018.

Les trois villes Mayence, Spire et Worms sont dominées par des cathédrales sublimes. La cathédrale St.-Martin-et-St.-Etienne à Mayence fut fondée en 975, consacrée en 1036 (présence de l'empereur Conrad II). La cathédrale de Spire (1030 – 1061) était le caveau d'empereurs et de rois, nef moyenne voutée modèle de l'architecture de l'Occident. Worms, Borbetomagus des Celtes, Civitas Vangiorum des Romains, était pendant l'ère antique finissante la capitale des Burgondes. La cathédrale impériale St.-Pierre fut édifiée sous l'impulsion de l'empereur Henri II (1000 – 1018).

Mainz · Landtag / Mainz · State Parliament / Mayence · édifice de la diète

Koblenz · Deutsches Eck / Koblenz · Deutsches Eck / Coblence · Deutsches Eck

Bad Kreuznach · Brückenhäuser / Bridge houses / pont avec deux maisons

Am Fuß der Loreley / At the foot of the Loreley / Le rocher Loreley

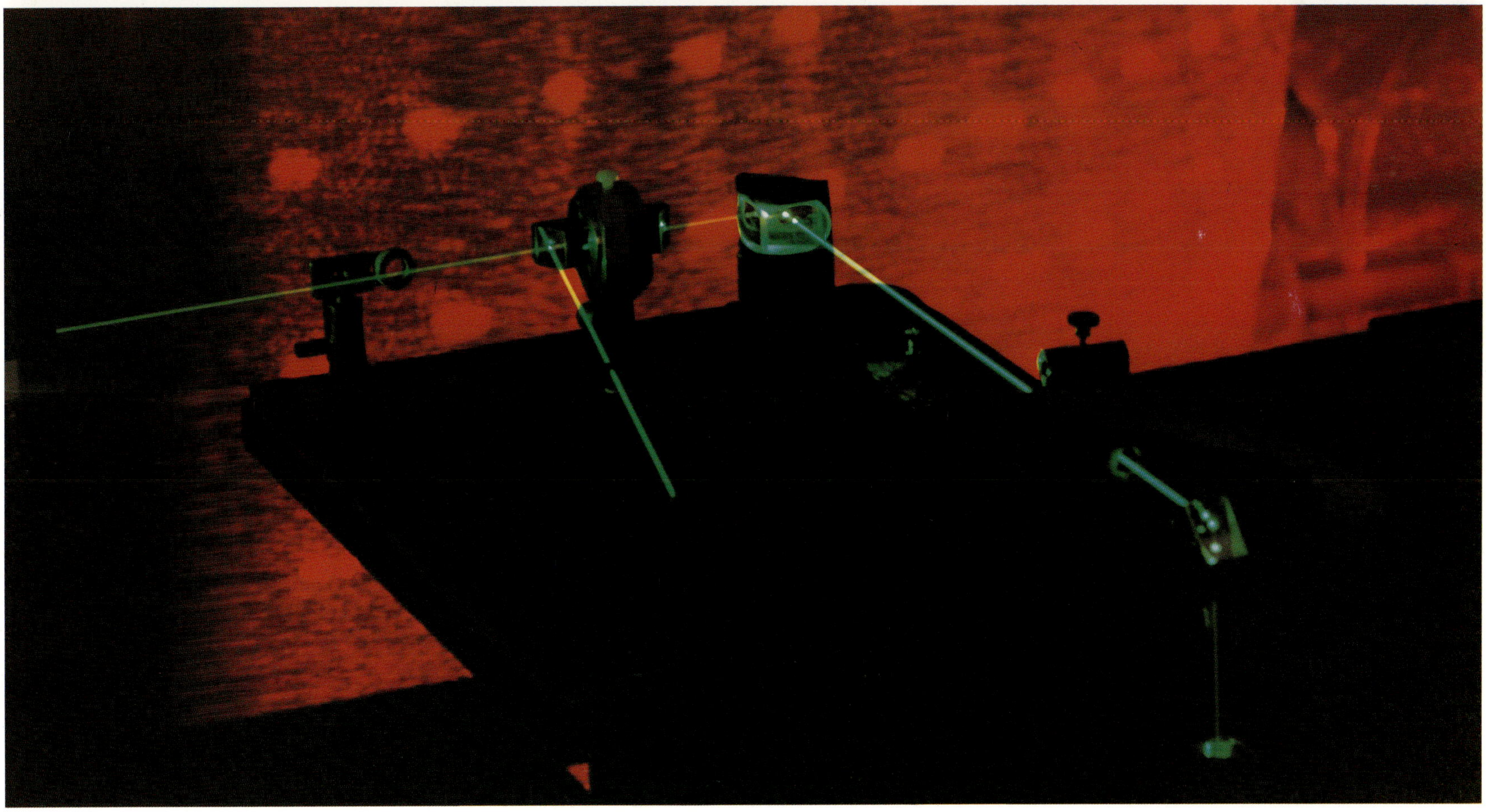

Die Badische Anilin & Soda-Fabrik AG, BASF, in Ludwigshafen ist neben Bayer und Hoechst der dritte große deutsche Chemiekonzern. Unser Bild zeigt aus den Laboratorien die Laserforschung.

The Badische Anilin & Soda-Fabrik AG, BASF, in Ludwigshafen, is the third of the German chemical giants, along with Bayer and Hoechst. The picture shows laser reserarch in the laboratories.

L'entreprise Badische Anilin & Soda-Fabrik (BASF) à Ludwigshafen fondée en 1865 est la troisième de l'industrie chimique allemande. Voilà le laboratoire de la recherche des rayons Laser.

Trier ist die älteste deutsche Stadt, gegründet um 15 v. Chr. von Kaiser Augustus als Augusta Treverorum. Das monumentale Stadttor, die Porta Nigra (oben), wurde gegen Ende des 2. Jh. als Schutz gegen die Germanen errichtet.

Trier is the oldest German city, founded around 15 b.c. by the Emperor Augustus as Augusta Treverorum. The monumental town gate, the Porta Nigra (above), was erected towards the end of the 2nd century as protection against Germanic tribes.

Trèves, Colonia Augusta Treverorum des Romains, est la plus ancienne ville de l'Allemagne, fondée env. 15 av. J.C. Une marque distinctive de la ville est la Porta Nigra en grès noirci.

Oben rechts: Wehlen/Mosel, Sonnenuhr
Unten: Bernkastel. Marktplatz mit Michaelsbrunnen

Top right: sundial in Wehlen on the Mosel
Below: Bernkastel. Market Place and Michael's Fountain

En haut à droite : Wehlen sur la Moselle, cadran solaire
En bas : Bernkastel, place du Marché et la « Fontaine de St.-Michel »

185

Moselschleife bei Eller und Ediger / A bend in the Mosel near Eller and Ediger / Une boucle de la Moselle aux environs d'Eller et d'Ediger

Moselschleuse bei Zeltingen
Mosel sluice near Zeltingen
L'écluse de la Moselle près de Zeltingen

Cochem an der Mosel
Cochem on the Mosel
Cochem sur la Moselle

Völklingen im Saarland / Völklingen in the Saarland / Völklingen, Sarre

Saarbrücken, Landeshauptstadt des Saarlands / Saarbrücken, State Capital of the Saarland / Saarbrücken (Sarrebruck), capitale de la Sarre

191

Petrochemische Anlage der BASF, Ludwigshafen / BASF petrochemical plant in Ludwigshafen / Usine de la fabrication pétro-chimique de la BASF, à Ludwigshafen

DER SÜDEN
THE SOUTH
ALLEMAGNE DU SUD

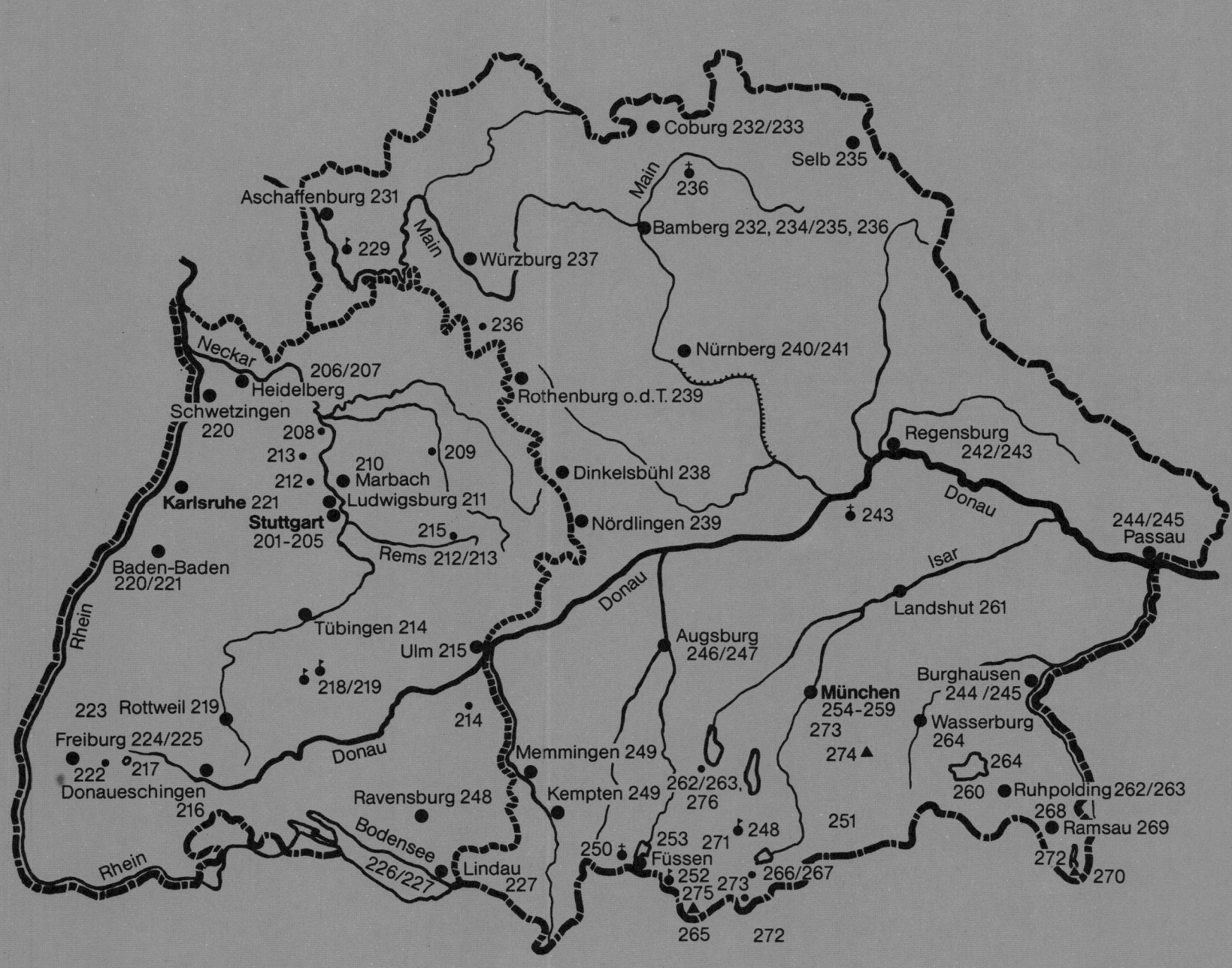

DER SÜDEN / THE SOUTH / DU SUD

Baden-Württemberg Der gesamte Südwesten der Bundesrepublik Deutschland gehört Baden-Württemberg, das seine politische Zusammensetzung der Zeit nach dem Zweiten Weltkrieg verdankt. Das dadurch entstandene großräumige Wirtschaftsgebiet hat den alten Traditionen neue Aspekte hinzugefügt, die in den seither vergangenen Jahrzehnten immer mehr Gewicht bekommen haben. Baden-Württemberg hat heute den Charakter eines Landes, das zwar aus unterschiedlichen Landschaften und Bevölkerungsgruppen zusammengesetzt ist, aber doch unübersehbar eine Einheit darstellt.

Die Grenze zu den Nachbarländern im Süden und Westen bildet vom Bodensee bis Lörrach und dann hinauf nach Mannheim der Rhein. Einzige Ausnahme ist der Schweizer Kanton Schaffhausen, der über den Fluß nach Norden greift. Im Osten und Norden hat das Land eine gemeinsame Grenze mit Bayern. Dabei wird im Norden der Main bei Wertheim streckenweise zur Grenzlinie. Außer den Grenzflüssen Rhein und Main haben für die Geschichte wie für die Wirtschaft des Landes besondere Bedeutung der Neckar mit seinen Nebenflüssen und die nach Osten fließende Donau, die bei Ulm das Land verläßt. Baden-Württemberg umfaßt Teile der Oberrheinischen Tiefebene und den gesamten Schwarzwald, der im Feldberg die höchste Erhebung des Landes aufweist. Die Mitte nimmt das Südwestdeutsche Schichtstufenland ein, das sich von der Schwäbischen Alb aus allmählich nach Norden senkt. Die Bevölkerung ist schwäbischen und alemannischen Ursprungs, im Norden fränkisch.

Hauptstadt des Landes ist Stuttgart, die „Großstadt zwischen Wald und Reben", die es seit je verstanden hat, Tradition und Fortschritt zu verbinden. Das Gesicht der Stadt wird daher ebenso von würdigen alten wie von richtungsweisenden neuen Bauten bestimmt. Im Mittelpunkt steht die zweitürmige Stiftskirche, die auf das 12. Jh. zurückgeht. Markanter Kontrapunkt ist die Calwer Passage, Stuttgarts neue Gute Stube, die in der Nachfolge der berühmten Passagen des 19. Jh. als verführerisches Einkaufszentrum entstanden ist. Hoch über die Stadt ragt der 216 m hohe Fernsehturm, eine der frühesten derartigen Anlagen in Deutschland.

Baden-Württemberg ist das am stärksten industrialisierte Land der Bundesrepublik. Nicht nur die Landeshauptstadt Stuttgart konzentriert eine geballte Wirtschaftskraft auf sich,

Baden-Württemberg Baden-Württemberg comprises the whole of South-West Germany and it owes its political structure to the period following the Second World War. The extensive economic area which has thus emerged has added new aspects to old traditions, and in the intervening decades the former have consistently gained in significance. Today Baden-Württemberg has all the character of a state which is, to be sure, composed of differing landscapes and population groups, but which is nevertheless quite clearly a single unit.

The Rhein forms the boundary to the neighbouring countries in the south and west, from Lake Constance to Lörrach and from there upwards to Mannheim. The only exception is the Swiss Canton Schaffhausen which extends to the north of the river. In the east and the north the State has a common frontier with Bavaria. In the north the River Main forms a stretch of boundary near Wertheim. Apart from the demarcation rivers Rhein and Main, the Neckar and its tributaries and the eastwards flowing Danube, which makes its exit near Ulm, are especially significant both historically and economically.

Baden-Württemberg takes in parts of the low-lying plateau of the Upper Rhein and the whole of the Black Forest, in which the Feldberg is the State's highest peak. The central area is the descending plateau of South-West Germany, from the Swabian "Alb" gradually downwards towards the north. The inhabitants are of Swabian, Allemannic and, in the north, Franconian origins.

The State Capital is Stuttgart, "Metropolis between Forest and Vines," which has always known how to blend tradition and progress. The city thus displays both old and venerable buildings and modern, progressive ones. Central point is the Stiftskirche with its twin spires, dating back to the 12th century. Its counterpoint is the "Calw Passage" (Arcade), Stuttgart's new attraction and a successor to the famous "Passages" of the 19th century, an enticing shopping centre. High above the town stands the 700 ft. high television tower, one of the first of such structures in Germany. Baden-Württemberg is the most highly industrialised state in the Federal Republic. This concentrated economic power is centered not only in Stuttgart, but also in countless other towns whose concentrated economic

Tout le sud-ouest de la R.F.A. fait partie de *Baden-Württemberg*, créé après la seconde guerre mondiale, lorsqu'on voyait clairement l'utilité économique et administrative de l'union des anciens Etats Bade et Wurttemberg. Les régions sont complémentaires : on y trouve des terres rurales, des pays touristiques et des centres industriels.

Le Rhin et le lac de Constance sont les frontières de Baden-Württemberg dans l'ouest et dans le sud, seulement le canton helvétique Schaffhouse traverse le Rhin. Dans le nord et dans l'est Baden-Württemberg est voisin de la Bavière, une partie de la frontière commune se trouve près du Main (dans les environs de Wertheim). Autres fleuves importants : le Neckar avec ses affluents et le Danube (jusqu'aux environs de la vieille ville Ulm). Baden-Württemberg comprend la plaine effondrée de Bade, que domine la Forêt-Noire (dont le plus haut mont est le Feldberg, 1495 m) et au nord du Danube un bassin sédimentaire (Jura souabe). C'est une région rude et pauvre avec quelques riches bassins ensoleillés. La plupart des habitants appartient aux Alemans ou aux Souabes. Dans le nord vivent des Franconiens.

La capitale est Stuttgart, la « métropole au milieu des forêts et des vignes », le centre culturel de la région où l'on trouve des échantillons de l'architecture ancienne et moderne ; Stuttgart a toujours su combiner la tradition et le progrès. Au milieu de la ville se trouve l'église collégiale de la Sainte-Croix, fondée au 12e siècle. Un bâtiment moderne c'est le « Passage de Calw », le nouveau salon de Stuttgart, un centre d'achats élégant dans la tradition des passages célèbres du 19e siècle. La ville est dominée par la tour de télévision (216 m de hauteur) sur le mont Hoher Bopser, qui a été construite ent 1954/56.

Stuttgart est aussi un centre industriel. L'industrie est très répandue en Baden-Württemberg. Le port fluvial de Mannheim est un des

sondern zahlreiche andere Städte haben nicht mindere wirtschaftliche Bedeutung. Hier sei vor allem Mannheim genannt, dessen Hafen im Winkel zwischen Neckar und Rhein sich zu einem der größten Binnenhäfen Europas entwickelt hat. Ein wichtiges Industrie- und Verwaltungszentrum ist Karlsruhe, das als Sitz des Bundesgerichtshofes und des Bundesverfassungsgerichts bundesweite Bedeutung hat.

Charakteristisch für das Land ist die breite Streuung der Industrie im gesamten Wirtschaftsgebiet. Während im Raum Heidenheim-Aalen-Schwäb. Gmünd-Göppingen-Geislingen eine Vielfalt von Industriezweigen arbeitet, finden sich in vielen kleineren Orten Firmen, deren Leistungsfähigkeit nicht unwesentlich zum Weltruhm der schwäbischen Industrie beigetragen hat. Da wird beispielsweise Papier in Oberlenningen gefertigt, optisches Gerät kommt aus Oberkochen, Uhren werden in Schramberg und Schwenningen gebaut, Musikinstrumente in Trossingen, in Künzelsau werden Bücher gebunden; im Einzugsbereich von Stuttgart gibt es Schuhfabrikation in Kornwestheim, Automobilherstellung in Untertürkheim und Büromaschinenbau in Sindelfingen. Auch die Schmuckindustrie in Pforzheim oder der Motoren- und Flugzeugbau in Friedrichshafen verdienen Erwähnung. Holzgewinnung und -verarbeitung ist naturgemäß im ganzen Schwarzwald zu Haus.

Neben dem Industriepotential trägt auch die Landwirtschaft das ihre zur wirtschaftlichen Kraft des Landes bei. Mehr als vier Zehntel der landwirtschaftlichen Nutzfläche sind Dauergrünland. Auch im Ackerbau spielen Futterpflanzen eine wichtige Rolle. In der südlichen Oberrheinebene, am Bodensee und nicht zuletzt am Neckar gedeihen ausgezeichnete Weine, die allerdings nur teilweise außer Landes gelangen. Bekannt sind die Bühler Zwetschgen, Schwetzingen ist berühmt wegen seines Spargels.

Wenn vom Wirtschaftsleben des Landes die Rede ist, darf auch der Fremdenverkehr nicht unerwähnt bleiben. Von Badenweiler im Südwesten über Freudenstadt und die große Kurstadt Baden-Baden bis nach Bad Mergentheim im Nordosten gibt es eine große Zahl anerkannter Kurorte, die ihren Ruhm dem Sprudeln von Heilquellen oder der ozonreichen Luft verdanken. Der gesamte Schwarzwald darf als eines der ausgedehntesten und meistbesuchten Erholungsgebiete gelten. Feldberg und Belchen, Kandel und Blauen bieten herrliche Fernsicht über den Schwarzwald. Die Schwarzwaldhochstraße, die den Nördlichen und den Südlichen Schwarzwald miteinander verbindet, ist eine der landschaftlich schönsten Straßen in Deutschland. Während sich westlich die Oberrheinische Tiefebene anschließt, setzt sich die Erholungslandschaft nach Osten über den Hegau mit seinen charakteristischen Kegelbergen bis zum Bodensee fort, dessen weiches, fast mediterranes Klima Vorzüge ganz anderer Art

vitality is in every way equal. The most noteworthy is Mannheim whose port at the juncture of the Rhein and Neckar has now become one of Europe's biggest inland installations. Karlsruhe is an important industrial and administrative centre which, as the seat of the German Federal Court and the Constitutional Court, has nation-wide significance.

A prime characteristic is the wide distribution of industry throughout the State. In the region Heidenheim — Aalen — Schwäbisch Gmünd — Göppingen — Geislingen a vast number of industrial sectors are involved, while in a host of smaller places there are undertakings whose efficiency has contributed in no lesser degree to the world fame enjoyed by Swabian industry. Examples are paper-making in Oberlenningen, optical instruments in Oberkochen, timepieces made in Schramberg and Schwenningen, musical instruments built in Trossingen and book-binding in Künzelsau. On the periphery of Stuttgart there is footwear manufacture in Kornwestheim, automotive production in Untertürkheim and office machinery production in Sindelfingen. Also worthy of note are the jewellery makers of Pforzheim and the aeroframe and engine-builders in Friedrichshafen. In the very nature of things wood production and woodworking are right at home in the Black Forest.

In addition to the industrial potential, agriculture contributes its share to the economic power of the State. More than two fifths of the agricultural area are permanent pasture. Fodder crops too are important in tillage. In the southern part of the Upper Rhein Plateau, on Lake Constance and, even more so, on the Neckar, exquisite wines are produced, although only some of these leave the area. Zwetschgen (a small plum) from Bühl are renowned, as also the asparagus from Schwetzingen.

In speaking of the economic life of the State, tourism should also not be overlooked. A vast number of acknowledged watering places extend from Badenweiler in the south-west through Freudenstadt and the big spa Baden-Baden to Bad Mergentheim in the north-east. They owe their repute either to bubbling mineral fountains or air rich in ozone. The whole of the Black Forest is one of the most extensive and popular of German recuperative and curative areas.

The Feldberg and the Belchen, Kandel and Blauen offer a magnificent panorama across the Black Forest. The Black Forest High Road, linking the north and south of the Black Forest, is one of the most picturesque routes in Germany. In the west it touches on the Lower Plateau of the Upper Rhein, while the region of the spas continues towards the East across the Hegau, with its characteristic cone-shaped peaks, and on to Lake Con-

plus grands de l'Europe. Les centres industriels les plus importants sont : Heidenheim, Aalen, Schwäbisch Gmünd, Göppingen et Geislingen, en plus Oberlenningen (papeterie), Oberkochen (instruments optiques), Schramberg et Schwenningen (montres), Trossingen (instruments de musique), Künzelsau (reliure), Kornwestheim (cordonnerie), Untertürkheim (automobiles) et Sindelfingen (machines de bureau). Un centre renommé de la parure est Pforzheim. La construction des avions est traditionelle à Friedrichshafen. La Forêt-Noire alimente les industries du bois et du papier. Karlsruhe, est un centre industriel et en même temps le siège de maintes autorités (cours de justice et de la jurisdiction et de la constitution).

Baden-Württemberg est aussi un pays rural. Les forêts sont coupées de pâturages (régions d'élevage perfectionné). La vigne croît sur les collines de la plaine de Bade, auprès du Lac de Constance et auprès du Neckar (un vendage extraordinaire, comparable à celui du Palatinat). On connaît les prunes de Bühl et l'asperge de Schwetzingen.

Baden-Württemberg est riche en villégiatures. Vous y trouvez beaucoup de stations climatiques et de bains : Badenweiler, Freudenstadt et Baden-Baden dans la Forêt-Noire ainsi que Mergentheim. Aux sommets des monts Feldberg, Belchen et Kandel on a une magnifique vue panoramique sur les vallées et hauteurs de la Forêt-Noire jusqu'au Rhin. Auprès de la voie Schwarzwaldhochstrasse on jouit d'un paysage pittoresque. Les monts du Jura souabe sont voisins de la rive nord du Danube, qui perce les parois des rochers entre Tuttlingen et Sigmaringen. Des rochers d'Urach on peut regarder le charmant pays du Neckar. La chaîne volcanique Kaiserstuhl et les roches isolés du Hégau sont riches en

anbietet. Die Insel Mainau zwischen Konstanz und Meersburg ist geradezu ein Blumenparadies.

Baden-Württemberg ist eine überaus reiche Kulturlandschaft mit Kunstschätzen und Baudenkmälern überall im Land. Eines der geistigen und künstlerischen Zentren des Abendlandes im frühen Mittelalter war die Insel Reichenau im Bodensee mit ihren Klöstern und Kirchen. Jahrhunderte später entstanden zahlreiche Münster und Dome, Kloster- und Pfarrkirchen, die wir heute noch bewundern, darunter als bedeutendste Schöpfungen die herrlich geschmückten Münster in Freiburg i.B. und Ulm. Die großartigen Klosterbauten von Hirsau und Alpirsbach, von Maulbronn und Blaubeuren und andere bestehen würdig neben ihnen. Einen besonderen Hinweis verdienen die barocken Kleinode von Neresheim und Birnau und Zwiefalten. Einzigartigen Rang nehmen die zauberhaften oberschwäbischen Klosterbibliotheken ein, in Wiblingen und Salem etwa oder in Schussenried, die Zentren mönchischer Gelehrsamkeit waren. Auch die profane Baukunst hat stolze Leistungen aufzuweisen. Mittelalterliche Wehrbauten wechseln ab mit barocken Schlössern. Kunst und Wissenschaft sind eng miteinander verbunden. Bedeutende Museen und Bibliotheken gibt es in vielen Städten. Unter den Hochschulen des Landes finden sich so ehrwürdige alte Bildungsstätten wie die Universitäten von Heidelberg (1386), Freiburg (1457) und Tübingen (1477). Aber auch Ulm und Konstanz als jüngste Universitäten des Landes haben sich rasch einen Namen gemacht. Die Geschichte des Landes ist aber nicht nur in Klöstern, Palästen und Universitäten dokumentiert. Gerade im schwäbischen Raum haben in den Städten von jeher auch die Bürger mitgesprochen. Ihr Mut und ihr Unternehmungsgeist fanden Ausdruck in prächtigen Wohnbauten und Rathäusern. Es ist kein Zufall, daß eine gar nicht kleine Zahl der ehemaligen Freien Reichsstädte im Gebiet des heutigen Landes Baden-Württemberg angesiedelt war. Ulm gehörte ebenso dazu wie Schwäb. Gmünd, die erste Stadtgründung der Staufer, und Schwäb. Hall, die frühere Münzstätte des Deutschen Reiches. Auch Heilbronn, Esslingen, Reutlingen fanden sich in dieser Eigenschaft.

Bayern Der Freistaat Bayern ist der Fläche nach das größte und was die Bevölkerungszahl angeht das zweitgrößte Land der Bundesrepublik Deutschland. Er erstreckt sich von den Bayerischen Alpen bis an den Fuß des Thüringer Waldes. Die Ostwestausdehnung reicht im Süden von Berchtesgaden bis Lindau, im Norden von Hof bis Aschaffenburg. Bayern hat Anteil an den Nördlichen Kalkalpen mit der Zugspitze als höchster Erhebung. Daran schließt sich die mählich zur Donau abfallende oberbayerische Hochebene mit ihren zahlreichen großen und kleinen Seen an. Jenseits der Donau liegen die bayerischen Mittelgebirge: zunächst Bayerischer

stance whose almost Mediterranean climate offers advantages of a different nature. Mainau Island, between Constance and Meersburg is almost a floral paradise.

Baden-Württemberg is an area rich in culture, in which art treasures and structural monuments abound. One of the West's spiritual and cultural centres in the early middle ages was Reichenau Island on Lake Constance with all its monasteries and churches. Centuries later countless Minsters, cathedrals, monasteries and parish churches arose which are today objects of admiration. To the fore among these are the exquisitely decorated Minster in Freiburg im Breisgau and Ulm. Ranking alongside these are the fabulous monasterial edifices Hirsch and Alpirsbach, Maulbronn and Blaubeuren as well as many others. The Baroque jewels at Neresheim, Birnau and Zwiefalten deserve special mention. The bewitching monastery libraries of Upper Swabia, as exemplified in Waiblingen and Salem, or in Schussenried, centres of monastic learning, deserve special ranking. Secular architecture too can show some outstanding achievements in the way of battlements from the middle ages and Baroque palaces.

Art and science are inextricably linked. There are important museums and libraries in many towns. Seats of learning in the State include such venerable university centres as Heidelberg (1386), Freiburg (1457) and Tübingen (1477). But also Ulm and Constance, the youngest universities in the State, have rapidly gained renown.

The State's history is, however, not only documented in monasteries, palaces and universities. In the Swabian region above all, the citizens of the big towns have always had a voice. Their courage and their enterprise found expression in magnificent dwellings and civic buildings. It is by no means a matter of chance that no small number of the former Free Reichs Cities were to be found in the region that is the present-day State of Baden-Württemberg. Ulm and Schwäbisch Gmünd, the first city founded by the Stauffers, are among them, as well as Schwäbisch Hall, earlier on the place where the Reichs' coins were minted. Heilbronn, Esslingen and Reutlingen also enjoyed this status.

Bavaria In terms of area the Free State of Bavaria is the biggest of the German Federal States; in terms of population it is the second biggest. It stretches from the Bavarian Alps to the foot of the Thuringan Forest. In the South it extends from Berchtesgaden to Lindau, and in the North from Hof to Aschaffenburg. Bavaria has a share of the northern limestone Alps whose highest peak is the Zugspitze. These gradually descend across the Upper Bavarian highlands with their countless small and large lakes to the Danube. On the other side of the river lie the central mountains (Mittelgebirge), consisting firstly of the Bavarian

passé historique. Le lac de Constance est d'une animation toute méridionale. Le célèbre parc de l'île Mainau dans le lac de Constance est un paradis de fleurs.

A la splendeur du paysage de Baden-Württemberg correspond la splendeur de ses monuments et œuvres d'art, nombreux témoins de toutes époques culturelles.

L'abbaye sur l'île Reichenau dans le lac de Constance était au Moyen-Age un des puissants centres spirituels et artistiques de l'Occident. A retenir parmi les nombreux monuments : La cathédrale de Freiburg (Fribourg en Br.) : une construction gothique imposante avec une puissante tour filigrane, les abbayes bénédictines de Hirsau, Alpirsbach, Neresheim et Blaubeuren ainsi que l'abbaye cistercienne Maulbronn, la fameuse église de pèlerinage marial Birnau à la portée des villes Überlingen et Meersburg et l'église abbatiale Zwiefalten. Les précieuses salles de bibliothèques de Wiblingen, Salem et Schussenried sont dignes d'être vues. Le pays est riche en châteaux forts moyenâgeux et en châteaux de plaisance baroques.

Les villes pittoresques sont des centres culturels et artistiques ; on y trouve des musées importants et des universités anciennes et célèbres : Heidelberg (fondée en 1386), Freiburg (1457) et Tübingen (1477). Des universités nouvelles se trouvent à Constance et Ulm.

Beaucoup de villes ont conservé leur aspect moyenâgeux. Ulm est un centre du commerce ancien. Esslingen, Heilbronn, Schwäbisch Gmünd et Reutlingen étaient des villes libres impériales. Schwäbisch Hall était l'ancienne Monnaie de l'empire allemand.

La *Bavière* est le plus vaste pays de la R.F.A. et prend le deuxième rang quant à la population (étendue dans la direction est-à-ouest : de Berchtesgaden à Lindau). Elle comprend le rebord des Préalpes calcaires (Alpes de Bavière : Zugspitze), le plateau subalpin bavarois (s'inclinant doucement vers le Danube et le bassin sédimentaire franconien. Au nord du Danube elle est formée de plateaux et de

und Oberpfälzer Wald, weiter Fichtelgebirge, Frankenwald, Spessart und Rhön, dazwischen der östliche Teil des schwäbisch-fränkischen Stufenlandes mit Frankenhöhe, Steigerwald und Fränkischer Schweiz. Die beherrschenden Flüsse sind die immer mehr wachsende Donau und der Main, dessen Quellflüsse sich südwestlich von Kulmbach vereinigen.

Die Landeshauptstadt ist München. Hier regieren Staatsregierung und oberste Landesbehörden. Die Stadt beherbergt innerhalb ihrer Grenzen mehr als ein Zehntel der bayerischen Gesamtbevölkerung. Sie hat seit je eine gewaltige Anziehungskraft für Zuwanderer. Kein Wunder, daß Museen und Theater, Bibliotheken und Hochschulen von internationalem Rang hier eine Heimat gefunden haben. Der Stadtkern gruppiert sich um den Marienplatz mit Mariensäule, Altem und Neuem Rathaus, Peterskirche, nicht weit der Liebfrauendom mit seinen beiden wuchtigen Türmen, dem Wahrzeichen der Stadt. Prächtige breite Straßen, die die Wittelsbacher Fürsten im 19. Jh. geschaffen haben, charakterisieren das Bild der Stadt, allen voran die Ludwigstraße, die an der Feldherrnhalle ihren Ausgang nimmt. Hier finden sich auch die Residenz und die eindrucksvolle barocke Theatinerkirche. Vor den Toren der Stadt liegen die Schlösser Nymphenburg und Schleißheim, auch sie Schöpfungen des Barock. Eines der markantesten Beispiele der Baukunst unserer Tage dagegen ist das Olympiastadion zu Füßen des Fernsehturms.

Nürnberg, die fränkische Metropole, zeichnet sich von alters her durch seinen Gewerbefleiß aus. Es ist kein Zufall, daß das mittelalterliche Nürnberg sich zu einer der bedeutendsten Freien Reichsstädte entwickelte. Hier wuchsen die herrlichen gotischen Kirchen St. Sebald und St. Lorenz, die Frauenkirche, der Schöne Brunnen. Hier war der originale Schauplatz der Meistersinger, hier lebten Hans Sachs, Albrecht Dürer. Heute ist Nürnberg eine Stadt, die einer vielfältigen Industrie Heimat bietet; neben den sprichwörtlichen Lebkuchen und Bleistiften haben vor allem Elektrotechnik, Maschinen- und Fahrzeugbau Gewicht. Nürnberg ist Sitz des bekannten Germanischen Nationalmuseums.

Augsburg, die Hauptstadt von Bayer. Schwaben, ist nicht nur eine der ältesten, sondern zugleich auch eine der bedeutendsten bayerischen Städte. Ein halbes Jahrtausend Freie Reichsstadt, zeichnet sich Augsburg zu Beginn der Neuzeit durch weitreichende Handelstätigkeit aus und wurde im Zuge dieser internationalen Beziehungen zu einem Zentrum des deutschen Geisteslebens. Die Renaissancehäuser der Maximilianstraße lassen an die großen Familien der Fugger und Welser denken, das berühmte Rathaus von Elias Holl gehört zu den schönsten seiner Art. Heute ist Augsburg Sitz vieler Behörden und einer Universität. Auch zahlreiche führende Industriebetriebe haben sich hier niedergelassen.

and Upper Palatinate Forest, then the Fichtelgebirge, the Franconian Forest, the Spessart and the Rhön, and in between the eastern part of the Swabian-Franconian rise, including the Frankenhöhe, the Steigerwald and the Franconian lake district, the so-called "Schweiz." The dominant rivers are the ever-broadening Danube and the Main whose tributaries unite to the South West of Kulmbach. The State Capital is Munich (in Ger. München). This is the seat of the State Legislation and the State Authorities. One tenth of the total Bavarian population lives within its boundaries. Munich has always attracted people from afar. No wonder then, that seats of learning, museums, theatres and libraries of international ranking have found a home here.

The heart of the city is concentrated round the Marienplatz and the Mariensäule (Marian Column), the Old and New Town Halls, the Peterskirche (Peter's Church), not far from the Liebfrauendom (Cathedral) whose two mighty spires symbolise the City. Magnificent wide streets, laid out by the Princes of Wittelsbach in the 19th century, set the picture of the City, first and foremost the Ludwigstraße, starting at the Feldherrenhalle. Also here are the Residenz and the impressive Baroque Theatiner Church. The Schlosses Nymphenburg and Schleissheim, also Baroque, stand at the gates of the City. One of the most expressive examples of present-day architecture is, in contrast, the Olympic Stadium beneath the television tower.

Nuremberg (Ger. Nürnberg), the Franconian Metropolis, has from time immemorial been noted for the industry of its citizens. It is no accident that Nuremberg was one of the most important of the Free Reichs Cities. Here are to be found the magnificent Gothic churches St. Sebald, St. Lorenz and the Frauenkirche, as well as the Schöner Brunnen (Beautiful Fountain). Here was the Meistersingers' first stage setting. Hans Sachs and Albrecht Dürer lived here. Nuremberg today boasts a host of industries. As well as the legendary Lebkuchen (a type of biscuit) and lead pencils, electro-technology and machinery and vehicle construction now have great weight. Nuremberg is the home of the well-known National Germanic Museum.

Augsburg, capital of Bavarian Swabia, is not only one of the oldest, but also one of the most important Bavarian towns. For five centuries a Free Reichs City, Augsburg had, at the dawn of our modern age, extensive trading activities, and thanks to this international contact it became a centre of German spiritual activity. The Renaissance houses on the Maximilianstrasse evoke memories of the great Fugger and Welser families, the famous Rathaus (Town Hall), by Elias Holl, is among the most beautiful of its genre. Today Augsburg is an administrative centre with a university. It also boasts numerous leading industrial undertakings.

petits massifs : Forêt de la Bavière, Forêt du Haut-Palatinat, Fichtelgebirge, Forêt de la Franconie, le plateau de la Franconie, Spessart et Rhön. Les fleuves les plus importants sont le Danube et le Main (avec leur affluents).

Munich, la capitale de la Bavière est un centre culturel et artistique, plus qu'un dixième des habitants de la Bavière se concentre a Munich. Le centre de la cité c'est la place Notre-Dame avec la colonne mariale et l'ancien hôtel de ville (en partie conservé) et le nouvel hôtel de ville non loin de la cathédrale Notre-Dame avec ses deux tours puissantes. La place fait partie de la zone réservée aux piétons. L'église des Théatins, une construction baroque domine la place de l'Odéon, où se trouve aussi le Hall des Généraux ; ici commence la rue de Louis (Ludwigstrasse). Vis-à-vis de l'église des Théatins se trouvent la résidence et le Jardin de la Cour. Hors murs : Les châteaux Nymphenburg et Schleissheim sont des échantillons coûteux de l'époque baroque. Un échantillon remarquable de l'architecture moderne est le stade olympique dominé par la tour de télévision.

Nuremberg, l'ancienne cité impériale (scène des « Meistersinger »), est depuis longtemps une ville commerçante, jadis rayonnante de gloire et de prospérité, dominée par le château fortifié. Eglises importantes : St-Sébald avec ses statuaires célèbres, St-Laurent et Notre-Dame devant l'église se trouve la « Belle Fontaine ». Le Musée National Germanique abrite l'héritage historico-culturel et artistique. Nuremberg n'est pas seulement la ville des pains d'épice et des crayons où vivaient Hans Sachs et Albrecht Dürer, aujourd'hui l'industrie mécanique et l'industrie électrique sont importantes.

Augsbourg (Souabe), était une ville libre impériale et depuis la Renaissance un centre culturel et artistique. Monuments intéressants : la cathédrale romanogothique, l'hôtel de ville (d'Elias Holl), la « Tour Perlach » et les maisons Fugger (un long et bel alignement de façades). Aujourd'hui Augsbourg est siège 'une université et de maintes autorités et une ville industrielle.

Die alte Kaiserpfalz Bamberg ist stolz auf den mittelalterlichen Dom mit dem berühmten Bamberger Reiter, auf die bischöflichen Gebäude und prächtige profane Bauten wie das Böttingerhaus und das Alte Rathaus.

Regensburg, die uralte Stadt an der Donau, spielte in der Geschichte des Deutschen Reiches eine wichtige Rolle. Im Reichssaal des Rathauses tagte bis 1806 der Immerwährende Reichstag. Beherrschendes Bauwerk der Stadt ist der gotische Dom. Älter noch als er ist die „Steinerne Brücke" über die Donau.

Die Bischofsstädte Würzburg und Passau mit ihren Kirchen und Schlössern machen deutlich, daß Bayern ungeachtet aller Köstlichkeiten der gotischen Baukunst — in Nürnberg, Bamberg und Regensburg, aber auch in der niederbayerischen Herzogstadt Landshut, in Dinkelsbühl und Rothenburg — ein Land des Barock ist. Überall in Bayern stehen große und kleine Kirchen und Schlösser, die ihren Rang nicht nur aus der Prachtliebe ihrer Bauherren und der Kunst ihrer Baumeister schöpfen, sondern auch aus dem ländlichen oder städtischen Ambiente, in das sie gestellt sind. Das mag die Wieskirche bei Steingaden sein oder die Klosterkirche von Weltenburg an der Donau. Dazu gehören auch das Markgräfliche Opernhaus in Bayreuth, die zauberhafte Amalienburg im Nymphenburger Park in München und die Klosterbibliothek in Metten nahe Deggendorf; dazu gehören vor allem die großen festlichen Kirchen von Ottobeuren, Vierzehnheiligen und Amorbach, die Schlösser von Pommersfelden und Ellingen.

Straßen und Schienen durchziehen das Land in allen Richtungen und verbinden die großen und kleinen Städte. Einer der Straßen sei hier besonders gedacht, nämlich der Romantischen Straße, die von Würzburg kommend und den nordöstlichen Winkel von Baden-Württemberg schneidend, vor allem durch Bayern führt. Sie ist einer der beliebtesten Touristenwege in Deutschland und bringt Ströme von Besuchern in die romantischen mittelalterlichen Städtchen mit ihren Kirchen und Rathäusern, mit schönen Bürgerhäusern und Brunnen. Rothenburg ob der Tauber zumal bietet mit Mauer, Türmen und Toren und malerischen Winkeln ein unvergleichliches Stadtbild. Auch Dinkelsbühl und Nördlingen sind wahre Kleinode unter den alten fränkischen Städten.

Die bayerische Wirtschaft hat sich seit dem Zweiten Weltkrieg zunehmend gewandelt. Während das Land früher von Land- und Forstwirtschaft geprägt wurde, hat heute die Industrie beherrschenden Einfluß. Zentren sind München, Augsburg, Nürnberg mit Fürth und Erlangen. Hier hat sich eine Vielfalt von Industrien etabliert, insbesondere auf dem Gebiet der Elektrotechnik, der Feinmechanik, des Fahrzeug- und Maschinenbaus. In den kleineren Städten dagegen dominieren bestimmte Industriezweige, so Porzellan in Selb, Kugellager in Schweinfurt, Glaswaren im Bayerischen Wald, Fahrzeugbau in Dingolfing

Old Imperial Bamberg is proud of its Cathedral from the Middle Ages with the famous "Bamberg Rider," as well as the Episcopal Building and magnificent secular edifices such as the Döttingerhaus and the Altes Rathaus.

Regensburg, age-old city on the Danube, played an important part in the history of the German Reich. The Permanent Reichstag convened in the "Reichssaal" of the Rathaus until 1806. The town's dominating structure is the Gothic Cathedral. Older still is the "Steinerne Brücke" (Stone Bridge) on the Danube. The episcopal cities Würzburg and Passau make it quite plain with their churches and castles that in spite of all the superb examples of the Gothic — in Nuremberg, Bamberg and Regensburg as well as in Landshut, Town of the Dukes, in Dinkelsbühl and Rothenburg — Bavaria is first and foremost Baroque country. Everywhere in Bavaria there are churches and castles, both small and large, whose status derives not solely from their motivators' love of pomp and the artistry of their architects, but also from the rural and urban environment in which they emerged. These may be the Wieskirche near Steingaden or the monastery chapel at Weltenburg on the Danube, as well as the Markgraf Opera House in Bayreuth, the enchanting Amalienburg in the Nymphenburg Park in Munich and the monastery library in Metten, near Deggendorf, and perhaps above all the huge ceremonious churches at Ottobeuren, Vierzehnheiligen and Amorbach and "Schlosses" Pommersfelden and Ellingen.

The State is criss-crossed in all directions by road and rail networks, linking both big and small towns. Well worthy of mention is the "Romantische Straße" (Romantic Road), emerging from Würzburg and cutting across the north-east edge of Baden-Württemberg back into Bavaria. It is one of Germany's most popular tourist routes, guiding streams of visitors through romantic towns of the middle ages with their churches and town halls, fountains and citizens' houses. The town wall, towers, gates and picturesque corners of Rothenburg ob der Tauber present an indelible picture. Dinkelsbühl and Nördlingen too are jewels among the old Franconian towns.

Since the Second World War the Bavarian economy has been increasingly changing. Agriculture and forestry, formerly dominant, are steadily yielding to the influence of industry. Its centres are Munich, Augsburg, Nuremberg and nearby Fürth and Erlangen. A multiplicity of industrial operations have established themselves, electro-technology, precision mechanics and vehicle and machinery construction to the fore. In the smaller townships specific industries set the scene, for example porcelain in Selb, glass in the Bavarian Forest, vehicle building in Dingolfing and In-

Bamberg renferme beaucoup de monuments du Moyen-Age : l'ancienne résidence englobant le palais impérial et la cathédrale avec le célèbre cavalier. Constructions baroques : L'ancien hôtel de ville et la maison Böttinger. Ratisbonne (Regensburg), ancienne ville fondée des Romains, rassemble en surabondance des monuments du Moyen-Age : la cathédrale St-Pierre, le vieux pont de pierre et l'ancien hôtel de ville (siège de la Diète Permanente jusqu'à 1806).

Beaucoup de villes bavaroises nous offrent de splendides exemples de l'âge gothique ; Nuremberg, Bamberg, Ratisbonne, Landshut sur l'Isar (siège des « riches ducs » de Bavière), Dinkelsbühl et Rothenburg. Würzburg et Passau avec les impressionantes résidences épiscopales nous montrent l'épanouissement à l'époque baroque. On trouve partout d'églises pittoresques et de châteaux somptueux : l'église de pèlerinage Wies près de Steingaden, la lumineuse église de l'abbaye bénédictine Weltenburg (près de Kelheim), l'opéra margravial de Bayreuth, Nymphenburg avec son splendide parc, les grandioses bibliothèques de Waldsassen, Metten, Fürstenzell et Ottobeuren et les rayonnantes églises d'Ottobeuren, de Vierzehnheiligen et d'Amorbach ainsi que les châteaux de Pommersfelden et d'Ellingen.

La Bavière dispose d'excellentes communications routières liant les villes pittoresques (par exemple la « route romantique », une des routes touristiques les plus fréquentées). La Bavière est riche en villes romantiques, dont le patrimoine médiéval est à peine diminué : Rothenburg sur la Tauber avec ses murailles et tours fortes, ses portes fortifiées et ses vieilles et pittoresques maison, Dinkelsbühl (Main franconien) et Nördlingen dans la plaine du Ries.

La vie économique a changé depuis la dernière guerre mondiale. Autrefois la Bavière vivait surtout des produits du sol (agriculture et exploitation des forêts). Aujourd'hui l'industrie est importante — centres industriels : Munich, Augsbourg et Nuremberg avec Fürth et Erlangen (industrie électrique et méchanique). Les petites villes excellent dans des fabrications traditionelles : industrie porcelainière à Selb, cuvettes à billes à Schweinfurth, verreries dans la Forêt de la Bavière, constructions de véhicules à Dingolfing et Ingol-

und Ingolstadt, Textilerzeugnisse in Aschaffenburg. Das bei Ingolstadt angesiedelte Ölraffineriezentrum ist durch Pipelines mit den Mittelmeerhäfen Triest und Genua verbunden. Alle diese industriellen Aktivitäten lassen allerdings auch heute noch der Landwirtschaft ihren Rang. Besonders in Oberbayern und im Allgäu ist die Viehwirtschaft bedeutend: 30 % der Milchprodukte und 70 % der Käseerzeugnisse in der Bundesrepublik kommen aus Bayern. Die Hopfenkulturen der Hallertau bringen 90 % der Bundesproduktion. Stets begehrt sind auch die Weine des fränkischen Anbaugebietes.

Zum Wirtschaftsleben Bayerns tragen auf ihre Weise zahlreiche Städte und Dörfer bei, die sich als Erholungsorte einen Namen gemacht haben. Das trifft keineswegs nur auf die Gebirgsorte zwischen Oberstdorf und Garmisch, zwischen Mittenwald und Berchtesgaden und auf die vielen Gemeinden im Voralpenland zu, sondern ebenso auf viele Orte im Bayerischen Wald, in der Fränkischen Schweiz, im Fichtelgebirge, auf die Staatsbäder Reichenhall, Kissingen und Brückenau.

golstadt, ball bearings in Schweinfurt, textiles in Aschaffenburg. The oil-refining centre around Ingolstadt is linked by pipeline to the Mediterranean ports Triest and Genoa.

Even today all these industrial activities still concede to agriculture its pride of place. In Upper Bavaria and the Allgäu in particular cattle raising is of great significance. Thirty per cent of German dairy products and seventy per cent of all cheese come from Bavaria. Ninety per cent of all hops come from the hop-fields of the Hallertau. Wines from the Main-Franconian area have their friends everywhere.

Countless towns and villages which have won renown as recuperative centres also contribute in their own way to Bavaria's economy. This holds not only for the high altitudes between Oberstdorf and Garmisch and Mittenwald and Berchtesgaden, as well as the numerous spots in the outcrops of the Alps, but also for many places in the Bavarian Forest, the "Franconian Schweiz" and the Fichtelgebirge, along with the State Spas Reichenhall, Kissingen and Brückenau.

stadt, industrie textile à Aschaffenburg. Les raffineries d'Ingolstadt sont liées par des pipelines aux ports de Trieste et de Gênes. A côté de l'industrie l'agriculture est prospère. Dans la Haute-Bavière et dans l'Allgäu l'élevage est très rationel (30 % du lait et 70 % du fromage de la R.F.A.). Les houblonnières de la région de Hallertau donnent 90% du houblon. Les vins de la Haute-Franconie sont renommés.

Les stations climatiques et de plaisance offrent de nombreuses possibilités de sports et chacun peut s'adonner à ses hobbies : alpinisme et sport d'hiver dans la région de Garmisch, Oberstdorf, Mittenwald et Berchtesgaden. Les amis de la nature trouvent des villages à l'écart dans la Forêt de la Bavière, dans la « Suisse de la Franconie » et dans la région Fichtelgebirge. Des stations balnéaires mondaines sont Reichenhall, Kissingen et Brückenau.

Stuttgart. Das Neue Schloß ist einer der großen und charakteristischen Bauten Stuttgarts. Die ehemalige Residenz der württembergischen Könige ist ein Spätbarockbau, der unter mehreren Baumeistern von 1746 an errichtet wurde. 1944 wurde das Neue Schloß zerstört, 20 Jahre später war der Wiederaufbau abgeschlossen.

The "Neues Schloss" is one of Stuttgart's biggest and most characteristic buildings. This former residence of the Kings of Baden-Württemberg is late Baroque and was completed by a number of architects from 1746 onwards. The "Neues Schloss" was destroyed in 1944. Twenty years later its reconstruction was completed.

Stuttgart. Le Château-Neuf fondé en 1746 était la résidence des ducs, électeurs et rois de Wurtemberg construit par plusieurs architectes, une construction baroque. Le Château-Neuf détruit en 1944 a été reconstruit après la guerre. La reconstruction durait à peu près vingt années.

Stuttgart, die Landeshauptstadt von Baden-Württemberg, ist der kulturelle Mittelpunkt Südwestdeutschlands: zwei Universitäten, Hoch- und Fachschulen, Musik, Theater und Ballett sowie bedeutende Museen charakterisieren den geistigen Rang der Stadt. Richtungweisend ist auch die neue Architektur, wie diese Doppelseite zeigt. Modernes Einkaufszentrum am Schloßplatz (oben).

Stuttgart, State Capital of Baden-Württemberg, is the cultural centre of South West Germany. It has two universities, high schools, technical schools, music, theatre and ballet which, along with important museums, set the seal on the city's spiritual status. Its modern architecture is also most expressive, as these two pages show. Above: modern shopping centre on the Schlossplatz.

Stuttgart, la capitale politique de Baden-Württemberg est le centre culturel du sud-ouest de l'Allemagne: on y trouve deux universités et des académies, des théâtres et des musées. La ville a toujours su combiner la tradition et le progrès. Voilà un échantillon de l'architecture nouvelle bordant la place du Château.

Der Fernsehturm am Hohen Bopser (482 m) ist nicht der höchste unter diesen himmelstrebenden technischen Wunderwerken, aber gewiß der schönste in Deutschland.

Anknüpfend an die Tradition der Passagen des 19. Jh. entstand mit der Calwer Passage ein reizvolles Einkaufszentrum.

The television tower on the Hoher Bopser (1,600 ft.) may not be the highest of these sky-scraping technical wonders, but it is certainly Germany's most beautiful.

The Calw Passage, an exciting shopping centre, is a link with the 19th century "Passage" tradition.

La tour de télévision sur le mont Hoher Bopser (482 mètres de hauteur) est une marque distinctive de la ville, une des plus belles tours de l'Allemagne.

Le « Passage de Calw » est un centre d'achats élégant dans la tradition des passages cèlébres du 19e siècle.

Daimler-Benz, oder volkstümlicher „Mercedes", ist ein Synonym für Wertarbeit „Made in Germany". Hier Aufnahmen aus dem Hauptwerk in Stuttgart-Untertürckheim.

Daimler-Benz, more commonly "Mercedes", is a synonym for German quality workmanship. Shown are views in the main works in Stuttgart-Untertürckheim.

L'usine Daimler-Benz (« Mercedes ») à Untertürckheim est très renommée. On y attache une grande valeur au « Made in Germany ».

Heidelberg, Universitätsstadt seit 1386, verkörpert in idealer Weise die Romantik in Deutschland. Hoch über dem Neckar gelegen das mächtige Schloß der Pfälzer Kurfürsten, das 1689 von französischen Truppen in Brand gesteckt wurde.

Der Brunnen im Schloßhof (rechts unten).

Lastkähne auf dem Neckar.

Heidelberg, a university town since 1386, embodies almost ideally all the romance of Germany. High above the River Neckar stands the imposing castle of the Prince Electors of the Palatinate. It was set on fire by French troops in 1689.

The fountain in the castle courtyard (bottom right).

Barges on the Neckar.

L'université de Heidelberg fondée en 1386 était célèbre dans le monde entier. La ville est dominée par le château somptueux des comtes palatins et des électeurs, périodes d'épanouissement : gothique et Renaissance (brûlé par les Français en 1689).

Puits dans la cour du château (à droite en bas).

Bateaux de transport sur le Neckar.

207

Bad Wimpfen · Altstadt und Blauer Turm / Old town and the "Blue Tower" / La cité et la « Tour bleue »

Schwäbisch Hall · Rathaus (vollendet 1735) / Town Hall (completed 1735) / Hôtel de ville (1735)

Marbach · Geburtshaus des Dichters Friedrich Schiller / The house where the poet Friedrich Schiller was born / Maison de naissance de Friedrich Schiller

Ludwigsburg · Schloß und Schloßpark / Schloss and Schlosspark / Château et parc (baroque)

Das Remstal, östlich von Stuttgart, ist ein Kernstück des Schwabenlands und Weinanbaugebiet / The Rems Valley to the south of Stuttgart belongs to the heart of Swabia and its vineyard

Markgröningen · Rathaus (15. und 17. Jh.) / Town Hall (15th and 17th century) / Hôtel de ville (15e et 17e s.)

gion / La vallée de la Rems, non loin de Stuttgart est un paysage pittoresque et un pays de vignobles

Besigheim/Enz · Blick auf die Stadt / View of the town / panorama

Tübingen · Blick von der Burg / View from the castle / Vue panoramique du château fort

Schwäbisch Gmünd · Kornhaus und Knöpflesturm / "Grain House" and "Knöpfles Tower" / Grenier à blé et la tour «Knöpflesturm»

Ulm · Donaufront mit Münster / The Danube and Cathedral / Bord du Danube et la cathédrale

Biberach a. d. Riß · Marktplatz / Biberach on the Riss · Market place / Biberach sur la Riss · place du Marché

Donaueschingen · Donauquelle / Danube source / Source du Danube

Donaueschingen · Schloß / Schloss / Château

Titisee im Schwarzwald zur Sommers- und zur Winterszeit / Lake Titi in the Black Forest in summer and in winter / Le lac Titisee dans la Forêt-Noire — été et hiver

Die großen deutschen Dynastien kamen aus dem Schwäbischen; die Staufer, die Welfen und die Zollern, diese später als Hohenzollern mit Preußen gleichgesetzt. Ein später Nachfahr der Zollern, der Preußenkönig Friedrich Wilhelm IV., ließ auf einem steilen Bergkegel am Südrand der Schwäbischen Alb (1850—1867) bei Hechingen die Stammburg der Zollern wieder neu erbauen, so, wie sich das 19. Jh. das Mittelalter vorstellte. Und dies alles zum Entzücken und Schauder vieler Hunderttausend Besucher jährlich (oben rechts und links).

The greatest of the German dynasties, the Staufer, the Welfen and the Zollern came from Swabia, the latter later melding into the Prussian Hohenzollerns. A later descendant of the Zollerns, Friedrich Wilhelm IV. of Prussia, had the main seat of the Zollerns, a castle, built on a steep mountain face near Hechingen (1850—1867) so reconstructed as to represent current concepts of the middle ages. This both attracts and repels hundreds of thousands of visitors annually (above left and right).

La Souabe était la patrie de quelques grandes dynasties allemandes : des Gibelins (Staufer), des Guelfes et des Zollern, qui étaient les ancêtres des Hohenzollern de la Prusse. Remarquablement situé sur un plateau au bord de la chaîne de montagnes Schwäbische Alb près du village Hechingen le château Hohenzollern est un reconstitution d'un château féodal en néo-gothique (1850—1867) édifiée sous l'impulsion du roi Frédéric-Guillaume IV avec incorporation de parties anciennes (en haut).

Balingen · Zollernschlößchen (rechts)
Rottweil · Erker eines Patrizierhauses in der Hauptstraße

Balingen · Zollernschlößchen" — "Little castle" (right).
Rottweil · Alcove in a patrician house on the main street.

Balingen, château « Zollernschlösschen » (à droite)
Rottweil, partie d'une maison patricienne

Baden-Baden · Kurhaus (oben)

Schwetzingen · Schloß (unten)

Karlsruhe · Schloß, gebaut nach einem Entwurf Balthasar Neumanns (rechts oben)

Iffezheim · Galopprennbahn bei Baden-Baden

Baden-Baden · Spa Casino (above)

Schwetzingen · Schloss (below)

Karlsruhe · Schloss, built to a design by Balthasar Neumann (above right)

Iffezheim · Racecourse near Baden-Baden

Baden-Baden, établissement des bains (en haut)

Schwetzingen, château (en bas)

Karlsruhe, château, dessin de Balthasar Neumann (à droite en haut)

Iffezheim, turf célèbre non loin de Baden-Baden

Hinterzarten ·
Kurort im Schwarzwald

Hinterzarten ·
Spa in the Black Forest

Hinterzarten · Station climatique
dans la Forêt-Noire

Schwarzwald
The Black Forest
Forêt-Noire

Schwarzwaldhaus im Gutachtal

Black Forest House in the Gutach Valley

Ferme dans la vallée de Gutach

Trachten aus dem Gutachtal

Tracht garments from the Gutach Valley

Costumes de la vallée de Gutach

Martinstor
Martin's Gate
Porte « Martin »

Die größte Stadt des Schwarzwaldgebietes ist die Universitätsstadt Freiburg. Zu Füßen des gotischen Münsters das spätgotische Alte Kaufhaus (oben), im Hintergrund ein altes Stadttor, das Schwabentor. Der Münsterturm (links) gilt als der schönste aller hochgotischen Kirchtürme.

SEITE 226/227
Insel Mainau/Bodensee · Das im 18. Jh. erbaute Schloß
Lindau · Hafeneinfahrt
Unteruhldingen · Rekonstruktion eines steinzeitlichen Pfahlbautendorfes

The university town Freiburg is the biggest town in the Black Forest region. At the foot of the Gothic cathedral is the old Late Gothic shopping place (above), behind is an old town gate, the Swabian Gate. The spire of the Minster (left) is said to be the most beautiful of all high Gothic spires.

PAGE 226/227
Mainau Island on Lake Constance. Schloss, built in the 18th century
Lindau · Harbour entrance
Unteruhldingen · Reconstruction of a village on pylons from the stone age

La plus grande ville de la Forêt-Noire est Freiburg, siège d'une ancienne université. Devant la cathédrale, dont la puissante tour et les vitraux sont des monuments de haute valeur artistique, on se trouve sur une très belle place bordée de l'ancien magasin et de maisons patriciennes.

PAGE 226/227
L'île Mainau dans le lac de Constance : le château (18e s.)
Lindau · entrée du port
Unteruhldingen · reconstitution d'un village néolithique sur un pilotage dans le lac

Gastlichkeit und ...
... Gemütlichkeit — zwei typisch deutsche Worte

Typical German hospitality and ... "Gemütlichkeit"

« Gastlichkeit » et ...
... « Gemütlichkeit » — deux mots typiques allemands

Mespelbrunn. In einem kleinen Seitenteil des waldreichen Spessart liegt versteckt das Stammschloß der Echter von Mespelbrunn. Begonnen wurde mit dem Bau des Wasserschlosses um 1560.

Mespelbrunn. Tucked away in a little side valley in the woody Spessart is the seat of the Echters of Mespelbrunn. The building of the moated castle began around 1560.

Mespelbrunn, château entouré de forêts dans un val solitaire du Spessart — un castel d'eau édifié à partir des environs de 1560.

Reiz des Fachwerkbaus: Das Rathaus, erbaut 1484, von Michelstadt (links) und Häuser in Miltenberg (unten rechts).

Einer der wenigen großartigen Renaissancebauten Deutschlands, das Schloß von Aschaffenburg, erbaut vom Festungsbaumeister Georg Riedinger.

Half-timbered charm: the Town Hall of Michelstadt, completed in 1484 (below), and houses in Miltenberg (below right).

One of the less outstanding of German examples of the Renaissance: the Schloss in Aschaffenburg, built by fortification architect Georg Riedinger.

La beauté des constructions à pans de bois : l'hôtel de ville de Michelstadt (1484) (à gauche) et la ravissante place du Marché de Miltenberg (en bas à droite).

Le château d'Aschaffenburg, construit par l'architecte G. Riedinger est un bel échantillon de l'architecture de la Renaissance.

231

Bamberg · Der Dom, errichtet 1237

Bamberg · Cathedral dating from 1237

Bamberg · Haute Franconie, la cathédrale (1237)

Coburg. · Aufgang zur Veste

Coburg · Ascent to the "Veste"

Coburg · Haute Franconie, château fort médiéval, montée

Coburg. Lutherzimmer auf der Veste Coburg; hier schrieb Luther den „Sendbrief vom Dolmetschen".

Coburg · Luther's room in the Coburg "Veste" where Luther wrote his "Edict on Interpreting"

Coburg, la chambre de Martin Luther dans le château fort

Bamberg · Marienaltar des Veit Stoß im Dom

Bamberg · Altar of Mary by Veit Stoss in the Cathedral

Bamberg · Haute Franconie, autel marial de Veit Stoss dans la cathédrale

Bamberg · „Klein Venedig" an der Regnitz
Selb · Teller aus der weltberühmten Porzellanmanufaktur Rosenthal

Bamberg · "Little Venice" on the Regnitz
Selb · Dishes from the world renowned Rosenthal porcelain manufactury

Bamberg · charmantes habitations anciennes sur les bords de la Regnitz
Selb · assiette de la manufacture porcelainière célèbre Rosenthal

Alljährlich wird im Juli in Dinkelsbühl die „Kinderzeche" gefeiert. Das Fest wird zur Erinnerung an ein Ereignis in Dreißigjährigen Krieg gefeiert, als die Stadt im Jahr 1632 vor schwedischen Plünderern bewahrt wurde.

The "Kinderzeche" (Tribute to the Children) is celebrated each July in Dinkelsbühl. It recalls an event during the Thirty Years' War when, in 1632, the town was saved from Swedish plunderers.

Dinkelsbühl est surtout charactérisé par son aspect moyenâgeux. Chaque année une fête commémorative rappelle un événement de la Guerre de Trente Ans. En 1632 la ville fut préservée du pillage par les Suédois.

SEITE 236/237
Die Wallfahrtskirche Vierzehnheiligen am Main in der Nähe von Bamberg
Weikersheim · Schloß
Würzburg · Mainbrücke mit Brückenheiligen, in der Bildmitte der Dom St. Kilian
Würzburg · Auf der Feste Marienberg

PAGE 236/237
The "Wallfahrtskirche" of the Fourteen Saints, on the Main near Bamberg
Weikersheim · Schloss
Würzburg · Bridge across the Main with saints, in the centre St. Kilian's Cathedral
Würzburg · On the "Feste Marienberg"

PAGE 236/237
L'église baroque de pèlerinage Vierzehnheiligen non loin de Bamberg
Weikersheim · château
Würzburg · pont sur le Main et la cathédrale St.-Kilian.
Würzburg · la citadelle Marienberg

Romantische Städte mit großer Vergangenheit. Das Rödertor unterbricht die heute noch intakte Stadtmauer von Rothenburg o. d. Tauber; im Vordergrund die Gerlachschmiede
Blick auf Nördlingen, einst freie Reichsstadt

Romantic towns with an impressive past. The Röder Gateway interupts the still intact town ramparts of Rothenburg ob der Tauber. In the foreground is the "Gerlach Smithy".
View of Nördlingen, former Free Reichs City.

Les villes romantiques conservées dans leur forme médiévale : La porte fortifiée Rödertor, l'enceinte et la pittoresque maison de la forge « Gerlachschmiede ». Panorama de Nördlingen, ancienne ville libre impériale.

Nürnberg · Die spätgotische Frauenkirche am Hauptmarkt ist ein Geschenk Kaiser Karl IV. an die Stadt (1355). Die 19 m hohe gotische Turmpyramide des Schönen Brunnens ist umgeben von Propheten, Evangelisten, Kirchenvätern und Kurfürsten.

Nuremberg · The Late Gothic Frauenkirche on the "Hauptmarkt" was a gift to the City from Kaiser Karl IV in 1355. The 62 feet high Gothic pyramide column of the "Schöner Brunnen" (Beautiful Fountain) is surrounded by Prophets, Evangelists, Church Fathers and Prince Electors.

Nuremberg · Notre Dame (1350–55) gothique tardif, type halle à 3 nefs est un don de l'empereur Charles IV. Devant l'église : la Belle Fontaine (19 m de hauteur) complétée ultérieurement de statues (prophètes, électeurs etc.).

Vor der Zerstörung im 2. Weltkrieg war Nürnberg weltberühmt für sein mittelalterliches Stadtbild. Veit Stoß, Albrecht Dürer, Meistersinger, Peter Henlein sind Namen, die einem spontan einfallen. Nach dem Krieg wurde die größte Stadt Nordbayerns behutsam restauriert und die schönsten Punkte aus alter Zeit wiederhergestellt. Unser Bild zeigt die romanisch-hochgotische Sebalduskirche, davor Henkersteg mit Weinstadl.

Before its destruction in World War II Nuremberg was renowned as a town out of the middle ages. Veit Stoss, Albrecht Dürer, the Meistersingers and Peter Henlein are all names which come instantly to mind. After the war this biggest North Bavarian city was carefully restored and the most beautiful old time features returned. Pictured is the Roman-High Gothic Sebaldus Church, in front of it the hangman's stand with wine tavern.

Avant les destructions de la seconde guerre mondiale Nuremberg était rayonnante de gloire, riche en maisons patriciennes et en hôtels particuliers anciens. Parmi les grands créateurs citons Albrecht Dürer, Veit Stoss et Peter Henlein. Après la guerre les monuments principaux ont été reconstitués. Le château fortifié domine toujours la vieille cité. Voilà St.-Sébald romano-gothique, Henkersteg et Weinstadl.

Regensburg · Die das Stadtbild beherrschenden Türme des Doms St. Peter sind im 19. Jh. vollendet worden, während mit dem Bau des übrigen Komplexes bereits 1273 begonnen wurde.

Regensburg · The spires of St. Peter's Cathedral, which dominate the panorama, were completed in the 19th century, although the building of the main body started in 1273.

Ratisbonne · ville danubienne dominée des tours de la cathédrale St.-Pierre, œuvre maîtresse du gothique, complétée au 19e siècle.

Die über die Donau führende Steinerne Brücke stammt aus dem 12. Jh.

The stone bridge across the Danube dates back to the twelfth century.

Le pont de pierre traversant le Danube fut bâti au 12e siècle.

Neun Stockwerke hoch ist der Goldene Turm, ehemals Wohnung eines Patriziergeschlechts.

The Golden Tower, once the abode of Patricians, is nine storeys high.

Uniques en Allemagne: les maisons-tours de familles nobles, voilà la « Tour d'Or ».

Inmitten der romantischen Felseneinsamkeit des Donaudurchbruchs westlich von Regensburg liegt das barocke Benediktinerkloster Weltenburg, eine Schöpfung der Münchner Brüder Asam.

In the midst of the romantic, cliff-lined passage of the Danube to the west of Regensburg is the Baroque Weltenburg Benedictine Monastery the work of the Asam brothers of Munich.

Probablement la plus ancienne des abbayes bénédictines de Bavière, Weltenburg près de Kelheim, est située dans un site incomparable à la percée du Danube (œuvre des frères Asam)

243

245

Augsburg, die traditionsreiche Hauptstadt Oberschwabens, ist neben München und Nürnberg die bedeutendste Industriestadt Bayerns. Im Vordergrund stehen Papier-, Textil- und Maschinenindustrie, wie hier der Schwermaschinenbau bei der Maschinenfabrik Augsburg — Nürnberg, M.A.N.

Rich in tradition, Augsburg, capital of Upper Swabia, is the third most important industrial town in Bavaria after Munich and Nuremberg. Paper, textiles and machine-building head the list. Shown is the heavy machinery plant of M.A.N., Maschinenfabrik Augsburg — Nürnberg.

Né d'une fondation romaine, Augsbourg (ancienne capitale de la Haute-Souabe), rassemblant en surabondance des monuments du Moyen-Age, est aujourd'hui une ville industrielle (papeterie, industrie textile et mécanique). Voilà l'usine M.A.N.

SEITE 244/245

Burghausen · Ehemalige kurfürstliche Residenz
Passau · Donaubrücke mit St. Michael
Burghausen an der Salzach · Burg
Passau · Dom St. Stephan

PAGE 244/245

Burghausen · Former residence of the Prince Electors
Passau · Bridge on the Danube and St. Michael's
Burghausen on the Salzach · Castle
Passau · St. Stephen's Cathedral

PAGE 244/245

Burghausen sur la Salzach · ancienne résidence électorale
Passau · pont sur le Danube et St.-Michel
Burghausen sur la Salzach · château fort
Passau · cathédrale St.-Etienne

Trotz schwerer Zerstörungen im Kriege finden sich in Augsburg noch viele Zeugnisse aus vergangener Zeit: Der Herkulesbrunnen auf der Maximilianstraße (Mitte oben und rechts) wurde 1610 errichtet; im Hintergrund die Kirche St. Ulrich und Afra. Die „Fuggerei", die erste Sozialsiedlung der Welt (1525), wurde von den Fuggern gestiftet und existiert heute noch (Mitte unten); dahinter das Rathaus, 1615—1620 vom Augsburger „Stadtwerkmeister" Elias Holl errichtet.

In spite of heavy war demage, Augsburg can still show a great deal of evidence of bygone times. The Hercules Fountain in the Maximilianstrasse (above centre and right) dates back to 1610. In the background is the Church of St. Ulrich und Afra. The "Fuggerei", the world's first social community, was donated by the "Fuggern", a merchants' consortium in 1525, and is still in existence (below centre). Behind is the Town Hall (1615—1620) by municipal architect Elias Holl.

En dépit de profondes destructions par fait de guerre Augsbourg est riche encore en monuments d'art et d'historie. A signaler particulièrement : (en haut) la « Fontaine d'Hercule » (1610), l'église St.-Ulrich-et-Ste.-Afra et (en bas) le plus ancien groupe social du monde : « Fuggerei » (1525) et l'hôtel de ville d'Elias Holl (1615/20).

Ravensburg · Marienplatz und Grüner Turm / Marienplatz and Green Tower / Place Notre-Dame et « Tour Verte »

Schloß Linderhof (1870) im Graswangtal / Linderhof Schloss (1870) in the Graswang Valley / Linderhof, château (1870) dans la vallée Graswang

Memmingen · Rathaus / Tower Hall / Hôtel de ville

Kempten · Kornhaus / Grain House / Grenier à blé du 18e siècle

Drachenflieger über dem Allgäuer Land / Hang gliding above the Allgäu Region / Allgäu, aérosportif volant

St. Koloman b. Füssen / St. Koloman near Füssen / L'église de pèlerinage St-Koloman

Sylvensteinspeicher im Isarwinkel / Sylvanite store in the Isar "Corner" / Le réservoir Sylvensteinspeichersee près de l'Isar

Die „Wieskirche" bei Steingaden (1745–54) / The "Wieskirche" near Steingaden (1745–54) / L'église de pèlerinage « Wies » près de Steingaden (1745/54)

Schloß Neuschwanstein, errichtet vom bayerischen König Ludwig II.
Neuschwanstein Schloss, erected by King Ludwig II of Bavaria
Le château Neuschwanstein près de Füssen, œuvre de Louis II

Rechts: Der Forggensee, ein Stausee des Lech, fügt sich harmonisch in die Landschaft
Right: Lake Forggen, a reservoir on the River Lech, harmonises beautifully with the landscape
A droite : Le lac Forggensee, un réservoir blotti harmonieusement dans le paysage

München · Marienplatz
München · Biergarten
München · Blick auf die „Weltstadt mit Herz"

Munich · Marienplatz
Munich · Biergarten
Munich · View of the "Metropolis with a Heart"

Munich · place Notre-Dame
Munich · jardin d'une brasserie
Munich · panorama de la « métropole cordiale »

SEITE 256

Schleißheim b. München · Neues Schloß
München · Olympiastadion

PAGE 256

Schleissheim near Munich · New Schloss
Munich · Olympic Stadium

PAGE 256

Schleissheim près de Munich · château
Munich · Stade olympique

255

SEITE/PAGE 257

München · Schloß Nymphenburg / Munich · Nymphenburg Schloss / Munich · château Nymphenburg
München · Fernsehturm / Munich · Television Tower / Munich · la tour de télévision

Moderne Weltraumtechnik entsteht vor den Toren Münchens bei Messerschmitt-Bölkow-Blohm (MBB) in Ottobrunn. Oben links ein Wettersatellit; Solargeneratoren in Kohlefasertechnik dienen zur Energieerzeugung für den Satelliten im Weltraum (oben und unten); das Bild auf der rechten Seite zeigt einen Nachrichten-Satelliten, der in deutsch-französischer Zusammenarbeit entsteht.

Messerschmitt-Bölkow-Blohm (MBB) à Ottobrunn près de Munich s'occupe de la technique moderne aérospatiale. En haut : un satellite météorologique. Des générateurs solaires pourvoient les satellites d'électricité. A droite : un satellite de communication, une coopération franco-allemande.

Modern space technology in the making at Messerschmitt-Bölkow-Blohm (MBB) in Ottobrunn just outside Munich. Above left is a weather satellite; carbon fibre solar generators serve to produce energy for satellites in space (above and below). The picture on the right shows a communications satellite, a German-French joint project.

Marquartstein · Zunftsäule
Marquartstein · Column of the Guilds
Marquartstein · colonne des métiers

Rechte Seite: Landshut. Burg Trausnitz; die Landshuter „Fürstenhochzeit" ist Deutschlands größtes historisches Fest und wird alle drei Jahre gefeiert.
Right: Landshut. Trausnitz Castle. The Landshut "Wedding of the Princes" is Germany's biggest historic festival, celebrated every three years.
A droite : Landshut sur l'Isar, dominé par la château féodal Trausnitz. La fête « Landshuter Fürstenhochzeit » (« mariage des princes ») est un événement pittoresque.

261

Oben: Raisting · Erdefunkstelle / Above: Raisting. Ground communications station / En haut : Raisting, grand poste radio-télégraphique

Unten: Ruhpolding in den Chiemgauer Alpen / Below: Ruhpolding in the Chiemgau Alps / En bas : Ruhpolding dans les Alpes de Chiemgau

Blick auf das Wettersteingebirge / View of the Wetterstein Mountains / Panorama de la montagne Wetterstein

Links oben: Frauenchiemsee, die zweitgrößte Insel im Chiemsee / Above left: Frauenchiemsee, the second-largest island on Lake Chiem / A gauche en haut : Frauenchiemsee, île dans le lac Chiemsee

Links: Wasserburg am Inn hat beinahe südländischen Charakter / Left: Wasserburg on the Inn appears almost sub-tropical / A gauche : Wasserburg sur l'Inn, petite ville d'une animation méridionale

"Lüftlmalerei", fröhlich bunte Malereien an den Hausfassaden im alpenländischen Raum. Hier ein besonders schönes Beispiel an einem Gasthof in Wallgau.

"High colours" — gay, colourful motifs on the fronts of houses high under the alps. Shown is a particularly fine example, an inn in Wallgau.

« Lüftlmalerei » (« peinture dans l'air »), peinture traditionelle, que l'on trouve sur les façades des maisons rustiques des pays alpins — décoration d'un hôtel, Wallgau.

Zu Gast im Wallgau: Eine Trachtenkapelle aus dem Tiroler Grödnertal.

On a visit to Wallgau: An orchestra in full "Tracht" from the Tyrolean Grödner Valley.

Musiciens du Tyrol dans la région de Wallgau.

Der Zauberwald am Hintersee
The "Bewitched Forest" on the Hintersee
La forêt « Zauberwald » près du lac Hintersee

Reiteralpe über Ramsau
The Reiteralpe above Ramsau
Le mont « Reiteralpe » dominant Ramsau

Ramsau im Berchtesgadener Land
Ramsau in the Berchtesgadener Land
Ramsau, station climatique à la portée de Berchtesgaden

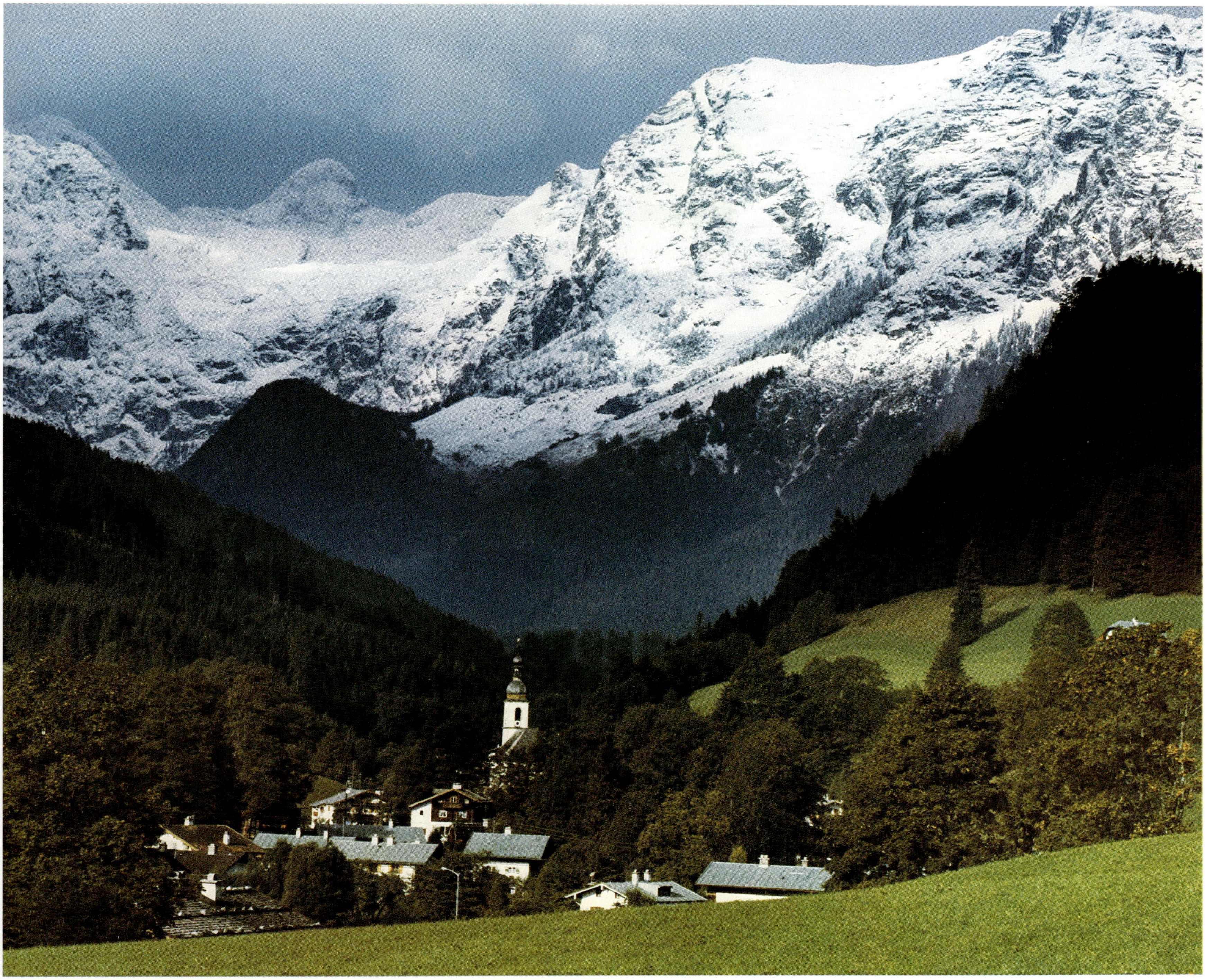

SPORTHOTEL-CAFE REHLEGG

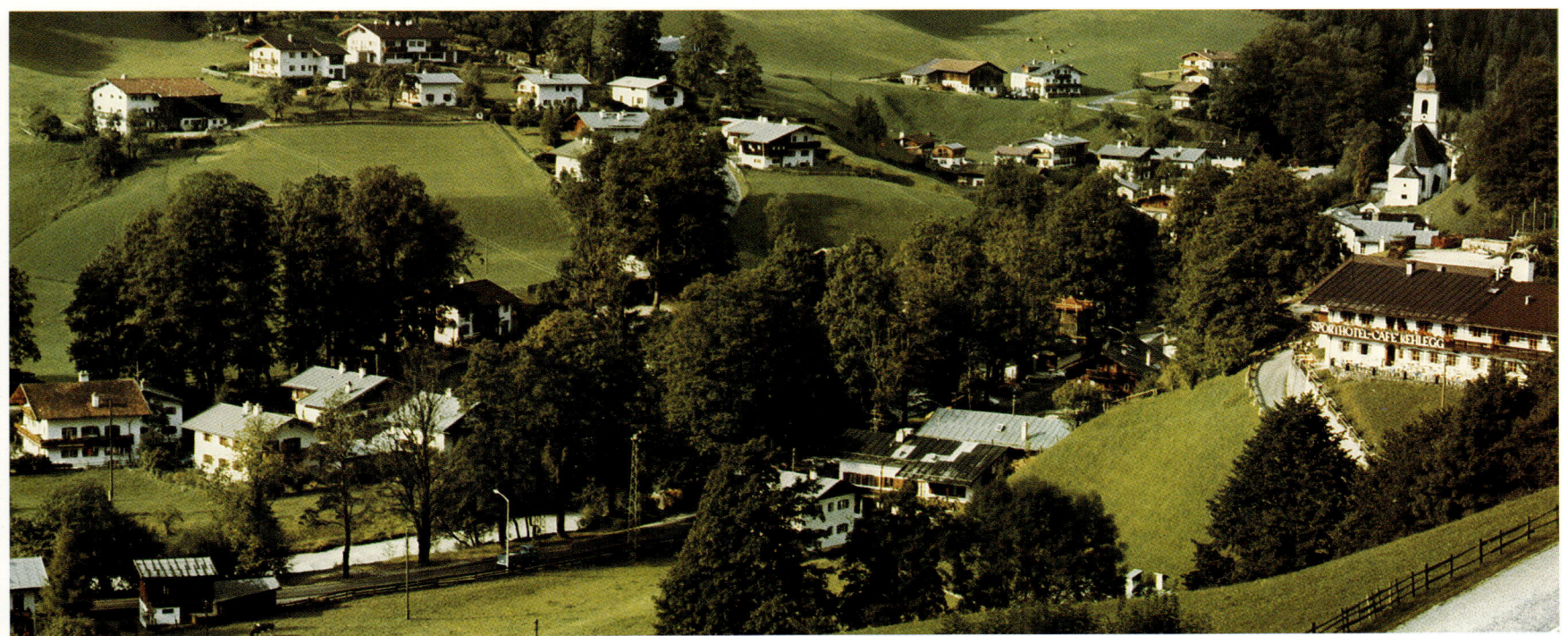

St. Bartholomä am Königssee. Im Hintergrund das Watzmannmassiv
St. Bartholomew's on Lake König. In the background is the Watzmann Massif
La chapelle St.-Bartholomä au lac Königssee dominée par la montagne Watzmann

Der Rießersee bei Garmisch-Partenkirchen
Lake Riesser near Garmisch-Partenkirchen
Le lac Riessersee près de Garmisch-Partenkirchen

Blick auf das Karwendelgebirge
View of the Karwendel Mountains
Karwendel, chaîne de montagnes

Schliersee · Pfarrkirche
Lake Schlier · Parish church
Schliersee · église paroissiale

Bootsfahrt auf dem Königssee mit Blick auf die Teufelshörner
Boat on Lake König and view of the Teufelshörner (Devil's Horns)
Promenade en bateau sur le lac Königssee, panorama des monts Teufelshörner

Mittenwald · St. Peter und Paul sowie Viererspitze
Mittenwald · St. Peter and Paul and "Viererspitze"
Mittenwald · St.-Pierre-et-St.-Paul devant un décor de montagne Viererspitze

Wetterstation auf dem Wendelstein in den Schlierseer Bergen
Meterological station on the Wendelstein in the Lake Schlier Mountains
Station météorologique sur le sommet du Wendelstein

Die Zugspitze, mit 2964 m Deutschlands höchster Berg
The Zugspitze, 9,730 feet, Germany's highest mountain
Zugspitze (2964 m), le plus haut mont de l'Allemagne

Die Windmühle auf der Eröffnungsseite des Bildteils gehört zu jenen Bauten, die wir als selbstverständlich in einer Landschaft akzeptieren, weil sie historisch sind. In einem modernen Industriestaat sind es jetzt andere Bauten, die Teil der Landschaft werden: Fabrikschornsteine, Kühltürme, Fernsehtürme oder wie hier die Erdefunkstelle Raisting (Obb.) der Deutschen Bundespost, die über Satelliten bis zu 1000 Ferngespräche gleichzeitig überträgt.

The windmill shown on the introductory page of the picture section is the sort of landscape feature we nowadays take for granted because of its historic connotations. Nowadays, in a modern industrial country, other types of structure are becoming a part of the landscape: factory chimneys, cooling towers, TV towers or, as in this case, the ground Federal Post Office's communications station at Raisting (Upper Bavaria), which can handle up to 1,000 overseas phone calls as simultaneously.

Le moulin à vent sur notre première illustration est un bel échantillon des bâtiments traditionels. Nortre chemin nous mène des origines de l'histoire jusqu'au dynamisme actuel, aux échantillons de l'architecture moderne, aux usines, raffineries, tours de sondage et tours de télévision, notamment au grand poste radio-télégraphique de Raisting, qui rend simultanément possible la transmission de mille communications téléphoniques.